Why Salvation?

Reframing New Testament Theology

Reframing New Testament Theology

Why Salvation?

JOEL B. GREEN

Nashville

Library of Congress Cataloging-in-Publication Data has been requested.

ISBN: 978-1-4267-5699-3

13 14 15 16 17 18 19 20 21 22—10 9 8 7 6 5 4 3 2 1

MANUFACTURED IN THE UNITED STATES OF AMERICA

Contents

Foreword

At first glance, the phrase "New Testament theology" seems clear enough. However, attempts to explain it immediately expose some speed bumps. Do we want to describe the theology we find in the New Testament? Construct a theology on a New Testament foundation? Or perhaps sketch an account of early Christian beliefs and practices from the New Testament era? This series of books frames the question in a different way: How do we take seriously that, together with the Old Testament, the New Testament has in the past and should in the present inform, form, and transform the church's faith and life?

Almost everyone will agree that the New Testament books concern themselves with *theology*. This truism is supported on almost every page as New Testament writers speak of God, the significance of Jesus of Nazareth for God's agenda for the world, the character of God's people, faithful life before God, and God's coming to set the world right.

How does the New Testament witness relate to the church's life today? This is less clear and therefore more controversial. The church affirms its allegiance to the God of whom scripture speaks and, therefore, ties itself, its faith and witness, to the Old and New Testaments. How the church's affirmations work themselves out in terms of engagement with the New Testament materials—this is the question.

Reframing New Testament Theology gets at this question by encouraging active, theological engagement with the New Testament itself. Readers will find among the books in this series an awareness of the obstacles we face—obstacles like the following:

- New Testament texts were written in another time and another place. In what sense, then, can we say that they were written *to* us or *for* us? After all, those first readers of Matthew's Gospel or the letter of James would be dumbstruck by the idea of streaming video in a church service, just as most of us lack any firsthand experience with anything analogous to the challenges of peasant farmers and fisherfolk in ancient Galilee.

- What of the sheer variety of voices we hear among the New Testament books? If we want the New Testament to help orient our thinking about mission or salvation, how do we make sense of the different perspectives we sometimes encounter? Do we accord privilege to some voices over others? Do we try to synthesize various viewpoints?

- New Testament writers raise issues that may seem foreign to us today and overlook some of our contemporary concerns. Our educational systems, political structures, immigration policies, knowledge of the universe, modes of transportation, and the countless other day-to-day realities that we take for granted separate us from the equally countless assumptions, beliefs, and behaviors that characterized people living in the ancient Mediterranean world. Faced with these differences, how do we work with scripture?

Additionally, our readers will find an awareness of a range of questions about how best to think about "New Testament theology"—questions like these:

- Since the "new" in "New Testament" presumes an "Old Testament," what status should our New Testament theological explorations assign to the Old Testament? How do we understand the theological witness of the New Testament in relation to the Old?

- Are we concerned primarily with what the New Testament writers *taught* (past tense) their first readers theologically, or do we want to know what the New Testament *teaches* (present tense) us? Is "New Testament theology" a descriptive task or a prescriptive one?

- Do we learn from the New Testament writers the "stuff" of Christian theology, or do we apprentice ourselves to them so that we might learn how to engage in the theological task ourselves? Does the New Testament provide the raw material for contemporary theology, or does it invite us into ongoing reflection with it about God and God's ways?

If contributions to this series demonstrate an awareness of obstacles and issues like these, this does not mean that they address them in a uniform manner. Nor are these books concerned primarily with showing how to navigate or resolve conundrums like these. What holds this series together is not a particular set of methodological commitments but a keen sense that scripture has in the past and should in the present instruct and shape the church's faith and life. What does it mean to engage the New Testament from within the church and for the church?

One further consideration: The church turns to the scriptures believing that the Bible is authoritative for what we believe and what we do, but it does so while recognizing that the church's theology is shaped in other ways too—by God's self-disclosure in God's "book of nature," for example—and in relation to the ecumenical creeds with which the church has identified itself: the Apostles' Creed, the Nicene Creed, and the Athanasian Creed. Not surprisingly, New Testament "theology" invites reflecting on, interacting with, learning from, and sometimes struggling with the scriptures, and doing so in relation to human understanding more generally as well as in the context of our common Christian confessions.

Intended for people interested in studying the New Testament and the nature of the Christian message and the Christian life, for classrooms, group interaction, and personal study, these volumes invite readers into a conversation with New Testament theology.

Joel B. Green
General Editor

Abbreviations

COQG	Christian Origins and the Question of God
CTI	Current Issues in Theology
DJG²	*Dictionary of Jesus and the Gospels*, rev. ed.
DPL	*Dictionary of Paul and His Letters*
DSE	*Dictionary of Scripture and Ethics*
ed.	edition; edited by; editor(s)
EDEJ	*The Eerdmans Dictionary of Early Judaism*
e.g.	*exempli gratia*, for example
GBS:OTS	Guides to Biblical Scholarship: Old Testament Series
HeyJ	*Heythrop Journal*
i.e.	*id est*, that is
JBL	*Journal of Biblical Literature*
LCL	Loeb Classical Library
MCT	The Matrix of Christian Theology
MNTS	McMaster New Testament Series
NDBT	*New Dictionary of Biblical Theology*
NET	New English Translation
NETS	New English Translation of the Septuagint
NICNT	New International Commentary on the New Testament
NIDOTTE	*New International Dictionary of Old Testament Theology and Exegesis*
NIGTC	New International Greek Testament Commentary
NIV	New International Version (2011)
NRSV	New Revised Standard Version
NTL	New Testament Library
NTOA	Novum Testamentum et Orbis Antiquus
NTT	New Testament Theology

OBT	Overtures to Biblical Theology
OTL	Old Testament Library
OTP	*Old Testament Pseudepigrapha*
PBTM	Paternoster Biblical and Theological Monographs
SABH	Studies in American Biblical Hermeneutics
SBLDS	Society of Biblical Literature Dissertation Series
SJLA	Studies in Judaism in Late Antiquity
SNTU	Studien zum Neuen Testament und seiner Umwelt
SNTW	Studies of the New Testament in Its World
SOTBT	Studies in Old Testament Biblical Theology
STI	Studies in Theological Interpretation
TBS.	The Biblical Seminar
TDOT	*Theological Dictionary of the Old Testament*
TECC	Theological Explorations for the Church Catholic
TJL	The Jesus Library
TLNT	*Theological Lexicon of the New Testament*
TSc	Theology and the Sciences
v(v)	verse(s)
VT	*Vetus Testamentum*
WUNT	Wissenschaftliche Untersuchungen zum Neuen Testament
WW.	*Word and World*

Introduction

I n his little book, *Theology: A Very Short Introduction,* David Ford observes that "salvation" is that point in the study of religions in general
and Christian faith in particular where all of the key issues converge.[1] How a
community views God, the character of the cosmos and of humanity, the nature of evil and sin, the process of healing and recovery of health, its own life
as a community, and its hope—these issues and more come into focus when
we address the theme of salvation. If we take seriously that the "theme" of a
text concerns what unifies its many, often distinct, and sometimes discontin-
uous elements,[2] then there is an important sense in which we are justified in
speaking of salvation as the theme of scripture. Here is the integrating center
of scripture, just as it is the coordinating center of theology.

Our understanding of salvation builds on a number of related concepts,
including, for example, *anthropology* (our understanding of humanity and the
human situation), *theology* (our understanding of God), *Christology* (our understanding of the person and work of Christ), *ecclesiology* (our understanding of the church), and *eschatology* (our understanding of the end to which
God's work is headed). If our exploration of the theme of salvation is to be
faithful to the New Testament and meaningful for our lives, it must be suf-
ficient to account for the human cry for healing what is wounded in personal,
communal, and even global terms, and it must provide a vision of salvation
that can be reckoned and related genuinely as good news. In fact, what we
find in scripture is a virtual choir of voices capable of multiple analyses of human need and the condition of our planet, with each witness underwriting
its own distinct, though not unique, soteriological vision. Our concern will
not be to jam each witness into a single box or to silence one voice in favor

of another, since it is precisely on account of its multiplicity that the biblical witness to salvation can address itself authentically to communities separated by experience and culture. These multiple voices, all in the same scriptural choir, can challenge and enable us to reach outside of ourselves to imagine transformed images of human health and vocation, and to foster in our communities the ability to generate language and practices of healing and restoration that reflect and embody the biblical hope of salvation.

In the same way, a biblical soteriology presupposes a *theology*, a certain God-portrait—rooted in history but stretching beyond history. Those who embrace Christian faith are not free to construct portraits of God willy-nilly, since what it means to be Christian is to locate ourselves in the ongoing story of God's relationship to the whole cosmos, and thus to all humanity, and especially to Israel, as this is narrated in the Old and New Testaments and revealed in the world of God's creation. Our understanding of God's character and activity is thus oriented around and shaped by the biblical narratives and the ongoing story of God's work with God's people. This story of God's project is grounded in Israel's scriptures, comes to decisive expression in Jesus Christ, continues into the present, and moves forward to the consummation of God's purpose and self-revelation in the end. Biblical notions of salvation presuppose at the same time that they demonstrate the creative and redemptive God, whose purpose scripture identifies as eternal and ongoing, now progressing toward the ends that God has determined. Consequently, we need a storied approach to our understanding of salvation, one that apportions profound significance to the canonical narrative of God and God's people. To be Christian is to belong to an ancient and ongoing story, whose aims, twists, and turns are shaped in relation to Israel's God. This is the God who provides an inheritance for his children, who calls for obedience and honor, and who promises faithfulness and love.

Since Aristotle's classical reflections on such matters, narratives have been categorized as having beginnings, middles, and ends. What of the narrative of salvation? Beginnings are capable of supporting and generating multiple narratives, and so it is with the Bible's beginnings. In the first century, for example, Pharisees and revolutionaries, Essenes and the Jewish elite in Jerusalem—these and other groups within Judaism could each read the story of the scriptures particularly as *its own* story. The same could be said of the early Christian movement. The book of Acts records speech after speech in which Jesus' witnesses work to interpret the gospel of Jesus as nothing less (and nothing more) than the continuation of the story of God's people related in Israel's scriptures. If we can take 1 Corinthians as exemplary, one of Paul's primary agendas in his work among predominately Gentile churches was to teach those Gentile Christians to read Israel's story as their story, or rather to read themselves into the story of Israel. In the same way, today, Muslims, Jews, and Christians each look to Abraham's story as the beginning of their story. But a particularly Christian reading of the biblical story identifies a narrative begun in creation that passes through Abraham, Sarah, and the exodus and that leads to and in an ultimate way is determined by the advent of Jesus of Nazareth, whom Christians name as Christ and Lord. In a handful of New Testament texts, Jesus is identified explicitly as "Savior," and still other texts present him in this role even when they do not employ the term. Any exploration of salvation in the Christian scriptures cannot escape the catalog of questions that accompany this designation of Jesus as Savior, which, together with the exodus, forms the midpoint of the narrative of salvation.

A focus on Jesus cannot, and is not meant to, bypass the role of the church, the community of God's people, either in salvation itself or in the identity of the church as a community of salvation. Neither is it meant to mask the degree to which God's purpose in salvation is not self-evident around us, in spite of our claim as Christians, based on good biblical warrant, that the age of salvation is already a present reality. Herein lies the importance of tying our understanding of the church to the message of salvation, of being clear in our grasp of the church's commitments and impulses to mission in the world, and of nurturing a robust hope in God's power to complete the work of salvation.

Roughly speaking, these concerns provide the outline of this study. Chapter 1, "Adam, What Have You Done?" explores selected testimony from the Old and New Testaments concerning the nature of humanity. Although our history has largely been one of differentiating ourselves from the animal world and locating ourselves in a place of preeminence with respect to the rest of the cosmos, we will see that scripture presents a perspective that is both more modest and less isolationist. "Marvelously set apart" we may be (Ps. 139:14), and crowned "with glory and grandeur" (Ps. 8:5), but the pressing image of humanity in scripture is that of creatures in need of and dependent on God for salvation. Chapters 2 and 3, "Yahweh, the Healer" and "Yahweh, the Liberator," respectively, turn to the primary character in the biblical story, God, and to God's quintessential role as Savior. With astonishing consistency, scripture presents Yahweh as the one who binds up and heals the wounded (to borrow the language of Job 5:17-18). In Israel's scriptures the almost invariable subject of the verb "to save" is Yahweh. Recounting in Exodus 14 the spectacular victory over the Egyptian army at the Reed Sea, the narrator summarizes, "The LORD rescued Israel from the Egyptians that day" (v. 30).

Likewise, in her song of praise in anticipation of the birth of her son, Jesus, Mary addresses herself to "God my savior" (Luke 1:47). It is therefore crucial to explore not only the Bible's presentation of God as healer and liberator (an identity that in the New Testament Yahweh shares with Jesus) but also to examine how the categories of "healing and health" and "liberator" illumine the biblical message of salvation.

Chapter 4 focuses on the question, how can I be saved? At stake here are two intertwined though distinguishable issues. First, how is salvation mediated? Second, how might people appropriate God's gracious work? In the first instance, our concern is a large one, moving across the biblical materials, as we examine how God draws near to save. The theology of the temple and sacrifice and the nature of Christ's work come into particular focus here. In the second part of this chapter, we turn more to the human side of the equation. I say "more" because even our responses to God's saving work are dependent on divine grace and illumination. Our interest here falls on changed hearts and changed lives, with the dispositions of our inner character indissolubly linked to our behaviors in the world, both necessary in the performance of salvation.

Where is this biblical story taking us? What is the "end" of salvation? This is the focus of the fifth and final chapter. Here we work to make sense of the sometimes disparate, sometimes otherworldly and fantastic images that comprise the biblical witness to the end. Because this view of the eschaton (that is, the end time) so prominently casts its shadow back on the whole of the biblical story, and thus on the lives of those for whom the Bible is scripture, our exploration of these issues is manifestly bound up with contemporary life. Thus, our more general concern in chapter 5 is the nature of Christian progress in and toward salvation and so, of the character of the community of God's people oriented toward God's historic and anticipated acts of salvation.

All of this talk of "understanding" and theological concepts should not fool us into thinking that the Bible invites us in some superficial sense to an examination of its contents as these relate to salvation. Even if the Bible can be examined in order to see what it says *about* salvation, this does not exhaust the message of scripture on the subject. With regard to salvation, we have to do not only with grasping theological issues but also with being grasped. Indeed, scripture's own theological agenda has to do above all with inducting us into and guiding us along the way of salvation. The words of the Bible themselves were generated, shaped, and have long been read and heard in the throes of the formation and transformation of God's people. Accordingly, when we embrace those words as scripture we find that we have signed up for a life of ongoing, personal, and social transformation.

These ruminations determine and speak to the basic character of this book as an invitation to a journey of salvation oriented toward increased understanding, to be sure, but also to transformed commitments, renewed allegiances, and fresh practices. To address the grand narrative of scripture in a way that takes seriously its essential focus on the journey of salvation is to open ourselves to fresh (and perhaps refreshed) perspectives on the world and on life in the world. I refer to a process of illumination that allows us new categories for conceiving the world, for making sense of our experiences, and for directing our lives. As Luke tells the story, this openness is demonstrated by those gathered in Jerusalem on that Day of Pentecost when the Holy Spirit was poured out on Jesus' followers. They inquire, "What should we do?" (Acts 2:37). Similarly, those who gathered around John the Baptist, whether the crowds in general or toll collectors or soldiers, inquire, "What should we do?" (Luke 3:10-14). Seeing the conventional definitions of their faith reframed in Peter's sermon at Pentecost or refocused by John's ministry of proclamation and baptism, these persons recognize not only the possibility of fresh answers to age-old questions but also the need for changed behaviors. The question takes expanded form in the words of the Philippian jailor, "What must I do to be saved?" (Acts 16:30, my translation). This pivotal question must be spelled out in terms of an awareness of God's enabling purpose and a recognition of God's gracious gift, to be sure, but also with reference to human response and participation.

Initial impetus for this study came from an invitation to contribute to a series on Understanding Biblical Themes (Chalice Press). I am grateful for the opportunity afforded by Abingdon Press to revisit and, at numerous key points, revise those earlier ruminations. I am also grateful to Timothy Reardon for his work on the indexes. Unless otherwise noted, all citations of scripture follow the Common English Bible (CEB).

Adam,
What Have You Done?

The title of this chapter derives from a Jewish text written about 100 CE called 4 Ezra, a series of interactions between Ezra and God, or between Ezra and God's angel Uriel.[1] Uriel has just revealed to Ezra the nature of rewards and punishments in the afterlife and announced that the end-time judgment is decisive—no more leniencies, no more offers of mercy, no more injustices. Aware of the ubiquity of sin, Ezra is appalled and responds, "It would have been better if the earth hadn't brought forth Adam, or when it had brought him forth, that it had forced him not to sin" (4 Ezra 7:116). He continues:

Adam, what have you done?! If you sinned, the downfall wasn't yours alone but also ours who are descended from you. What benefit is it to us that we are promised an immortal time, but we have done works that bring death? What good is it to us that everlasting hope has been predicted for us, but we have utterly failed? What good is it that safe and healthy dwelling places are reserved, but we have behaved badly? What good is it that the glory of the Most High will protect those who have conducted themselves decently, but we have conducted ourselves indecently? What good is it that paradise will be revealed, whose fruit remains uncorrupted, in which there is plenty and healing, but we won't enter it, for we have visited unseemly places? What good is it that the faces of those who practiced abstinence will shine brighter than stars when our

1

faces are blacker than darkness? While we were alive and doing evil, we didn't think about what we would suffer after death. (7:118-126)

Written toward the end of the New Testament era, this Jewish text presents a telling interpretation of the human dilemma: God has purposed good things for humanity, but humanity will not experience those good things on account of the pervasiveness of sin. The first human, Adam himself, marks the downfall of all who descended from him. Adam is not the only culprit, however, since humans after Adam have "done works that bring death," "utterly failed," "behaved badly," "conducted ourselves indecently," and "visited unseemly places." As their conversation continues, Ezra is finally won over to Uriel's perspective so that his address to Israel in chapter 14 draws out the divine perspective for God's people. After rehearsing briefly the exodus story, Ezra proclaims, "If then you will rule your mind and instruct your heart, you will be kept alive, and after death you will attain mercy. Judgment comes after death, when we are restored to life, and then the names of the just will appear and the deeds of the wicked will be exposed" (14:34-35). The solution to Israel's plight, then is "to rule your mind and instruct your heart," that is, to keep Torah, "the Law of life" (14:30).

We can grant that evolutionary biology complicates the picture of human origins assumed by 4 Ezra and other similar, ancient texts. Chromosomal mapping suggests that men today share a common male ancestor who lived in Africa some 125,000 to 156,000 years ago, and women today share a common female ancestor who lived in Africa between 99,000 and 148,000 years ago. These findings also indicate that these two ancestors did not know each other and, in fact, were two of thousands of people alive at the time.[2] The judgments of evolutionary biology do not undercut Ezra's basic concern, however. As work at the interface of theology and science has emphasized, we can and should take seriously the situation to which Ezra gives voice: All humans are unified in sin.[3] Even if we can no longer claim that all human beings trace their parentage to a lone sinner at the beginning of the world, we can nonetheless recognize and grapple with both the inevitability and universality of sin. Things are not as they should be, and this sets the biblical and theological context for reflecting on salvation.

In this chapter, we begin our thinking about salvation, or soteriology (from the combination of two Greek terms: σωτηρία, *sōtēria*, *"salvation"* + λόγος, *logos*, "understanding"), by focusing on the *need* for salvation. We will first reflect theologically on the biblical story as a whole before turning more specifically to some New Testament voices. We will find agreement with

Ezra regarding the inevitability and universality of sin, but disagreement with him concerning the answer to the human dilemma.

Beginning at the Beginning

Simply put, "salvation" is the comprehensive term for all of the benefits that are graciously bestowed on humans by God. This definition focuses on two poles: God as the benefactor and humanity—and, indeed, the whole of creation—as the beneficiary of God's good gifts. Our primary concern in this chapter is with the human situation. What it means "to be saved," to be engaged in propagating and embodying the message of salvation, and to make one's way on the journey of salvation—these questions are tied to the larger question of what it means to be human. And, of course, even asking whether we need salvation presumes an understanding of what it means to be human. What is our call or vocation simply because we are members of the human family?

We should not be surprised by this emphasis on the anthropological focus of salvation, but neither should we exaggerate it. The initial account of creation in Genesis 1 reaches its crest in the creation of humankind. In the initial recounting of God's work on each day of creation, the narrator has employed a consistent literary pattern:

1. Introduction: "God said . . ."

2. Command: "Let there be . . ."

3. Report: "And that's what happened."

4. Evaluation: "God saw how good it was."

5. Time Marker: "There was evening and there was morning . . ."

Following this sequence of events, the light, the sea, the sky, vegetation, and eventually "every kind of living thing" appear on days one to five. Orderly creation comes into being in an orderly fashion. That the work of creation reaches the height of its crescendo in the creation of humanity is signaled not only by its being reserved for the sixth and final day but also by the narrator's departure from the orderly cadence he has established. The work of this day is not just "good," but "supremely good" (Gen 1:31).

Similarly, in Psalm 8, a psalm that extols human dignity in the context of divine glory, the psalmist claims of human beings,

3

You've made them only slightly
    less than divine,[4]
    crowning them with glory and grandeur.
You've let them rule over your handiwork,
    putting everything under their feet—
        all sheep and all cattle,
        the wild animals too,
        the birds in the sky,
        the fish of the ocean,
        everything that travels the pathways of the sea.
    Lord, our Lord, how majestic
is your name throughout the earth! (Ps 8:5-9)

On the one hand, this psalm, which serves as a kind of commentary on Genesis 1, sharply contrasts God's majesty with human insignificance. The psalmist expresses bafflement that Yahweh's splendor does not completely overshadow the possibility of his attending to mere earthlings: "What are human beings that you think about them; what are human beings that you pay attention to them?" (Ps 8:4). On the other hand, the psalmist recognizes that the human family finds its true identity only in relation to God and in relation to God's creation. Moreover, in a world that marked differences between royalty and commoners on the basis of family lineage (the accidents of birth, so to speak), Psalm 8 attributes nobility to every person. The prominent place of humankind in relation to the rest of creation is accentuated at the same time that human beings are positioned clearly in relation to God and the heavenly council. Even the nobility of humanity is cause for glorifying God.

Although these texts provide good reason for a soteriology focused on humanity, there is more to the story. From the standpoint of the biological sciences, the identity of human beings with other mammals, and indeed with all other animals and the whole creation, has become more and more evident in the past two or three centuries. This scientific analysis is not alien to the accounts of creation in the Bible, for there too the human creature is depicted very much at home in the cosmos. Humans are situated in relation to other living creatures in almost every way, so that the fate of the one is tied to the fate of the other. In the New Testament, Paul presumes this relationship in his portrait of the consummation of history, insisting that the restoration of all creation is intimately linked to the salvation of God's people:

The whole creation waits breathless with anticipation for the revelation of God's sons and daughters. Creation was subjected to frustration, not by its

own choice—it was the choice of the one who subjected it—but in the hope
that the creation itself will be set free from slavery to decay and brought into
the glorious freedom of God's children. (Rom 8:19-21)

And the book of Revelation cannot imagine the final deliverance of God's
people without at the same time envisioning cosmic restoration: "a new heaven and a new earth" (Rev 21:1).[5]

As important as it is that we account for the cosmological scope of God's
salvation, it remains nonetheless true that the focal point of the mural of salvation painted by the biblical writers is occupied by humankind. Theologically, this is the consequence of what distinguishes the human creature from all
other creatures. Evolutionary biology, which might be thought to emphasize
more the sameness of *homo sapiens* in relation to other animals, nonetheless
allows for difference. From the perspective of the natural sciences, the distinguishing marks of the human person would include at least the following: the
development of consciousness; the capacity for human relatedness, including
individuality within community and the ability to consider the likely feelings
and thoughts of others; self-consciousness; and the capacity to make decisions
on the basis of self-deliberation and assessment of the possible outcomes of
the options considered, to plan and take action on the basis of those decisions, and to take responsibility for those decisions and actions.[6] Biologist
Francisco J. Ayala summarizes the defining elements of the human family
with reference to the human capacity for ethics—referring not to a particular
ethical schema, but rather to "the proclivity to judge human actions as either
good or evil"; cognitive scientist Warren S. Brown highlights the human capacity for and experience of rich, textured forms of personal relatedness.[7] As
Brown makes clear, however, such qualities as I have listed are not distinctive
of the human family, as though no such qualities were to be found among
nonhuman animals. It is, rather, that these capacities are present in the human family in ways that significantly exceed what is found among nonhuman
species. From the perspective of the Genesis account, human distinctiveness
is charted in terms of the creation of humankind in the image of God, human
"dominion" in relation to the rest of the world, and the call to obey God.

Humanity in Contemporary Perspective

How do we come to terms with a scriptural portrait of the human person? The first obstacle we face is that we already possess views of personhood
or the self. Our assumptions about what it means to be human are often

unacknowledged and are therefore taken for granted simply as the way things are. Accordingly, it is easy to find in the Bible reflections of our own views, particularly if we are unaware that they are just that, *our own views.*

For this reason, it may be helpful to describe first how many of us have learned to construct what it means to be human. In his penetrating analysis of contemporary human identity in the West, philosopher Charles Taylor finds that personal identity has come to be based on presumed affirmations of the human subject as autonomous, disengaged, self-sufficient, and self-engaged. It is true, of course, that Taylor's findings are more telling for some parts of the population than others; some of us come from more community-oriented subcultures. Joe M. Kapolyo reflects on what it means to be human from an African perspective, for example, and Ismael Garcia writes from a Hispanic context, and both lean toward priorities less interested in dividing an individual into social, physical, or spiritual "parts" and more concerned with life as an undivided unity; less concerned with thinking about human nature one person at a time and more concerned with communality, interdependence, and participation.[8] At the same time, we should observe that the cultural forces Taylor describes are powerful ones, so much so that even community-based peoples may find their numbers infiltrated, however slowly, by these alien norms.

For Taylor, the development of this account of personal identity in the West can be traced from Augustine in the fourth to fifth centuries, through the major European philosophers of the seventeenth and eighteenth centuries (e.g., Descartes, Locke, and Kant), into the present. What he finds is a "self defined by the powers of disengaged reason—with its associated ideals of self-responsible freedom and dignity—of self-exploration, and of personal commitment." These provide a launching point for our modern conception of "inwardness."[9] Modern identity is thus shaped by such assumptions as the following:

- human dignity lies in self-sufficiency and self-determination

- identity is grasped in self-referential terms: I am who I am

- persons have an inner self, which is the authentic self

- basic to authentic personhood are self-autonomy and self-legislation

The upshot of this is a portrait of the human person that can be understood, as it were, one person at a time, with an individual's interior life of cardinal importance.

Although Taylor does not major much on the idea of a human "soul," it is nonetheless interesting that the view of human identity he sketches is one cultivated easily in the metaphysical garden of a Plato or a Descartes. Taylor does identify the precondition for the modern emphasis on the human sense of the "authentic, inner person" in Plato's concept of the "soul" (ψυχή, *psychē*), however, and the Christian tradition has tended to agree.

Given this portrait of humanity, how might "salvation" be understood? Perhaps it is not surprising that views of the human person like these have tended to emphasize the personal decisions of individuals and to center on transformation of the "inner person." Consider the famous and influential definition of "conversion" put forward by William James:

> To be converted, to be regenerated, to receive grace, to experience religion, to gain an assurance, are so many phrases which denote the process, gradual or sudden, by which a self hitherto divided, and consciously wrong inferior and unhappy, becomes unified and consciously right superior and happy, in consequence of its firmer hold upon religious realities. This at least is what conversion signifies in general terms, whether or not we believe that a direct divine operation is needed to bring such a moral change about.[10]

Salvation, then, is the resolution of a person's inner, subjective crisis—with its emphasis on individual experience rather than corporate life (or people in relation to all of creation), just as the locus of religion is a feeling-based, interior experience. Following James, A. D. Nock's classic study of conversion reaches a similar conclusion: "By conversion we mean the reorientation of the soul of an individual, his deliberate turning from indifferent or from an earlier form of piety to another, a turning which involves a consciousness that a great change is involved, that the old was wrong and the new is right." Nock goes on to write of "a passion of willingness and acquiescence, which removes the feeling of anxiety, a sense of perceiving truths not known before, a sense of clean and beautiful newness within and without and an ecstasy of happiness."[11] What is needed in this case is a "change of heart." According to Francis Crick, who together with James Watson is responsible for deciphering the structure of DNA a half century ago, these ideas are focused in a religious belief held today by billions of human beings.[12] As we shall now see, though, there is little about this portrait of the human person, or the soteriology that it underwrites, that is particularly biblical.

7

What Is Humanity?

Recall the words about humanity in Genesis 1–2:

God created humanity in God's own image, in the divine image God created them, male and female God created them. God blessed them and said to them, "Be fertile and multiply; fill the earth and master it. Take charge of the fish of the sea, the birds of the sky, and everything crawling on the ground." Then God said, "I now give to you all the plants on the earth that yield seeds and all the trees whose fruit produces its seeds within it. These will be your food. To all wildlife, to all the birds of the sky, and to everything crawling on the ground—to everything that breathes—I give all the green grasses for food." And that's what happened. God saw everything he had made: it was supremely good. There was evening and there was morning: the sixth day. (1:27-31)

This is the account of the heavens and the earth when they were created. On the day the Lord God made earth and sky—before any wild plants appeared on the earth, and before any field crops grew, because the Lord God hadn't yet sent rain on the earth and there was still no human being to farm the fertile land, though a stream rose from the earth and watered all of the fertile land—the Lord God formed the human from the topsoil of the fertile land and blew life's breath into his nostrils. The human came to life. The Lord God planted a garden in Eden in the east and put there the human he had formed. In the fertile land, the Lord God grew every beautiful tree with edible fruit, and also he grew the tree of life in the middle of the garden and the tree of the knowledge of good and evil. . . . The Lord God took the human and settled him in the garden of Eden to farm it and to take care of it. The Lord God commanded the human, "Eat your fill from all of the garden's trees; but don't eat from the tree of the knowledge of good and evil, because on the day you eat from it, you will die!" Then the Lord God said, "It's not good that the human is alone. I will make him a helper that is perfect for him." So the Lord God formed from the fertile land all the wild animals and all the birds in the sky and brought them to the human to see what he would name them. The human gave each living being its name. The human named all the livestock, all the birds in the sky, and all the wild animals. But a helper perfect for him was nowhere to be found. So the Lord God put the human into a deep and heavy sleep, and took one of his ribs and closed up the flesh over it. With the rib taken from the human, the Lord God fashioned a woman and brought her to the human being. The human said, "This one finally is bone from my bones and flesh from my flesh. She will be called a woman because from a man she was taken." This is the reason that a man leaves his father and mother and embraces his wife, and they become one flesh. The two of them were naked, the man and his wife, but they weren't embarrassed. (2:4-25)

A close reading of these texts leads to two immediate and overarching affirmations, *continuity* and *difference*—the continuity of humanity with all other animals and, indeed, with the rest of creation; and the difference between humanity and other animals.

Broadly speaking, Christians have been quick to grasp the latter, slow to recognize the former. We prefer to locate the human being—ourselves—in a place of incontestable honor at the center of creation. As a result, we have found ourselves humbled by scientific discovery—in the modern age, first by Copernicus, who demonstrated that our planet and thus we who inhabit it are not the center around which the universe pivots; second, by Darwin and evolutionary biology, who located *homo sapiens* within the animal kingdom with a genetic makeup that strongly resembles the creatures around us; and third, more recently by the neurosciences, with their tightening of the mind-brain link, which renders more and more improbable the need for the concept of the human soul as a separate entity capable of its own, independent existence.[13] As theologian Wolfhart Pannenberg recognized, recent advances with regard to the close mutual interrelations of physical and psychological occurrences have raised serious questions in the face of traditional ideas of a soul distinct from the body that is detached from it in death. He inquires, "When the life of the soul is conditioned in every detail by bodily organs and processes, how can it be detached from the body and survive without it?"[14] Humans, according to the biblical account of beginnings, are clearly like other living things in being created by God and thus in their relation to him. Like them, humanity is formed from the stuff of the earth.

Moreover, the Genesis narrative presents the sexes in a relationship of mutuality, parity, and egalitarianism. The male and female are created together and share in the common role of "filling the earth" and serving as its stewards. With the language of "partnering," the narrative provides no rationale for hierarchy or other differences of status or role. Not even the term "helper," used in reference to woman in Genesis 2:18, suggests any notion of "subordination" or servility, since elsewhere in the Old Testament the term is used of God (e.g., Gen 49:25; Exod 18:4). In the same way, the Genesis account says nothing that would provide for the human exploitation of nature. Vegetation is for both humans and nonhuman animals (Gen 1:30), who share with humans the command to reproduce, increase, and fill the seas and the earth (Gen 1:22). The additional vocation given humanity, "to master"

9

the earth and "to take charge of" it (Gen 1:26, 28), should be understood in the context of a creation account in which there is no hint of either chaos or combat. True, the creation account imbues humanity with a regal identity and a royal task, but this is nobility granted without conquest; it is nobility worked out in coexistence with all life in the land, and in the cultivation of all life. Similarly, Psalm 8:7 portrays humanity in a stance of dominion over creation, as though standing over its defeated enemies, but lacking any suggestion of military action, invasion, or colonization. Manage and care without conquest or domination—the human family has this responsibility in relation to God's creation because this is how God has made us.

Thus are humans *like* other living things. They are also unlike all other living things in that humanity is made in God's image. Of all the creatures mentioned in Genesis 1–2, only humanity is created after God's own likeness, in God's own image *(imago Dei)*. Humanity alone receives from God this divine vocation.

Humanity in God's Image

"God created humanity in God's own image, in the divine image God created them" (Gen 1:27). The relative succinctness of this text from Genesis has presented a stumbling block to its interpreters, who grasp for insight from the larger context of Genesis 1 to clarify the nature of this "image." In fact, the *imago Dei* tradition has generated diverse interpretations among Jews and Christians—ranging widely from some physical characteristic of humans (such as standing upright) to a way of knowing (especially the human capacity to know God), and so on. Clearly, humanity is thus defined in relation to God in terms of both similarity and difference: Humanity is in some sense "like" God, but humanity itself is not divine. Humanity stands in an ambivalent position—living in solidarity with the rest of the created order and yet distinct from it on account of humankind's unique role as the bearer of the divine image, called to a particular and crucial relationship with Yahweh and yet not divine.[15]

What more can be said? Within its immediate setting in Genesis 1, "the divine image" in which humanity is made is related to the exercise of dominion over the earth on God's behalf. This only presses for further clarification, though, since we must then ascertain what it means to exercise dominion in this way, that is, in a way that reflects God's own ways of interaction with God's creatures. Additionally, a narrow emphasis on "taking charge" does not really grapple with the profound word God speaks over humanity and about humanity, namely, that human beings *in themselves* (and not merely in what they do) reflect God's image.

What is this quality that distinguishes humanity? The Christian tradition has often identified this quality with the human soul, as though the soul were the instantiation of God's image in the human creature. This view runs aground both exegetically and biologically. We turn to the exegetical question momentarily, but here might simply query how, given the findings of evolutionary biology, it is possible to imagine that members of the species *Homo sapiens* possess a "soul," but nonhuman animals do not. (And what about other, now-extinct members of the genus *Homo*, say, *Homo habilis* or *Homo neanderthalensis*? Did they possess the soul that distinguishes the human family from the rest of creation?) To the contrary, God's words in Genesis 1 affirm the creation of the human family first and foremost in its relation to himself, as his counterpart, so the nature of humanity derives from the human family's relatedness to God. God's image, then, is fundamentally relational (or covenantal), and takes as its ground and focus the graciousness of God's own covenantal relations with humanity and the rest of creation. The distinguishing mark of *human* existence when compared with other creatures is thus the whole of human existence (and not some "part" of the individual). Humanity is created uniquely in relationship to God and finds itself as a result of creation in covenant with God. Humanity is given the divine mandate to reflect God's own gracious love in relation with God, within the covenant community of all humanity, and with all that God has created.

The individual human person, by herself or himself, is not a reflection of the Godhead, as though the human person were complete in herself or himself. God's words at the creation of humankind are spoken not over a human person, but over אָדָם, *adam*, that is, over humanity, the entire human family. According to Genesis 1:26-27, God (singular) created humanity (singular) as women and men (plural); God created humanity (singular) as a "them" (plural). In Christian terms, then, we reflect the community of the Triune God not so much as individuals but as the human community, whose life is differentiated from and yet bound up with nature, and whose common life springs from and finds its purpose (or *telos*) in God's embrace.

The Divine Image Elsewhere in Scripture

Outside of Genesis, creation in God's image is barely mentioned in scripture. On this basis, we might imagine that this affirmation has had or should have little influence on the faith of God's people. From the standpoint of a theological reading of the Bible as a whole, however, we should not underestimate the importance of Genesis 1. Study of narratives in general has emphasized the importance of beginnings for the way they establish the concerns, needs, and parameters within which the subsequent story can develop. From this narratival perspective, the creation of humanity in the divine image, and the recounting of this reality in the opening chapter of the Bible, is crucial for the way it sets out for the whole of scripture, and for the whole of life, the cornerstone presupposition of all reflection on humanity. In ancient buildings the cornerstone was cut to a true 90-degree angle and was used to align the rest of the foundation stones to ensure that the building would be solidly built and would endure. With the metaphor of a "cornerstone presupposition," then, I mean to draw attention to how the divine image determines how humanity is to be measured, so to speak. It establishes at the outset of the biblical narrative the peculiar "need" for humans to realize their humanity as bearers of God's image. The being and doing of humans throughout scripture, and subsequently, is thus to be measured by this single standard: whether and/or to what degree humans fulfill their vocation to bear the divine image. Creation in the divine image thus entails gift and vocation, identity and call.

The nature of humanity is tied to God's image also in Genesis 5:1-3; 9:5-6, Psalm 8, and in two New Testament texts, 1 Corinthians 11:7 and James 3:9. That this affirmation can be found after Genesis 3, traditionally taken as the account of humanity's "fall," is especially important, because this means that the introduction of sin does not result in the disinheritance of the rest of humanity from its defining quality, creation "in God's own image." In James 3, the writer seems to shake his head in disbelief at the way humans use their tongues: "With it we both bless the Lord and Father and curse human beings made in God's likeness." This text suggests the degree to which the identity of humanity as bearers of the divine image lies in the background of biblical faith more generally. It also draws a straight line from our actions toward one another to our behavior toward God; in other words, the theological affirmation of the creation of humanity in the divine image is a basic datum in ethical reflection.[16] And it reminds us that creation in God's image is a theological statement about the whole of humanity—and not only regarding those who lived "in the beginning" nor those who would later be called out as God's people, Israel. Inside and outside Israel, inside and outside the church, we encounter people, all of whom are created "in God's own image."

The language of "God's image" is also used of humanity in other Jewish texts from the Second Temple period, and, in the New Testament, preeminently of Jesus Christ. In the New Testament, Paul's thought is closest to the interpretation of the *imago Dei* expressed in the Wisdom of Solomon. The phrase is used there with reference to the actual expression of God's image in a human life rather than to human capacity or potential. Paul goes on to develop the motif of Christ as God's image (2 Cor 4:4; Col 1:15; cf. Phil 2:6) and, as its corollary, the conformation of human beings into Christ's image (Rom 8:29; 1 Cor 15:49; 2 Cor 3:18). One might say on this basis that Christology is first anthropology, since we find in Christ the measure of authentic personhood.

What about the "Soul"?

The affirmation of human beings as bearers of the divine image in Genesis, together with the interpretation of the *imago Dei* tradition at the hands of Paul, points unquestionably to the uniqueness of humanity when compared with all other creatures. However, this tradition does not locate this singularity in the human possession of a "soul." Instead, it emphasizes the human capacity and call to relate to Yahweh in covenant and to join in companionship within the human family and in relation to the whole earth in ways that reflect God's loving-kindness.

Admittedly, the Christian tradition has often tied human uniqueness to the soul, a theological move that depends on the prior identification of "God's image" with the human "soul." In the English-speaking world, this decision may appear to be supported by Genesis 2:7, which reads in the Authorized Version as follows: "And the Lord God formed man of the dust of the ground, and breathed into his nostrils the breath of life; and man became a living soul." That last word, "soul," is a translation of the Hebrew term נֶפֶשׁ, *nepeš*, which is the same term used only a few verses earlier with reference to "every beast of the earth," "every fowl of the air," and "every thing that creepeth upon the earth," that is, to everything "wherein there is life *(nepeš)*" (Gen 1:30, again following the AV). Interestingly, however, this observation alone demonstrates that "soul" is not for the Genesis story a unique characteristic of the human person, since the same term is used both of humanity and of all wildlife. Accordingly, one might better translate Genesis 2:7 with reference to the divine gift of life: "the human being became fully alive" (my translation), or "the human came to life" (CEB).

In the first-century world of Roman antiquity, it was not the New Testament writers who identified God's image with the human soul but the Alexandrian Jew Philo. Working with language and categories inspired by Plato, Philo identified the "rational soul" with the human mind, separate from the human body. Working under the assumption that Moses authored the book of Genesis, Philo writes of Genesis 1:

> Accordingly, the great Moses has not spoken of the rational soul as it resembled in its species any created thing, but he has called it the image of the divine and invisible God, looking upon it to be a glorious and carefully wrought image, the seal of God, the character of which is the everlasting Word; for, says he, "God breathed into his face the breath of life." (*Concerning Noah's Work as a Planter* 2.5 §§18-19, LCL)

How does Philo reach this conclusion? He thinks of the creation of the human being as having occurred in two stages: Genesis 1:26-27 reports the creation of the invisible, immortal person (i.e., the human soul), whereas Genesis 2:7 reports the creation of the visible, mortal human being (i.e., the human body). In hindsight, it seems obvious that Philo puts forward this reading in order to make the creation story intelligible to others like himself who were nurtured in the philosophical world that we now call Middle Platonism. Accordingly, it is fascinating that (1) this reading spread into the early church where it would have a remarkably far-reaching influence on Christian understanding of the human person, even though (2) this reading is difficult to square with what the text of Genesis actually says.[17]

Genesis does not define humanity in essentialist terms, as though the important question had to do with a human's "parts," the metaphysical essences that make up a human. This question was important to Greek philosophy and to the major philosophical schools in the Roman Empire, and it would occupy the spotlight again in Descartes's work; however, this question is not the driving concern behind the creation material in Genesis 1–2. There we find humanity understood above all in relational terms, identifying the human family foremost as Yahweh's partner, and then identifying the communal, intersexual character of personhood, the quality of care the human family is to exercise with regard to the earth as God's representative, and the unassailable vocation of humans to reflect in their relationships God's own character.

Painting the Human Person

Recall the human qualities that Taylor identified in his exploration of *Sources of the Self:* human individuality and autonomy, and the nature of the individual as self-legislating, self-sufficient, and self-engaged. How might this compare with the portrait that emerges from scripture? Were we to summarize what we find in the Genesis story of humanity's origins, and add to it central emphases found throughout the Old Testament, we might compile a list that looks like this one, proposed by Robert A. Di Vito:

- the construction of the self as ineluctably nested in social relationships and, then, the importance of relational interdependence for human life and identity

- a premium on the health and integrity of the human community

- the assumption that a person *is* one's behavior—that is, that one's deepest commitments are unavoidably exhibited in one's practices—so that attention focuses on "embodied life," disallowing the possibility that the "real" person might be relegated to one's interior life

- the call to live out the human vocation as this is drawn from a vision of Yahweh's own character, God's "difference" (or holiness) in relation to the cosmos[18]

If human beings were to reject their identity and vocation as humans expressed in these terms, and thus be found in need of restoration to their true selves, what would salvation look like? What soteriology might result? Given widespread views of the human person in the modern West, salvation refers especially to a person's interior life, to one's capacity to enter into and enjoy a relationship with God; moreover, salvation is often taken as the means by which the human "self" is able to cross over the bridge between this life and the next. By way of contrast, the portrait of human nature we have seen thus far from scripture would support soteriological interests in human restoration to covenantal relationship to God, recovery of human community in its vitality, and the reintegration of one's self as a person fully embodied in relation to others and to the world in which life with and before God might be lived.

Again, the need for salvation articulated in these terms would arise *if* humanity were to reject the gift of its particularity as bearers of the divine image and its call to be fully human. What happens as we turn the page in the narrative of human beginnings in Genesis?

The "Fall" and the Human Situation

Within the good order of creation, God had carved out a space for Adam, a Garden, within which "the LORD God grew every beautiful tree with edible fruit." Here, too, grew the tree of life and the tree of the knowledge of good

15

and evil (Gen 2:8-9). This is the Garden from which, by the end of Genesis 3, the man and woman will have been expelled. The chain of encounters leading to expulsion has attracted interpretations of all kinds, from theologically laden analyses of "the fall" to Sigmund Freud's assessment that the latent content of Genesis 3 concerns an adolescent's erotic attachment to his mother's affections (i.e., the Oedipus complex).[19] Our interest falls on the ramifications of this account for the unfolding story of humanity and its significance for the journey of salvation.

A Snake in the Garden

Genesis 3 opens as follows:

> The snake was the most intelligent of all the wild animals that the LORD God had made. He said to the woman, "Did God really say that you shouldn't eat from any tree in the garden?" The woman said to the snake, "We may eat the fruit of the garden's trees but not the fruit of the tree in the middle of the garden. God said, 'Don't eat from it, and don't touch it, or you will die.'" The snake said to the woman, "You won't die! God knows that on the day you eat from it, you will see clearly and you will be like God, knowing good and evil." The woman saw that the tree was beautiful with delicious food and that the tree would provide wisdom, so she took some of its fruit and ate it, and also gave some to her husband, who was with her, and he ate it. Then they both saw clearly and knew that they were naked. So they sewed fig leaves together and made garments for themselves. During that day's cool evening breeze, they heard the sound of the LORD God walking in the garden; and the man and his wife hid themselves from the LORD God in the middle of the garden's trees. The LORD God called to the man and said to him, "Where are you?" (Gen 3:1-9)

The terms of the temptation faced by the woman in the Garden are startling. First, in representing God as forbidding the consumption of any of the Garden's fruit, the snake engages in a ridiculous exaggeration. If they could not eat, how could they survive? Second, the snake proposes that partaking of a particular tree will transpose humans into being "like God." Yet, as bearers of the divine image, humankind is already "like God." This strongly suggests that the snake has put forward an alternative, and misleading, concept of God. Indeed, the very presence of the snake, one of the wild beasts (Gen 2:19-20), in the Garden, a place of ordered, domesticated habitation, together with his opening characterization as one who engages in premeditated scheming (Gen 3:1), urges that we hear his claims as ill formed, deceptive, out of place. Third, what the woman sees is a tree "beautiful with delicious food" (Gen 3:6), yet the man and woman already inhabit a world surrounded by "every beautiful tree with edible fruit" (Gen 2:9). These three points help us focus on the snake's two-pronged portrayal of the character of God and what it means "to be like God": "You will see clearly and you will be like God, knowing good and evil" (Gen 3:5). It may be startling to discover that the words spoken by the snake have some truth about them; having eaten of the fruit of the forbidden tree, "they both saw clearly" (Gen 3:7), just as the snake predicted.

This is the point in the story where things begin to unravel, since the wisdom promised by the snake and desired by the man and woman is not the wisdom that resides in life before Yahweh. Rather than becoming gods, the man and woman become aware of their nakedness—a condition signifying in the biblical and later Jewish traditions the gravest dishonor (see 2 Sam 6:20; Rev 16:15). Clearly, being "like God" in the sense promised by the snake was not as they had expected.

The snake led the woman to consider the apparent arbitrariness of God's prohibition regarding the tree in the middle of the Garden, and proposed that the life God set before them was deficient in some important way. Partaking of the fruit, they would begin their apotheosis, their heavenly journey, their divinization. At its center, the temptation they faced and into which they entered was a denial of their creaturely status before God, the gift of their nobility within creation and the vocation to be human in dependence on God. The ensuing narrative is overtaken with references in the first person—"I," "I," "I"—documenting a tragic crescendo of self-aggrandizement, self-legislation, self-orientation, and self-dependence. The alluring fruit morphs into bitter disappointment. With their newfound enlightenment, they are newly introduced to a need they had not previously known, their need for a covering for their nakedness, their shame.

Genesis 3 introduces into the biblical narrative no particular vocabulary of sin, such as "disobedience" or "transgression" or "doing evil," but the concept of sin is very much on display. Sin is portrayed as the use of God's good gift of freedom of decision to decide against God. Old Testament theologian H. D. Preuss adds that sin is here "understood as the failure to recognize the authority of God and as preferring to discuss the divine word rather than observe it"—perhaps to deflect its applicability to themselves or to question its fairness or goodness. This behavior is the denial of human responsibility to God, the willful attempt for humans to make themselves lord of their own lives.[20]

Sin, the Human Epidemic

What are the outcomes of this misrepresentation of the divine command, this disobedience to Yahweh, this denial of the place of the human in the cosmos? Reading the story that unfolds is like watching interlaced rows of dominoes fall or the ripples in a pool after a rock is dropped into it. First, sin proves to be contagious, with sin leading to sin, from one sinner to the next (Gen 3:6). The human couple learns shame and vulnerability, leading not to efforts at reconciliation with God but to further alienation, even to the point of hiding from Yahweh's presence. In Psalm 8, God's attention to the human family is astonishing but welcome. To humanity in the Garden, however, Yahweh's voice seems menacing. Having refused to heed Yahweh's voice regarding the tree (Gen 2:17), they now hear that voice differently, not as an invitation to relationship but as a threat. Moreover, the woman and man both learn to deflect responsibility—the man blaming the woman, the woman the snake; they now regard themselves as victims of others' influence. Alienation extends from the human-divine relationship to all forms of relatedness, between persons and between humankind and the whole earth. Thus far, Genesis has held in balance a liberal dose of human freedom to organize the world in relation to God's creatures with the vocation set before humanity by God. Human self-determination destroys that balance, leading to a freedom that exceeds its grasp and a harmony set aside in favor of struggle, hierarchy, and drudgery.[21]

What is lost in the Garden, then, is the humanness of humanity. Lost is the fullness of what it means genuinely to be human in the context of the ordered creation within and in relation to which God has formed the human creature. As a result, in a very real (though perhaps unexpected) sense, the woman's prediction, that partaking of the fruit of the forbidden tree would result in death (Gen 3:3), was realized. This is because, in Israel's scriptures, death is never a phenomenon focused merely on biological cessation, but marks especially the severance of all relationships—relationships with God and with every person and with everything in the cosmos. This is why Ray Anderson can observe that "death is a threat to personhood, not merely a fact of natural life."[22]

Genesis 3 is only the beginning, however. The narrative goes on to enumerate one episode of sin and alienation after another. Cain's murderous act results in his exile (Gen 4:1-16); a restless, godless society emerges (Gen 4:17-24; 5:28-29); global violence leads to global destruction (Gen 6:1-9:18); sin among Noah's family leads to the enslavement of one people by another (Gen 9:17-27); and, finally, humanity is implicated in the imperialism of conquest, giving rise to a tower made to touch the heavens (Gen 11).[23] Sin even of this magnitude cannot irreparably mar the divine purpose in creation, however. Even the words of God spoken to a rebellious humanity on the plains of Shinar, construction zone of the infamous Tower of Babel, are nothing less than a reiteration of Yahweh's words in creation, to multiply and spread throughout the whole earth (Gen 1:28; 9:7; 11:6-9). Here in the opening chapters of Genesis, therefore, we find the basic pattern of the ongoing saga: God acts and speaks; humanity refuses its vocation, responds in disobedience, and experiences the consequences of its sin; God acts and speaks again, now in forgiveness and reconciliation.

Tracing the story from Genesis into the rest of the Old Testament, we discover that sin has infiltrated human existence. This is not because sin is hereditary. In fact, sin's etiology is typically not a matter of speculation, though there is occasional reference to the fountainhead of human weakness (e.g., Job 4:20; 25:6; Pss 78:38-39; 103:13-14). More common is the rehearsal of those simple words associated with David's own confession, following his transgression of the law against adultery: "I've sinned" (2 Sam 12:13);[24] or by the people at signal points of turning back to God: "We've sinned."[25] New Testament witnesses agree with this emphasis on the universality of sin. "All have sinned and fall short of the glory of God" (Rom 3:23), Paul writes, and, according to the Gospels of Matthew and Luke, Jesus teaches his followers, all of them, to pray for forgiveness of sins (Matt 6:12; Luke 11:4). Given the breadth of the notion of "conversion" in the ancient Roman world, to signal a moving deeper into one's own religion as well as to embrace a new religion,[26] the universality of sin is highlighted too by the call to repentance, set before Jews and Gentiles alike in the missionary preaching of Acts (e.g., Acts 2:38; 17:30).

In Need of Salvation: New Testament Voices

Enough of the story has been told that we can sense something of the anguish in Ezra's voice as he contemplates the human dilemma, "Adam, what have you done?" That these words are written in a Jewish text from the end of the New Testament era suggests their relevance for our reading of the New Testament, though it must be admitted that the New Testament writers rarely put things in just this way. In the Gospels, for example, Adam is mentioned only once, in the record of Jesus' genealogy in Luke 3:8, not to draw attention to Adamic sin but to emphasize Jesus' solidarity with all humanity. In the New Testament, apart from letters attributed to Paul, Adam is otherwise mentioned only in the letter of Jude, and then only to provide an anchor for situating Enoch chronologically (v. 14). If not in terms of Adam, how do the New Testament materials reflect on the nature of sin and its relation to the need for salvation?

Mark's Gospel

We can allow the Gospel of Mark to introduce two important claims regarding the human dilemma shared more widely in the New Testament. First, for Mark's Gospel, the key players in the drama of salvation include more than God and human beings; Satan and his minions are also at work. Immediately after Jesus' baptism, he is tempted by Satan (Mark 1:12-13). Satan works against those who hear the good news (Mark 4:15), and one of Jesus' own disciples can serve as the mouthpiece of diabolic patterns of thinking about Jesus' messianic career (Mark 8:32-33). Demons or evil spirits can dominate people, rendering them helpless or uncontrollable, even to the point of self-harm (e.g., Mark 1:21-28, 32; 5:1-20; 7:24-30; 9:14-29). Whatever else might be said of God's saving initiative, then, it must address cosmic powers of evil. It is critical that Mark portrays Jesus' encounter with the demonized not as a struggle for power but as a demonstration of Jesus' authority. After all, Jesus is God's anointed king (that is, the Messiah), God's Son (Mark 1:1), whose arrival marks the decisive disclosure of God's authoritative rule and the debunking of all false rules and rulers. This means that Jesus' ministry is one of dispelling the reach of Satan's domain; in fact, responding to the charge that Jesus is in league with the prince of demons, Jesus casts his entire ministry as an assault on Satan's authority (Mark 3:22-26).

References to the devil and his lackeys appear throughout the New Testament. The book of Revelation is particularly interesting in this regard, since it makes clear that this-worldly authorities, powers, and institutions working at cross-purposes with God's saving agenda are actually animated by "the great dragon," that "old snake, who is called the devil and Satan, the deceiver of the whole world" (Rev 12:9; see especially Rev 13). What is transparent in Revelation is also evident in Paul's letters and in 1 Peter. In their lists of "thrones," "rulers," "authorities," and "powers,"[27] these letters unveil the spiritual dimension of what we might otherwise have imagined are the mundane social and political configurations of influence and control—systems, institutions, social rules, and cultural practices—that seem to govern our lives, and not always for the better. For Paul and Peter, these "authorities" occupy a place on a continuum between their enfleshment in human beings and institutions and their autonomous existence as disembodied heavenly beings (e.g., angels and demons). These creatures breathe life into and influence social structures and organizations with malevolent capacities and aims. Accordingly, the Gospels can speak of competing kingdoms, God's versus the devil's (e.g., Luke 4:5-6, 43), and Paul can refer to the actions of "the god of this age" (2 Cor 4:4).

First, then, for Mark, the drama of salvation includes more than God and human beings. Second, Mark's Gospel opens by recalling Israel's salvation, understood in terms of Israel's restoration from exile, the fulfillment of Isaiah's expectation of God's kingdom (Mark 1:1-15). Mark grounds "the good news about Jesus Christ, God's Son" in Isaiah (Mark 1:1-3, combining language from Isa 40:3-5; Exod 23:20; Mal 3:1). He also encapsulates the whole of the preface to his Gospel with references to "good news" (Mark 1:1, 14-15), embedding the story of Jesus in Isaiah's announcement of good news: "Here is your God!" (Isa 40:9) and "Your God rules!" (Isa 52:7). This is significant above all for the way it ties Jesus' ministry into Israel's life as this is known in the Old Testament and Second Temple literature. Mark thus shows how Jesus' ministry signals the actualization of Israel's anticipated new exodus.[28] It is also significant for the way it shapes our reading of John the Baptist's ministry, with its emphasis on human repentance and confession of sins, and God's forgiveness of sins (Mark 1:4-5). Israel's exile was broadly understood as the result of Israel's sin, particularly the sin of idolatry. Return from exile, then, would require the renewal of the relationship between God and God's people. Against this backdrop, the phrase "forgiveness of sins" is another way of saying "end of exile": God has acted to restore God's people and in faith God's people have embraced God's royal authority.

The importance of this motif elsewhere in the New Testament is easy to document, though typically in hindsight. That is, New Testament texts do not so much refer to Israel's dilemma as one of exile as they might refer to salvation as God's decisive act to restore God's people. For example, Matthew 1:1-17 organizes Jesus' ancestry around the exile, leading to the climactic announcement that Mary's baby is to be called Jesus "because he will save his people from their sins" (Matt 1:21). In Luke's birth account, Zechariah presents the work of Jesus in terms reminiscent of exodus:

> Bless the Lord God of Israel because he has come to help and has delivered his people. He has raised up a mighty savior for us in his servant David's house, just as he said through the mouths of his holy prophets long ago. He has brought salvation from our enemies and from the power of all those who hate us. He has shown the mercy promised to our ancestors, and remembered his holy covenant, the solemn pledge he made to our ancestor Abraham. He has

21

granted that we would be rescued from the power of our enemies so that we could serve him without fear, in holiness and righteousness in God's eyes, for as long as we live. (Luke 1:68-75)

The perspective of Luke-Acts is also important for the way it uses phrases like "forgiveness of sins," "the resurrection," and "the hope of Israel" to make explicit the ripple effect of Israel's restoration to include good news for Gentiles as well (e.g., Luke 24:46-49; Acts 4:2; 28:20). Restoration from exile lies in the background of Romans 8 and Galatians 3–4, and both 1 Peter and James characterize their audiences as God's restored people who nonetheless remain in exile as they wait for the glorious return of the Lord Jesus (e.g., Jas 1:1; 1 Pet 1:1-2).[29]

Reverberations of the exodus tradition in Mark's Gospel help to emphasize the situation in which God's people find themselves and, by way of implication, their need for God to act mightily and decisively to bring about a new exodus. Consider, for example, references to people as hard-hearted (Mark 3:5; 6:52; 8:17). This phrase depends on an ancient psychology that locates emotions, understanding, and volition in the heart so that it could explain why people fail to understand or they resist the truth. The classic illustration of an unyielding heart is found in the exodus story. Egypt's pharaoh resisted God's purpose for the Israelites on account of his hard heart, a condition that resulted from both his own choices and God's sovereignty (e.g., Exod 4:21; 8:15). The phrase is also used of Israel, however (e.g., Ps 95:8). To mix metaphors, we can say that in Mark's narrative hardness of heart refers above all to a lack of perception. This is consistent with Mark's accounts of blindness and recovery of sight (8:22-25; 10:46-52). Working at two levels at once, these texts underscore the character of Jesus' healing ministry and identify the need among God's people for salvation, symbolized now as illumination (cf. Isa 40:5; 52:8).

Otherwise, the vocabulary of sin is not used much in Mark's Gospel. In Mark 2:1-12, forgiveness of sins and healing are correlated. In Second Temple Judaism, sickness or illness was sometimes, though not necessarily, understood to have been caused by sin; always, though, God was the ultimate source of healing.[30] In Mark 2:15-17, Jesus dines with tax collectors and sinners, then draws a three-part analogy: He is like a physician, the righteous are like the healthy, and sinners are like the sick. Using the terms of the analogy, Jesus announces that he has "come to call not the righteous but sinners." Given Old Testament texts like Hosea 6:6, Jesus' statement is probably an indication of priority rather than negation: "I have come primarily to call

sinners," we might paraphrase.[31] Here "sinners" refers to those who live on society's margins, outside the community of God's people, on account of their
failure to keep Torah and, as in this case, because of their association with
outsiders like those despised tax collectors. Mark 14:41 is similar in its use of
the term "sinners" as a stand-in for those who live apart from Torah, that is,
Gentiles. In these texts, we find little reflection on the human situation per se,
though we do recognize that the cosmic and corporate dimensions of human
need introduced in Mark 1 (see above) reach into the nooks and crannies of
the day-to-day lives of individuals. We might anticipate, then, that salvation
must be similarly wholistic in its cosmic, corporate, and personal aspects.

The only attempt to identify the origin of sin in Mark's Gospel comes in
Jesus' instructions to his disciples concerning what contaminates a person in
God's sight. Regarding purity rules, the Pharisees and legal experts in Mark's
Gospel emphasize washing hands, cooking and eating utensils, and sleeping
mats (Mark 7:3-4). By way of contrast, Jesus emphasizes the human heart:
"It's from the inside, from the human heart, that evil thoughts come: sexual
sins, thefts, murders, adultery, greed, evil actions, deceit, unrestrained immorality, envy, insults, arrogance, and foolishness. All these evil things come
from the inside and contaminate a person in God's sight" (Mark 7:21-23).
We can identify in this passage three important structural features: (1) references to "evil intentions" (or "thoughts") and "evil things" bracket the list
(Mark 7:21, 23); (2) Jesus remarks twice that sins come "from inside" a person (Mark 7:21, 23), then defines "the inside" as "the heart" (Mark 7:21); and
(3) the list itself begins and ends with sins associated in Jewish tradition with
rejection of God: "sexual sins," often collocated with idolatry (Mark 7:21),
and "foolishness," that is, the prideful rejection of God (Mark 7:22).[32] Jesus'
teaching about sin does not focus on Jews in particular, or on Jewish religious
practices per se. Instead, he absorbs the Pharisees and legal experts' concerns
into a universal claim about humans, Jew and Gentile: Sin arises from the
center of a person's understanding and will, and the principal sin, the one that
gives rise to the rest, is rejection of God in favor of other gods. This means
that humans are responsible for their own evil designs and behaviors.

James

We find in the letter of James a related approach to the etiology of sin.
From a wide-angle perspective, we may observe, first, James's interest in cata-
loging sinful patterns of thinking and acting—partiality, for example, or faith
that does not express itself in faithful activity (Jas 2). The basic problem for

James is double-mindedness (Jas 1:8; 4:8). People try to have it both ways, as though they could be friends with the world and friends with God at the same time, forgetting that, in the ancient world, "friendship" signified unity of heart and mind. In the words of the Roman philosopher Cicero (106–43 BCE), friendship is "nothing other than the agreement over all things divine and human along with good will and affection" (*On Friendship* 6.20). Accordingly, double-mindedness is tantamount to unfaithfulness, or adultery: "You unfaithful people! Don't you know that friendship with the world makes you an enemy of God?" (Jas 4:4).

Focusing our lens more tightly, the opening verses of James 1 identify the human dilemma in terms of two distinct responses to the pressures of living as God's people in a world unfriendly to God's ways. Those who stand firm reach maturity and lack nothing; they are "blessed," they are "tried and true," and will receive God's reward of life (Jas 1:2-4, 12). Others embrace their own cravings, though, and this leads to sin and death (Jas 1:14-15). James locates the opportunity to sin, then, at the intersection of human response:

$$\text{Endurance} \rightarrow \text{Genuineness} \rightarrow \text{Life}$$

$$\nearrow$$

$$\text{Evil things} \rightarrow \text{Testing/Temptation}$$

$$\searrow$$

$$\text{Craving} \rightarrow \text{Sin} \rightarrow \text{Death}$$

We should note that, for James, "craving" or "desire" is not the neutral term sometimes associated with modern reflection on human sin. Patricia A. Williams, for example, writes from a sociobiological perspective about how, in the absence of natural controls, desire can morph into "inordinate desire": "Only inordinate or inappropriate desires can be sinful. Inordinate and inappropriate desires spring from natural ones that become distended and distorted in various ways and for various reasons."[33] As in moral discourse more generally, "desire" for James has the sense of "evil desire." In fact, in James 1:14, James has metaphorically associated "craving" or "desire" with powerful enticements: an irresistible lure for snagging fish and an overwhelmingly seductive woman.[34]

Elsewhere, James unveils what is at stake by laying out the cosmic context within which human responses arise. The tongue is like "a small flame" that can "set a whole forest on fire," but "the tongue itself is set on fire by the flames of hell" (Jas 3:5-6). And the command to "resist the devil" (Jas 4:7) makes sense only in a context in which it is assumed that the devil is active in human affairs. God, however, is the giver of all good gifts, of everything we need (Jas 1:5, 17). Two kinds of wisdom are available—from above ("pure, and then peaceful, gentle, obedient, filled with mercy and good actions, fair, and genuine") and from below ("natural and demonic," "jealousy and self-ish ambition," "disorder and . . . evil") (Jas 3:15-17). Situated in this cosmic arena, humans have two paths before them, but their proclivities are shaped by what the wider Jewish tradition referred to as the evil inclination.[35] It is "craving," this evil inclination, that gives rise to the double-mindedness with which James is concerned.

"Craving" is not the sum of the human situation for James, however. Tucked away in his brief treatise on the tongue is an indictment that is at the same time tragic and hopeful: "No one can tame the tongue, though. It is a restless evil, full of deadly poison. With it we both bless the Lord and Father and curse human beings made in God's likeness" (Jas 3:8-9). As in Genesis 9:6, the formation of humans in the divine image entails a moral imperative, in this case, against cursing human beings. That we might curse those who with us share in God's image is tragic; that sinful proclivities do not evacu-ate God's likeness from the human family recommends against a posture of despair, even if James says little about how people, left to their own devices, might step outside of their evil inclinations.[36]

To summarize James's logic, the demands of exilic life open possibilities for uninhibited human craving, the result of which is sin and death. The problem does not lie in exilic life itself, however, nor can one place before God or the devil the blame for unbearable temptations. The problem is in-ternal, not external, to the human person; as John Wesley discerned, "We are therefore to look for the cause of every sin, *in*, not *out of*, ourselves."[37]

Romans

Within the thirteen New Testament letters attributed to Paul, sin comes under the microscope especially in Romans. In these letters, "sin" (ἁμαρτία, *hamartia*) appears sixty-four times—thirty-nine in Romans and thirty in Ro-mans 5–7. The verb "to sin" (ἁμαρτάνω, *hamartanō*) occurs fourteen times in Paul's letters, six in Romans and four in Romans 5–7. And the adjective "sinful," or in its substantival form "sinner" (ἁμαρτωλός, *hamartōlos*), ap-pears eight times in the Pauline letters, four in Romans and three in Romans 5–7. Clearly, then, the apostle's vocabulary of "sin" congregates above all in these three chapters of Romans.

What is most remarkable about Paul's understanding of "sin" in these texts is that it has less to do with what humans do and more to do with a power that is itself active. Sin "entered the world" (5:12), where it exercised power like a master or king. For example:

- we were "slaves to sin" (6:6, 16, 17-18, 20)

- sin wants to "rule your body" (6:12)

- sin would use your body "as weapons to do wrong" (6:13)

For Paul, sin is like a power that must be overcome. For this reason, whether in Romans or elsewhere, Paul is little concerned with "forgiveness of sins" (see Rom 4:7; Eph 1:17; Col 1:14). If sin is a slave-master, people do not need to be forgiven; they need to be freed.

Earlier, Paul had spoken of sin's ubiquity—what we might call "original sin"—while contrasting the deeds of Adam and Christ (5:12-21). Paul's explanation is reminiscent of what we found earlier in 4 Ezra (as well as other Jewish texts from the Second Temple period[38]): sin is like a communal virus that spreads to everyone, with the result that everyone is implicated in sin (cf. 3:23). Following a mistranslation of the phrase ἐφ' ᾧ (*eph' hō*), some have imagined that the entire human family sinned in the one person Adam ("in whom all sinned"). Typically, though, the Greek phrase in question is taken as a marker of cause, leading to the translation "because all sinned" (e.g., NET, NIV, NRSV).[39] That is, Paul's affirmation of sin's universality derives from his view that Adam's sin set in motion a chain of effects, one sin marching forward to the next, not because sin is integral to the human condition but because all humanity followed Adam in his sinfulness. Paradoxically, then, human sinfulness is a sign of both human helplessness and culpability, so the power of sin as the author of human behavior is not a manifestation of human perversity but of human frailty.[40]

Does portraying "sin" in almost personal terms as a taskmaster negate human choice and culpability? Since Paul regards human beings as responsible for their behavior, his position acknowledges the human freedom to choose. At some theoretical level, we might suppose, sin remains an option, a road that need not be taken. But what sort of choice is this? If the human family, globally and historically, has embraced sin and consequently has been given over by God to further sin (1:18-32), what range of options remains genuinely open to us? If the values and practices honored in the universe of our lives (that is, the ideals and modes of conduct that characterize our world's systems and institutions) are set in opposition to God's ways,[41] then the pull of sin's gravity does actually seem to be inescapable. Genuine choice can come only in the context of authentic options, and this highlights the importance for Paul of proclamation and community. Another vision of the world is needed, one that reminds us that rebellion in Eden may be our common heritage but not necessarily our defining influence. Here, we are invited to community life oriented toward resisting evil and sin and to practices of faith, hope, and love that remind both church and world that we were created for more than this.

For Paul, sin is a refusal to acknowledge one's creaturely status before God, a refusal to glorify God as God, a refusal fully on display in Adam's refusal to heed God's prohibition to self-indulgence (1:18-32). Pursuing wisdom apart from God, knowledge apart from life, humans exchange creature for creator, engage in idolatry, and journey down a road that leads to a form of existence that can only be labeled as "subhuman." This is an important point, for it is easy today to imagine that participation in sin is a natural part of our lives. "We are only human," after all, or so we are told. Long ago, however, Tertullian observed the oxymoron in the idea of "natural sinfulness": "The corruption of nature is another nature" (*De anima* 41; *ANF* 3:220). Sinful humanity is human nature "reversed."[42] Even when sin seems our natural companion, sinfulness is actually a denial of that humanity to which we are called.

At the same time, our experience is that sinfulness is inherent to our self-awareness and seems to flow out of "the way the world is." Here we look into the mirror of the paradox of our humanity. Here we see God's pronouncement over our creation that humanity is "supremely good," imbued with the vocation of nobility in relation to the earth. And yet there is also the sobering recognition of our limits and proclivity to expressions of evil, socially and personally. Reflecting backward on his own rise to power as an officer in the Soviet army, the Nobel prizewinner Aleksandr Solzhenitsyn wrote, "Pride grows in the human heart like lard on a pig"—this, as he came to realize that the demonic system that robbed him of so much of his life, that left him cruelly imprisoned, was not an invention of Soviet Russia but the progeny of the human heart.[43] And yet the witness of the Genesis text also embraces humanity in God's own work of creation and caring. Just because Adam and Eve were expelled from the Garden does not mean that the Garden should not continue to help define our reason for being, our vocation, the world toward which we orient our lives. We were made for more than this.

Yet, this is not often our experience. We easily find ourselves on a staircase spiraling downward from one landing to the next, each a new expression of sin's mastery in our lives. Theologian Ted Peters names seven of these.[44]

The first is *anxiety*, the fear of loss and especially the fear of losing ourselves, ultimately in death. We experience anxiety as the "sting of death" in our lives and combat it with illusions of immortality. We want to deny death, that is, to deny that we have limitations, that our abilities and even our existence has boundaries. The temptation to "be like God" is rooted here, in our unwillingness simply and fully to be human, to be creatures whose lives are finite and dependent on God.

The second is *unfaith*, the failure to trust. Failing to trust God, we refuse to live in his care and assume we must care for ourselves. We find that we are unable to trust our neighbors, whose own existence is troublesome to us, not least when their lives interrupt our own or when their success or failures threaten us. Like gods, we control our own lives, mirroring the whims of the mythical gods of old, manipulating people and events to our own ends.

The third is *pride*, where our tendencies toward the divine come to the surface, when our "me," "my," and "mine" occupy center stage. This might be manifested in heightened self-control, in machismo, and in prejudice, but also in refusing the social spotlight and in playing the role of the victim. Peters observes that characteristic of the proud is the capacity to ignore the suffering and needs of others. National or ethnic or even religious pride is a possible manifestation of sin.

The fourth is the *desire to possess*, and includes craving, lust, envy, greed, and coveting. The desire to possess is also a group or national phenomenon as well as an individual one and is the false solution to the sinful need to shore up one's own resources and to pretend that one is self-sufficient. Sin parades as self-promotion, self-provision, self-determination, and self-perpetuation.

Fifth, pride and the desire to possess lead to *self-justification*, which is nothing less than the desire to possess what only God possesses, namely, goodness. We turn to the mirror to define what is right and good. The measuring stick of all life is my life. Those who do not measure up must be cut down (whether in gossip, slander, or some other form of violence) for there is nothing that makes us look so good as the failure of others. Even God becomes susceptible to the outworkings of our self-justification. Having established the benchmark for what is good, we scold God for not measuring up. Having determined what it must mean to love, we wonder why God can be so unloving. Having set the meaning of justice, we question why God is unjust. Self-justification is self-delusionment, a lie about ourselves that we embrace, which gives us license to speak violent words and do violent acts against those who are not "us," and who therefore do not measure up.

Sixth, then, is genuine *cruelty*, where people who had no empathy for those in pain actually inflict pain—whether physical or social or emotional or spiritual, whether to humans or to other creatures. Is this not the work of a god, wielding the power of life and death over others?

Finally, sin is *blasphemy*, the use of God and the things of God in self-justification. The holy writings support our position and our actions, we say. God has commanded us to kill, we allege. "Who are you to question a servant of God?" we ask. The word of the cross, which calls into question all pretensions to power and status, is replaced with our own words. Nothing can call us into question, just as nothing can give hope to those who suffer under our behavior, since we have drafted God to our own ends.

This catalog is helpful for its focus on human motivations and allegiances, even if we might want to explore the relation of these images to others, such as sin-as-idolatry. In fact, as we have begun to see, the Old and New Testaments contain an abundance of terms and phrases for conceiving the condition that characterizes our lives: slavery, hard-heartedness, lostness, friendship with the world, ungodliness, wickedness, unrighteousness, living according to the sinful nature, the reprobate mind, the darkened heart, lacking worship, enemies of God, dead in one's trespasses and sins, children of (the first) Adam, lacking God's glory, and more. Sin parades in many guises! In part, this is because people at different times of social and psychological development manifest and experience sin in different ways. It is also because people dwell in different social environments, with some terms and phrases more appropriate in one environment than in another.

This catalog has its limitations too since it construes sin primarily in terms of self-promotion or self-assertion. In recent decades, a number of theologians have observed that sin can be manifest in different ways among marginalized persons and communities. Sin might take the form of a numbing of the self rather than as self-assertion or as a failure to embrace one's personhood rather than as a predisposition to extend it at the expense of others. Manipulation of others and other coercive behavior, moreover, can be performed by those who seem to be powerless as well as those whose power is more visible and muscular. Seen in this way, "pride," for example, is more pervasive among humans than its popular identification with *machismo* or conceit might suggest. Although sin might be expressed as machismo, it also has its shadowy side, as people at all points of the continuum of power and privilege refuse to embrace either *only* or *fully* their places as full members within the human family.

29

We see more clearly from this way of putting the matter that "acts of disobedience" are deeply rooted in the sick soil of widely held convictions about the nature of our humanity that run counter to those of God. It is in this important sense that we recognize the significance of the notion of original sin; after humanity's first refusals to serve God as God, sin is at work even before we sinned. Our actions do not introduce evil into the world. Sin arrived before we did. Its power surrounds us and draws us into itself.

This reality does not spell the loss of our freedom to choose, but it does suggest the degree to which our choices are circumscribed already by the worlds in which we live. Contrary to the claims of the snake in the Garden, the concepts of good and evil do not exist in a vacuum. These are not "objective" realities, but have meaning in relation to some instrument of measuring. Living in a world that measures "the good" always in relation to "my" interests or the interests of "my group" or of "people like me" coerces us with choices that perpetuate disobedience, estrangement, disharmony, alienation. What of "the good" as defined by God's own words spoken over creation? Like those who live with lifelong disease, we have adjusted our existence, our contentment, our happiness to account for our maladies. We can scarcely imagine what the freedom to choose God's "good" would be, so much have we adapted ourselves to estrangement and alienation. We are in need of the medicine of liberation. We need salvation. We need a savior.

Epilogue

God spoke the first and second words. The first was creative, the second evaluative. Surveying the horizons of the cosmos, inspecting the living creatures, God saw that it was "good." Surveying his work on the day of humanity's appearance, God's word was "supremely good." But these are not the only words spoken, and we are not far into the Genesis story before God is under evaluation by those into whom he breathed life itself. Found wanting in the human grasp for self-authorization and self-rule, God's ways are renegotiated, set aside. And so begins the miserable procession from sin to sin, with the whole human family implicated in clearing its own path, a way marked by disobedience and alienation, by sin. Offered and accepted as a path to enlightenment, it turns perversely toward the darkness. Thankfully, the last word has not yet been spoken.

chapter two

Yahweh, the Healer

Perhaps the most enduring portraits of Jesus place him in any number of poses but often with hand outstretched to touch the sick with the power of divine healing: Jesus the healer. Such images are among the most memorable and pervasive in the Gospels. Together, Matthew, Mark, Luke, and John write dozens of healing stories, including the raising of the crippled, the cleansing of lepers, exorcism for the demonized, recovery of sight to the blind, even raising the dead, and more.

What has this to do with the biblical theme of salvation? This is a thoroughly modern question, one that would not likely have occurred to most who lived in Jesus' day. If in the last three centuries we in the West have learned to drive a wedge between the craft (and, more recently, the business) of healing on the one hand, salvation on the other, we should not imagine that such distinctions would have come easily to inhabitants of either ancient Israel or the first-century Mediterranean world.[1] Scripture as a whole presumes the intertwining of salvation and healing.

Scripture as a whole interprets the image of Yahweh the savior as Yahweh the healer, the New Testament portrays Jesus as healer, the larger Roman world of Jesus' day conceived of salvation as healing, and God's people are called to be a community of healing and health. These realities underscore the need to consider how salvation and healing are related and to examine particularly the biblical presentation of Yahweh the Healer.

31

Salvation is an enormously wide-ranging concept in the biblical materials, and the biblical writers use a diverse assortment of terms to give it focus. In this chapter and the next, I want to explore two capacious ways in which scripture portrays Yahweh as Savior—in this chapter, Yahweh the Healer; in the next, Yahweh the Liberator. These two images may appear to stand in opposition, but they are actually complementary and even overlap. Scripture can refer to a single saving act of Yahweh at one point with the language of liberation, at another with the language of healing. Setting these two portraits side by side will give us insight into the character of the same God and into the same saving work of this God, albeit from different perspectives and with different emphases. It will also allow us to sketch some of the other, related ways in which salvation is represented in the scriptures, such as reconciliation, justification, "new creation," and forgiveness. We begin with salvation as healing and with the pervasive and profound image of Yahweh as healer in Israel's scriptures.

Salvation as Healing: Setting the Context

In the New Testament world, the Greek terms associated with "salvation"—σώζω (*sōzō*, "to save"), σωτήρ (*sōtēr, "savior"*), σωτηρία (*sōtēria*, "salvation"), and σωτήριον (*sōtērion*, "saving")—related generally to rescue from misfortune of all kinds: shipwreck, the ravages of a journey, enemies in times of conflict, and so on. By far, however, the most common use of these terms in the larger Greco-Roman world was medical. "To save" was "to heal." People might even refer to their physicians as "saviors." People other than physicians, who contributed to the welfare of a city, for example, could also be thought of as salvation-bringers.

A wide gulf separates the world of Jesus and Paul from our own world when it comes to thinking about what counts as salvation and who might be regarded as a savior. Miracles of healing in the Roman Mediterranean were claimed by and for "holy men." We might expect this, but be caught off guard by evidence that miracles of healing were also attributed to kings, emperors, and military leaders. Here is solid testimony that "salvation" cannot be relegated to the sphere of the ethereal, as though it were concerned merely with "things of the spirit" or especially otherworldly in its focus. Deliverance from the enemy was as much a political statement as a spiritual one (or as much a spiritual as a political one), so that recovery of health in the case of an individual or a people could be cataloged as "salvation" or "rescue" or "peace" or "healing." The Roman world knew nothing of our modern assumptions regarding the separation of church and state, about the separation of spiritual things from political, or even concerning the separation of private from public life. A characteristically ancient and integrated view is on display in this text, written by the Alexandrian Jew Philo (ca. 20 BCE–50 CE), *The Embassy to Gaius,* concerning the Emperor Augustus (63 BCE–14 CE):

> And again the great regions which divide the inhabited world, Europe and Asia, were contending with each other for sovereign power . . . so that the whole human race exhausted by mutual slaughter was on the verge of utter destruction, had it not been for one man and leader, Augustus whom men fitly call the averter of evil. This is the Caesar who calmed the torrential storms on every side, who healed pestilences common to Greeks and barbarians, pestilences which descending from the south and east coursed to the west and north sowing seeds of calamity over the places and waters which lay between them. (*The Embassy to Gaius* 144–45, LCL)

Philosophers too could be spoken of as though they were "physicians," whose teaching was to heal the vices of their auditors and to promote the good health of virtue. Galen (129–199/216? CE), the celebrated physician whose medical theories and practices dominated from the second century into the seventeenth century, entitled one of his books *That the Best Physician Is Also a Philosopher.* Continuing the metaphor, a philosopher might call for a change of diet and medicine, or even the surgical knife or hot iron to cauterize a wound. Corruption of inner character demanded radical intervention! The Roman philosopher Seneca (first century CE) says of himself, "I myself am to be cauterized, operated upon, or put on a diet" (*Moral Letters* 75.6–7).

Of course, in the Greco-Roman world, healing could refer more narrowly to physical restoration, and in such cases healing was one of the benefits of salvation. Among the deities, Hercules, Asclepius, and Isis were particularly known for their healing ministrations. Though exalted from mortal existence to the Greek pantheon, Hercules remained compassionate toward humanity and acted on its behalf to heal diseases of all sorts, including raising the dead. The goddess Isis was well-known for her healing and was recognized as queen of the universe, dispenser of life, healer, and bringer of salvation. Devotees of Asclepius labeled their god "Savior." He was the god of healing, who, it was presumed, guided the hands of the physicians. *Hygeia,* personified Health, was said to be his daughter.

Acts of healing were not limited to the gods. Indeed, worship of Jesus as Lord was challenged in the Roman world by the ever-expanding worship of the emperor. Rome's emperors could be recognized as bringing salvation (health, prosperity, peace, security) to the known world. Their saving work was regarded as proof of their enjoying the blessings and support of the gods, so that, again, religion and politics become mutually informing and supportive of one another. The Latin historian Tacitus (ca. 56–ca. 118 CE) credits Vespasian (9–79 CE) with acts of healing; these were interpreted by the emperor and, perhaps more importantly, by the masses, as demonstrations of the lofty esteem in which Vespasian was held by the gods.[2]

Stories and ideas like this would not have seemed foreign to readers of Israel's scriptures, which were available in Greek translation from the third and second centuries BCE onward. In the Old Testament, the language of "salvation" might refer to deliverance, healing, health, and prosperity. Sometimes the connection is explicit, as in this prophetic word of Jeremiah: "LORD, the hope of Israel, all who forsake you will suffer disgrace; those who turn away from you in the land will be written off, for they have abandoned the LORD, the fountain of living water. Heal me, LORD, and I'll be healed. Save me and I'll be saved, for you are my heart's desire" (Jer 17:13-14). Like water to the thirsty (Isa 12:3), salvation addresses the threat of sin (Isa 64:5) and sickness. Says Yahweh, "Because my people are crushed, I am crushed; darkness and despair overwhelm me. Is there no balm in Gilead? Is there no physician there? Why then have my people not been restored to health?" (Jer 8:21-22). At other times, images of healing are associated with the language of rescue and relief:

> The LORD your God is in your midst—a warrior bringing victory. He will create calm with his love; he will rejoice over you with singing. I will remove from you those worried about the appointed feasts. They have been a burden for her, a reproach. Watch what I am about to do to all your oppressors at that time. I will deliver the lame; I will gather the outcast. I will change their shame into praise and fame throughout the earth. At that time, I will bring all of you back, at the time when I gather you. I will give you fame and praise among all the neighboring peoples when I restore your possessions and you can see them— says the LORD. (Zeph 3:17-19)

For Isaiah, salvation is peace with other peoples, harmony within the cosmos (e.g., Isa 2:1-5; 11:1-9).

This broader perspective on healing as one paradigm for grasping the meaning and experience of salvation may seem odd to those of us weaned on the dominant medical practices and health care systems of the modern Western world. It is easy for us to misconstrue the nature of healing in scripture by reading into the Bible alien notions of health and disease. We do this by focusing too narrowly the reach of "healing." In this respect it is worth remembering, first, that humanity was created in God's image (Gen 1:26-27), which entails relationships of mutuality and harmony within the human community as well as with God and the rest of God's good creation. If this gives us a strong sense of what it means to be "healthy," then "healing" could scarcely be limited to the physical body, as it often is in Western conceptions of biomedicine. Instead, "healing" must entail restoration to health in its fullest sense.

For example, when in Acts 3 Peter reports the healing of the lame beggar at the temple gate, he observes that "the faith that comes through Jesus gave him complete health right before your eyes" (3:16). The term ὁλοκληρία (*holoklēria*) refers to "health" in this all-encompassing sense, taking into account Luke's presentation of this man's new ability to walk and his newfound social and religious well-being. Note that, once he is raised up, this man is able to enter God's house, the temple, with joy: "walking, leaping, and praising God" (3:8). We may hear an echo of Isaiah 35:6, signifying how the healing of this man epitomizes the advent of the age of salvation, when the exiles are regathered and God's people restored.

Second, we should remind ourselves that, even today, different cultures think of health, sickness, and healing in different ways, and this would certainly be true when we move from increasingly pervasive, Western, biomedical understandings of healing and health to the ancient Mediterranean world. In this regard, at least for most of us, reading biblical accounts of healing must be undertaken as an exercise in intercultural communication.

If "sickness" is any unwanted condition of self or substantial threat of unwanted conditions of self,[3] then notions of health and sickness are not "givens," as though all people at all times and in all places might represent themselves as healthy or sick in the same way. Rather, ideas and experiences related to "health" and "sickness" are immediately tied to how a people measures human well-being. It follows from this that accounts of sickness and hopes for health might take on different forms, as one moves from culture to culture. One system for classifying these accounts among medical anthropologists distinguishes between diseases, illnesses, and disorders:

- *Disease accounts* identify disease as an abnormality located within the body, at or beneath the skin, and apart from the mind. The problem lies in the structure and functions of bodily organs or systems. In this case, healing requires physical or biomedical intervention.

- *Illness accounts* take into account the body but also one's networks of relationships and interactions with one's larger social environment. The body is not discounted, but neither is the person reduced to his or her body. Instead, a person is located within a larger web of meaning, beyond a more narrow biomedical concern with body parts and bodily systems, including the embodied lives of persons in community. Within this paradigm, "healing" requires interventions that also address the nesting of persons with other people.

- *Disorder accounts* do not neglect the body and one's networks of relationships and interaction with one's larger social environment, but they attend also to one's relationship to the world at large—the cosmos, which is experienced as unbalanced, out of order. The recovery of well-being in this case would be tantamount to "putting the world back together," or otherwise redressing a cosmic imbalance.[4]

Of course, as medical anthropologists are quick to point out, this classification represents ideal groupings that, in the lived experience of a people, may overlap. Nevertheless, it provides a helpful grid for making sense of the representation of salvation as healing in the world of the Bible.

It almost goes without saying that modern people in the West tend to think in terms of disease accounts. We tend to think of diseased individuals (rather than communities), what we label as "ailments" generally fall in the category of the physical or bodily, and cures are typically found in different forms of biomedical intervention (e.g., a painkiller, a hearing aid, a transplant, an antidepressant, a pair of crutches, a surgical implant). Happily, in recent decades, more constructive attention has been given to the significance of mental health, but for the population as a whole the psychological constitutes a sphere of life separate from the physical. Only with slight hyperbole can Trinh Xuan Thuan remark, "To this day, the brain and mind are regarded as two distinct entities in Western medicine. When we have a headache, we consult a neurologist; when we are depressed, we are told to see a psychiatrist."[5] Given this understanding of things, it is no surprise that we and our contemporaries share a tendency toward segregating healing (biomedical) from salvation (spiritual).

More pressing is how this understanding of reality, this life-world, artificially truncates our experience of well-being. Deeply committed to a biomedical model of health and healing, we focus our concerns and hopes on the life of one individual at a time. In such a world, the maintenance of human life and the reduction of physical suffering, at any cost, becomes the overriding concern. Physical health—with its often contrived notions of what is or ought to be "normal," and what is or ought to be "good-looking"—supplants any full-bodied (that is, *fully embodied)* sense of salvation.

People in the world of the Bible, and certainly within the biblical accounts, tended to think of sickness in more *wholistic* ways. For them, the source of sickness rested not only in the bodies of the sick but also and sometimes especially in their social environments and in the larger universe. In this case, healing might entail restoring a person to community, some form of bodily intervention, the redress of cosmic imbalances—or, more typically, some combination of all of these. For example, in his study of healing in Second Temple Judaism, Larry Hogan identified multiple causes of illness: (1) God, who causes illness in order to accomplish his own purposes (to discipline, for example, or to punish); (2) divine intermediaries (e.g., God's angels); (3) evil spirits or demons; (4) astrological phenomena; (5) sin; and (6) natural causes. In light of this catalog of the origins of illness, the list of possible remedies is not surprising: (1) faith and prayer; (2) virtuous living; (3) exorcism; (4) physicians and practitioners of folk medicine; (5) magic.[6] The result of Hogan's investigation is a complex of overlapping categories and factors, none of which can be clearly distinguished from the others. Whatever the cause and whatever the remedy, human ailments have to do with humans, understood wholistically, and not with parts of humans.

A cross-cultural perspective on sickness and healing is important in making sense of many healing accounts in the Old and New Testaments, as well as when thinking about the relation of healing to salvation more generally. For example, in the Bible "leprosy" is rarely if ever true leprosy, caused by the bacterium *Mycobacterium leprae* and found in modern medical reference books under the heading "Hansen's Disease." Rather, "leprosy" refers to any of a number of skin conditions that, when diagnosed by a priest, might render a person "unclean." According to Leviticus 13–14, leprosy is a sign of God's curse on a person; hence, someone diagnosed as a leper is marked as contagious and so forced to the margins of human community. In this case, then, the contagion is not a virus or bacterium, but a socioreligious contamination. No one would catch a skin disease from this kind of "leper," though one could become religiously unclean through interpersonal contact. In fact, when restored to health these lepers are not said to be "healed" but, rather, are "made clean." What we find here, then, is a valuable example of how, within the world of the Bible, religious, social, and physical maladies coalesce in a single symptomology. In the Gospels, Jesus' intervention in cases of "leprosy" (CEB: "skin disease") is classified as "cleansing" because religious impurity (and not a biological disease) has become the primary presenting problem. Intervention is followed by such instructions from Jesus as those found in Luke 5:12-14: "Go and show yourself to the priest and make an offering for your cleansing, as Moses instructed." In these instances, the priest functions not as a healer but as a kind of community health consultant tasked with mediating the (former) leper's return to normal interactions among God's people.

In the same way, accounts of exorcism correlate spiritual, social, mental, and physical factors, both in the presentation of the disorder and in its resolution. The Gerasene demoniac lived not in a house but among the tombs (as though he were in quarantine, ritually unclean, isolated from human community, homeless, as though he were dead), was naked and uncontrollable (and thus lacking personal identity and status as a human being), and his speech moves back and forth between "I" and "we" statements (crisis of personal identity). Following exorcism, he is sitting at the feet of Jesus (submission, like a disciple), clothed and in his right mind (returned to status as a human, with personal identity intact), and Jesus returns him to his home to declare what God had done for him (restored to his community, with a vocation) (Luke 8:26-39).

In more straightforward accounts too, such as the healing of the woman with a hemorrhage (Mark 5:25-34), what might first be categorized as physical recovery (biomedical) is plainly bundled together with social and spiritual restoration. This is also true for the larger view of life wherein healing and sickness are indicators of Yahweh's favor and displeasure. Although one could never argue that health is necessarily the direct result of God's favor, nor that sickness is necessarily the direct result of divine punishment, it is nevertheless true that for ancient Israel there could be a causal link from sin to sickness. (For examples, see Deut 28; 1 Kgs 13:1-25; Prov 3:28-35; 11:19; 13:13-23; 1 Cor 11:29-30. This theological position is eloquently represented by Job's interlocutors in Job 8:1-22; 11:6; 22:1-30, though this logic is otherwise undermined in Job's story.) In John 9:1-7, the disciples assume the causal relation of sin to physical disorder, but Jesus makes no general pronouncement on the subject; elsewhere, his actions presuppose the commensurability of healing a man's paralysis and forgiving his sin (Mark 2:1-12).

One more illustration: In Matthew 4:23, the evangelist summarizes Jesus' ministry with these words: "He announced the good news of the kingdom and healed every disease and sickness among the people." Accordingly, Matthew 5–7 comprises the first major teaching block in Matthew's Gospel ("he announced the good news of the kingdom"), and this is followed immediately with two chapters, Matthew 8–9, in which miraculous events are lined up, one after the other, to show how he "healed every disease and sickness among the people." Matthew thus demonstrates Jesus making available God's regal presence and power to those dwelling on the margins of Jewish society in Galilee. We read accounts that focus on a leper, the slave of a Gentile army officer, an old woman, the demonized, a paralytic, a tax collector, a young girl, and the blind. As Matthew recounts the restoration to physical health of those who are diseased, he simultaneously chronicles the restoration of persons to status within their families and communities, the faith-full reordering of life around God, and the driving back of demonic forces. The spectrum of images that converge in Matthew's recounting includes examples like these:

- Cleansing a leper allows him new access to God and to the community of God's people (8:1-4).

- Healing a paralytic is like forgiving his sins (9:2-8).

- Extending God's grace to tax collectors and sinners illustrates the work of a physician (9:9-13).

- Recovery of sight functions as a metaphor for the exercise of the insight of faith (9:27-31).

Here, then, is further evidence of the essential point: We must reject all attempts to divorce physical from spiritual or psychological ailments, or communal from physical disorders. People do not come in "parts," so "healing" must be understood in this more comprehensive way. A more wholistic approach to healing is demanded by the evidence. This is why "healing" serves so well as a way of articulating the biblical message of salvation.

Yahweh, the Healer

The relationship of reflection more specifically on healing and health and grappling with a larger perspective on salvation as healing is grounded both in the integrated categories we have begun to sketch and, even more so, in scriptural testimony to Yahweh. In Israel's scriptures, physicians are typically regarded as poor substitutes for God (e.g., 2 Chron 16:12; Jer 8:22–9:6) and magic was categorically excluded as an option (e.g., Lev 19:26-28; Deut 18:10-14; Ezek 13:17-18). When in the early second century BCE Ben Sira makes a place for physicians, he does so under the umbrella of God's sovereignty in matters related to healing and health. "Honor doctors for their services, since indeed the Lord created them," he writes; and again, "The Lord created medicines out of the earth, and a sensible person won't ignore them"

(Sir 28:1, 4). God's role as healer can be demonstrated in the hands of physicians and their medicaments.

Throughout Israel's scriptures, Yahweh's identity as healer is paramount: "I am the Lord who heals you" (Exod 15:26). The context of this, Yahweh's self-description at this early point in Israel's life, is crucial, for it follows the narration of the incredible lengths to which Yahweh has gone to liberate Israel from Egypt. "I am your healer," Yahweh declares, drawing attention to God's powerful intervention on Israel's behalf, a power that has just been celebrated in the Song of Miriam: "Sing to the Lord, for an overflowing victory! Horse and rider he threw into the sea!" (15:21); this healing is then demonstrated in God's provision of sweet water in the desert (15:25). Poetic language celebrates Yahweh's royal authority over Israel's enemies and the natural world, and acclaims the gift of salvation, and all of this is epitomized in the metaphor of healing.

In this same setting, Yahweh communicates his will, setting before his people an agreement: "If you are careful to obey the Lord your God, do what God thinks is right, pay attention to his commandments, and keep all of his regulations, then I won't bring on you any of the diseases that I brought on the Egyptians. I am the Lord who heals you" (15:26). The remedy God provides Israel generates a covenantal relationship: Israel must attend to God's voice and heed his commands; for God's part, rather than afflict his people with disease, as he had done with the Egyptians, he will lavish them with health.

The Psalms similarly deploy the language of healing metaphorically to speak of God's blessings:

> Let my whole being bless the Lord
>   and never forget all his good deeds:
>   how God forgives all your sins,
>   heals all your sickness,
>   saves your life from the pit,
>   crowns you with faithful love
>   and compassion,
>   and satisfies you with plenty of good things
>   so that your youth
>   is made fresh like an eagle's.
> The Lord works righteousness;
>   does justice for all who are oppressed. (Ps 103:2-6)

Praise the LORD!
>Because it is good to sing praise to our God!
>Because it is a pleasure
>>to make beautiful praise!

The LORD rebuilds Jerusalem,
>gathering up Israel's exiles.

God heals the brokenhearted
>and bandages their wounds.

God counts the stars by number,
>giving each one a name.

Our Lord is great and so strong!
>God's knowledge can't be grasped! (Ps 147:1-5)

Note the constellation of images within which Yahweh's healing work is found. The concept of "healing" as divine gift rubs shoulders with Yahweh's care for and sovereignty over the cosmos, working justice on behalf of the oppressed, extension of love and mercy, renewal of the fatigued, forgiveness, and restoration. Healing is God's setting things right.

Again in the Torah, as proof of his singular status, Yahweh declares, "I'm the one who deals death and gives life; I'm the one who wounded, but now I will heal" (Deut 32:39). Here is generous testimony to God's fidelity:

But the LORD will acquit his people, will have compassion on those who serve him, once he sees that their strength is all gone, that both prisoners and free people are wiped out. The Lord will ask, "Where are their gods—the rocks they trusted in—who ate up the fat of their sacrifices, who drank their sacred wine? They should stand up and help you! They should protect you now! Now, look here: I myself, I'm the one; there are no other gods with me. I'm the one who deals death and gives life; I'm the one who wounded, but now I will heal. There's no escaping my hand." (Deut 32:36-39)

This is the blessing reserved for those who acknowledge that Yahweh alone is God, who devote themselves wholly to him. This motif surfaces in a similar way in the Writings, as in 2 Chronicles 7:11-14: If God's people will turn to him in prayer and humility, God will bring forgiveness and healing to their land. Yahweh binds up and heals the wounded (Job 5:17-18).

God's role as healer is even more pervasive among the prophetic writings, where appeals are made so that God might come and heal both people and the nation. Hezekiah petitions God that he might restore his health (Isa 38:1-6), and Ezekiel portrays Yahweh as healer of the lost, the sick, and the weak (Ezek 34:16). Yahweh's servant, Isaiah writes, will bring about the healing of

41

God's people (Isa 53:5). The prophet anticipates "the day that the Lᴏʀᴅ bandages the people's brokenness and heals the wounds inflicted by his blows" (Isa 30:26). The day is coming, Isaiah announces, when God "will come to save you." The restoration of God's people is vividly linked to images signifying the restoration of health: "Then the eyes of the blind will be opened, and the ears of the deaf will be cleared. Then the lame will leap like the deer, and the tongue of the speechless will sing" (Isa 35:4-6). It is no coincidence that we find in the Gospels and Acts that these acts of healing—indeed, as we will see momentarily, sometimes described with the very vocabulary of restored health and celebration—signify the advent of the anticipated era of salvation.

In the New Testament, healing is one of the means by which God's royal rule is decisively disclosed. As God's coregent, Jesus the anointed king engages in ministries of healing and exorcism and, in doing so, he reveals the nature of the kingdom in relation to the marginal, the vulnerable, and the suffering. In Jesus' healing ministry, the scriptural portrait of Yahweh the healer is extended. Jesus' followers participate in the work of healing too, and Jesus' delegates demonstrate that God has drawn near with power to heal. According to Peter's address at Pentecost, God worked deeds of power, wonders, and signs through Jesus (Acts 2:22), and this is preparatory to Peter's announcement of Jesus' status as God's coregent (Acts 2:33). Similarly, "the Lord confirmed the word about his grace by the signs and wonders he enabled [Paul and Barnabas] to perform" (Acts 14:3). Others may participate in God's healing activity, then, but this does not detract from the more fundamental affirmation that Yahweh is the one doing the healing. Indeed, the phrase so popular in Acts, "signs and wonders," is borrowed from Israel's scriptures where it refers above all to God's role in liberating Egypt. In the exodus story, as in Acts, "signs and wonders" broadcast the actualization of God's saving purpose, God's "healing," on behalf of God's people.[7]

Jesus Exercises God's Power to Heal

The portrait of Jesus as healer is central to the Synoptic Gospels: Matthew, Mark, and Luke. When we take into account that they sometimes contain multiple versions of the same episode, the list of independent accounts comprises six episodes of exorcism and seventeen accounts of healing (including three accounts of resuscitation). Jesus' ministry in these Gospels is distinguished by his typical behavior as a healer and his portrayal as one who exercises in a direct way God's saving power. He does not ask God to intervene on behalf of those in need of a miracle but pronounces their healing directly, in speech-acts that assume his authority to do so. He often emphasizes the component of faith in his healing ministry—so much so this becomes one of Jesus' characteristic declarations: "Your faith has healed you."[8]

In the Gospels, Jesus often heals merely by pronouncement, though the evangelists also mention his laying on of hands or touching the sick in relation to healing. This was a boundary-crossing gesture of compassion that reflects the extension of God's own hand to act in creation and deliverance. That this practice is continued by Jesus' emissaries in Acts identifies them as instruments of divine power.

According to the Synoptic Gospels, some who recognize Jesus' status as a healer do not see in his work divine credentials. Instead, they attribute his ministry of exorcism to his association with Satan. In dialogue with those people, Jesus interprets his ministry of exorcism as a sign of the Spirit's work in his mission and a demonstration of God's kingdom at work among them (Matt 12:24-33; Mark 2:22-30; Luke 11:14-26). Here, as elsewhere, the healing ministry of Jesus is portrayed as a sign of God's kingdom, the presence of the divine blessings of salvation available in Jesus' ministry.

Accordingly, Jesus' healing ministry marked the coming of the new aeon, the long-awaited era of salvation. Isaiah 35:1-7 promises the coming of God in history to bring salvation and judgment, promising, among other things, that "the eyes of the blind will be opened, and the ears of the deaf will be cleared." Similarly, in its Greek version, Isaiah 61:1 anticipates the end-time restoration of God's people as a time when the blind would receive their sight:

> The Spirit of the Lord is on me because he has anointed me to bring good news
> to the poor.
> He has sent me to heal the brokenhearted, to proclaim release to the captives
> and recovery of sight to the blind. (LXX, my translation)

The relevance of this repeated Isaianic vision rests in its implicit and explicit use by the New Testament evangelists to interpret the significance of Jesus' ministry as a healer. Mark 7:37, for example, records how the crowds were astonished by a healing miracle, and responded in words echoing Isaiah 35:5-6: "He even makes the deaf to hear and gives speech to those who can't speak." Matthew 11:2-5 and Luke 7:18-22 (see Luke 4:18-19) recall in an explicit way Isaiah's language and eschatological vision, and in doing so communicate both that Jesus is God's Anointed One and that with Jesus' advent the new creation that actualizes Isaiah's vision is unfolding. Jesus' perspective in Luke 11:20, though not tied into Isaianic expectations, is nevertheless comparable:

"But if I throw out demons by the power of God, then God's kingdom has already overtaken you."

Jesus' healing activity thus points beyond itself to the transformed nature of the times, to the new era introduced in Jesus' coming. God's redemptive purpose is being realized; God's kingdom is being unveiled. Today, some of us might imagine that the real significance of Jesus' healing ministry lies primarily in its miraculous character and so we might wonder at these manifestations of supernatural power. In the Gospels, though, their real importance lies elsewhere, in their witness to the reality that, in Jesus' advent and presence, the era of salvation has arrived, calling on and enabling people to live life faithfully before God.

In the Synoptic Gospels, Jesus' healing is pivotal to understanding the character of his ministry, demonstrating as it does the nature and presence of God's kingdom. It is worth remembering, though, that this presentation of the nature of Jesus' ministry and God's program is not always welcome. In fact, one of the corollaries of Jesus' disclosure of God's kingdom is that all pretend-kingdoms, all authorities and powers hostile to God's ways, likewise have the curtain drawn back on their true nature. Those trying to make a name for themselves in the world and to fit into its designs are not likely to nurture hope for a messianic kingdom that will transform and renew everything. Healing is welcome only when illness is recognized, and when that illness represents an unwanted condition. Only those who experience the pain of brokenness are likely to be hungry for restoration. Civil religion, whether in the time of the Roman Empire or more modern days, is more likely to quash announcements of God's end-time rule than to support them. Religious institutions sometimes find themselves doing the same, in order to recommend themselves as representing authentically God's interests on earth. Thus, for the Jewish leaders in Jerusalem, Jesus' healing activity marks him as a false prophet who manipulates God's people and subverts God's way, and is thus deserving of death (Luke 23:1-5).

In Jesus' execution, marked as a false prophet accused of steering the people away from God through miracles of healing, we find a shocking reminder that not all people and institutions welcome salvation with open arms. Some actually work against it, or deny it altogether.

The People of God as Community of Healing

Yahweh's portrait as original giver and ongoing restorer of human life is both central to and pervasive in Scripture. This is true with respect to individuals (whose recovery is set within the network of their relationships with others and with God, and nested within God's good creation) but also of God's people, who depend on him for life and renewal of life. Within this biblical story, Jesus' appearance, healing practices, and the gift of his life on behalf of others signal the decisive revelation of God's rule. As exalted Lord, Jesus is coregent with God and dispenses the divine blessings of salvation, including both restored health (for which prayers are to be offered on behalf of the sick) and the Holy Spirit (who enables gifts of healing).

What of other, human agents of healing? Priests in the Second Temple period were less healers and more community health consultants, who might be called on to verify a healing or cleansing. Old Testament prophets were sometimes portrayed as agents of healing, however. Elijah was instrumental in restoring a widow's son to life (1 Kgs 17:8-24), for example, and Elisha instructed Naaman, commander of the Syrian army, how to be cured of leprosy (2 Kgs 5:1-15). According to Luke 4:25-27, Jesus mentions both of these episodes by way of explaining the nature of his own mission. In the New Testament, during the course of Jesus' ministry, his disciples participate in his ministries of healing and exorcism, for example, in Mark 6:7-13: "They cast out many demons, and they anointed many sick people with olive oil and healed them" (Mark 6:13; cf. Matt 10:1-14; Luke 9:1-6; 10:1-11). In Acts the ministries of the apostles, as well as of Stephen, Paul, and Barnabas, are characterized by signs and wonders, including healing. Their healing practices are performed explicitly in Jesus' name (e.g., Acts 3:1-10; 9:34; 16:16-18). This is evidence in support of the affirmation that, vindicated as Lord through his exaltation to the right hand of God, Jesus pours out the benefits of salvation (see Acts 2:33-36). Both Peter and Paul actually repudiate any notion that they have power to heal apart from Jesus (Acts 3:12-16; 14:14-15). For Luke, the healing activity of persons like Stephen or Peter functions not only to convey the blessings of salvation available through the risen Lord but also to verify that people like Stephen and Peter are the Lord's authorized emissaries (e.g., Acts 14:3).

In 1 Corinthians 12, Paul lists the gifts of healings and working of miracles as manifestations of the Spirit's work in the life of the church. The use of the plural, "gifts of healings" (1 Cor 12:9, my translation of χαρίσματα ἰαμάτων, *charismata iamatōn*), suggests that each occasion of healing is a manifestation of this gift, as opposed to an individual's claiming to possess permanently the power to heal. In 2 Corinthians, Paul speaks of his having performed "the signs of an apostle" (12:12; cf. Rom 15:18-19; 1 Thess 1:5), which presumably would have included healing, but it is otherwise worth reflecting on how reticent Paul is to speak of such matters autobiographically. This is because his own weakness is an occasion for identifying with Jesus' suffering and for communicating the gospel's power (e.g., Gal 4:13; 2 Cor 12:7).

James directs those who are sick to call for the elders of the church to pray over them, anointing them with oil in the name of the Lord (Jas 5:14-16). We find no hint here of "healing" as a spiritual gift or that James anticipates the presence of "healers" in the church. "Elders" likely refers to congregational leaders generally rather than to any specific office. Though these leaders are tasked with praying for the sick, it is the Lord who restores health (Jas 5:15). James does not assume that illness is necessarily caused by sin, but does allow that sin may be a factor. In any case, sin must be confessed and it will be forgiven. It is worth drawing attention to the multifaceted perspective on healing and health we find in this text, which links sin, sickness, prayer, the use of a medicament, restoration of the community's integrity, and healing—all, of course, under the umbrella of the church's service in the Lord's name. Healing in this case is embedded in congregational life, not the task or experience of isolated individuals.[9]

This cursory sketch gathers some of the more explicit evidence to indicate the role of God's people, both individually and collectively, in the healing work of God. Easily overlooked in such a survey is the importance of the witness to wholeness and integrity, including the health of the community, implied in such texts. Let us return to the letter of James, where "salvation" is portrayed as restoring health in its expansive fullness.

> If any of you are suffering, they should pray. If any of you are happy, they should sing. If any of you are sick, they should call for the elders of the church, and the elders should pray over them, anointing them with oil in the name of the Lord. Prayer that comes from faith will heal the sick, for the Lord will restore them to health. And if they have sinned, they will be forgiven. For this reason, confess your sins to each other and pray for each other so that you may be healed. The prayer of the righteous person is powerful in what it can achieve. (Jas 5:13-16)

Restoration of health is concerned with physical wellness, to be sure (Jas 5:15), but not in a way that can be segregated from life more fully (Jas 1:21; 5:20). Indeed, the interweaving of healing and forgiveness (Jas 5:16) speaks to a vision of personhood that is wholly integrated. Likewise, life before God is worked out within a web of relationships within the Christian community, characterized by peace, care, and forgiveness (Jas 2:13; 3:13, 17; 4:11-12; 5:16, 19).

Again, James does not equate sickness and sin, nor does he claim that sickness derives from sin. His perspective, rather, is that what sickness is to the human body so sin is to the church. Consequently, "healing" cannot be focused on a single person or on a single aspect of life. In fact, it is not too much to say that James presents ill health among individuals within the church as a test of the church. Our first instincts might be (and often are) to quarantine the sick. Typically, those who are not well—the weak, the hurting, the lonely, the diseased—become the targets of growing isolation, usually through implicit acts or simple neglect. If we do not isolate the sick by deliberately locating them in rooms to themselves, but rather by adopting behaviors that hold them at arm's length, does this make their segregation any less real? Will the community, and particularly its leadership, answer the summons of the sick, and gather around them with faith and prayer? Or will the sick find themselves progressively excluded from a community fearful of its own boundaries, its own survival? Reflecting the character of God who is merciful and rich in compassion, the community of healing is one that is able to pray and confess sins together, confident in God's goodness.

Salvation as Healing: Expanding the Horizons

"Healing" has already proven to be a remarkably rich metaphor for working out the nature of salvation in the biblical materials. Not only is it deployed in this way in both the Old and New Testaments, but when explored from the perspective of medical anthropology, the concept of healing has an impressive elasticity that endorses its usefulness for our purposes. The promise of "healing" presumes a shared definition of health and recognition of sickness, as well as the gracious presence of a healer. From scripture itself, we receive an all-encompassing perspective on human health in the cosmos and in relation to God, as well as well-developed ways of identifying the sickness that spreads like a cancer throughout the human family, even eating away at the world that humans call home. The term generally given this sickness in the Christian tradition is "sin," though, as we saw in chapter 1, the term itself too easily limits conversation and masks the multivalent ways in which humans—individually, collectively, and systemically—neglect, deny, refuse to embody God's creative purpose. In this view, healing does not allow a person or his or her salvation to be reduced to "parts," as though inner and outer life could be separated. What is more, in a significant sense, healing does not allow us to think of the restoration of individuals, as it were, one at a time. Instead, it pushes our categories always to consider the human community and, indeed, God's creation, both as

47

the expanding contexts within which sickness and healing are experienced and for their roles in promoting and securing human health. Persons are not saved in isolation from the world around them. For healing, attention falls above all on the power and initiative of Yahweh, who declares himself to be Healer, and on Jesus, Yahweh's coregent, through whom God's renewing beneficence is available. Finally, the metaphor of healing serves as an invitation to God's people, not only to be recipients of God's gifts of salvation, but also to serve as healing agents, to be a community of compassion and restoration.

Scripture develops the metaphor of healing as it spells out the nature of God's salvation, but employs other, allied concepts as well. In part, this is because all metaphors reveal some aspects of the reality to which they point while concealing others. More words are needed if we are to grasp as fully as possible the richness of God's beneficence. In part, this is because different people in different times and places need to have the nature of salvation spelled out in different terms—in language that speaks clearly and meaningfully to their realities. The message of salvation requires a context for its articulation, and different contexts invite different articulations. It remains in this chapter, then, to comment briefly on several additional biblical motifs associated with the theme of salvation, and especially on some that share kinship with the concept of healing.[10]

Reconciliation

The scriptures use the language of "reconciliation" infrequently. Related words appear only twenty-five times in the whole of the Old and New Testaments. However, this should not keep us from noting, first, the important contexts in which the word group does appear (e.g., Rom 5:1-10; 2 Cor 5:18-21; Col 1:15-20); and, second, how often the concept is present even when the term is missing. If Genesis 3 ends with God and the first humans on less-than-friendly terms—with humanity having actually recoiled in shame from God's presence—then it makes sense of much of scripture to locate its narratives and theology within the larger plotline of God's ongoing initiative to restore what has been broken. As Paul phrases it, "If we were reconciled to God through the death of his Son while we were still enemies, now that we have been reconciled, how much more certain is it that we will be saved by his life?" (Rom 5:10); and, again: "God was reconciling the world to himself through Christ" (2 Cor 5:19).

Reconciliation is a concept broad enough to embrace relationships among people and between humanity and God, as well as the relationship of the human family to the created order. The chronic division between Jew and Gentile is addressed in the cross of Christ so that the dividing wall of separation has been razed (Eph 2:11-22). The broken relationship between a slave and his master is not only bridged but, even more significantly, the newly restored relationship should take on a different form, with slave and master comporting themselves from now on as brothers (Philemon). Indeed, in his missive to Philemon, Paul undercuts the moral basis of slavery through a well-crafted appeal to the gospel of reconciliation. Under the umbrella of reconciliation even the cosmic powers, regarded as God's creation but now out of step with God's purposes, are restored to their purpose (Col 1:15-20). Proclamation of reconciliation cannot be severed from acts of reconciliation. Consequently, the message of salvation lays a claim on the everyday lives of people who are called to moral sensitivity and vigilance rooted in a life lived for others (2 Cor 5:14–6:13).

We should note, finally, that Paul does not develop the motif of reconciliation in mutual terms, as though the need for divine-human reparation were equal. "The world" may be estranged from God, and in need of restoration, but God is not estranged from the world. Thus, it is the world that stands in need of God's re-creative activity (hence, the language of "new creation" in 2 Cor 5:17; Gal 6:15).

New Creation

The language of "new creation" is rare in the Old and New Testaments too, but the idea is not. One need only recall Isaiah's classical formulation of hope and promise, where enmity between animals and humanity is overturned:

> The wolf will live with the lamb, and the leopard will lie down with the young goat; the calf and the young lion will feed together, and a little child will lead them. The cow and the bear will graze. Their young will lie down together, and a lion will eat straw like an ox. A nursing child will play over the snake's hole; toddlers will reach right over the serpent's den. They won't harm or destroy anywhere on my holy mountain. The earth will surely be filled with the knowledge of the LORD, just as the water covers the sea. (Isa 11:6-9)

That this text is found in a larger passage related to the righteous rule of the messianic king (Isa 11:1-5) plays an important role in Mark's Gospel, where Mark comments on Jesus' temptation in the wilderness: "He was in the wilderness for forty days, tempted by Satan. He was among the wild animals, and the angels took care of him" (Mark 1:13). The time is coming—indeed,

49

it has already begun in Jesus' career—when the paradise of creation will be restored.[11] Of course, this hope comes to its most profound expression in the image of "a new heaven and a new earth" found in Isaiah 65:17 and, then, in John's Revelation (Rev 21:1). On this point, it is crucial to remember that, in scripture, "new" often has the sense of "renewed," so that we should think in terms of both continuity and discontinuity: God's restoration will both embrace and transform the cosmos.

Closely aligned with the imagery of "new creation" are other images—including *new birth* (1 Pet 1:3, 14; 2:2-3), being *born anew* or *from above* (John 3:3, 7), *adoption* (Rom 8:14-17), and rebirth and *renewal* (Titus 3:5). James, too, refers to God as having given "us birth by his true word" (Jas 1:18). A parallel image from rabbinic discourse concerning proselytes to Judaism helps to clarify what is at stake here: "One who has become a proselyte is like a child newly born" (*b. Tebam.* 22b).[12] Although each of these New Testament texts supports different emphases, we can identify some common motifs:

- Human dependence on divine initiative for salvation. The metaphor itself assumes as much, since people do not give birth to themselves. Transformation comes in accordance with God's mercy and by means of Jesus' resurrection (1 Peter). God saved us through new birth and renewal (Titus). To be born anew is to be born from above, that is, born from God (John). God's children are those who are led by God's Spirit; one does not adopt oneself, but is adopted by God (Romans).

- Salvation is personalized in terms of a makeover of what it means to be human. People participate in—one might even say that they are caught up into—the eschatological renewal of the cosmos.

- Those who are reborn find themselves in a new family, incorporated into God's household. This has immediate and sweeping ramifications for one's identity and inheritance and for the patterns of faithful behavior appropriate to this new community. Distinctions among people are dissolved because, within God's people, all are siblings.

- One's relation to life's realities is read according to radically different patterns of thought, from a different standpoint within God's family and in relation to God's drawing into the present the reality of end-time salvation. People have not relocated to another world, but they now view the world through faith-full eyes. Indeed, being born from above is the prerequisite to seeing (understanding, experiencing) God's kingdom at all (John). What Peter announces is simply the conversion to new ways of thinking, feeling, believing, and behaving.

As Paul phrased it, "If anyone is in Christ, that person is part of the new creation. The old things have gone away, and look, new things have arrived!" (2 Cor 5:17).

Forgiveness

Wherever reconciliation is found, forgiveness is close at hand, not because reconciliation and forgiveness are synonymous, but because forgiveness is a precursor to reconciliation. That is, forgiveness is a necessary precondition to reconciliation. This distinction is crucial insofar as it underscores the nature of the problem and, thus, the character of the solution. Sin and its effects are taken with real seriousness in scripture. Forgiveness is extended not simply to persons, but to persons and peoples *who are mired in sin*. In order for full fellowship to be restored, sin and its effects must be recognized, forgiven, canceled out. Although there may be forgiveness without reconciliation, there is no reconciliation without forgiveness.

We find examples of interpersonal forgiveness among women and men in the Old Testament (e.g., Gen 50:17; Exod 10:17). By and large, though, God is the one who forgives. In fact, it is within God's character that he is the source of forgiveness: "Compassion and deep forgiveness belong to my Lord, our God, because we rebelled against him" (Dan 9:9). Says the Lord, "I, I am the one who wipes out your rebellious behavior for my sake. I won't remember your sin" (Isa 43:25). This is not to say that God is obligated to forgive, nor that the granting of forgiveness is automatic. Rather, forgiveness flows out of Yahweh's character, his compassion and patience. "Who is a God like you, pardoning iniquity, overlooking the sin of the few remaining for his inheritance? He doesn't hold on to his anger forever; he delights in faithful love" (Mic 7:18).

Jeremiah anticipates the time when God would renew the covenant with his people, forgiving their iniquity and remembering their sin no more (Jer 31:34). According to Matthew's Gospel, the advent of this era is announced in the Last Supper, as Jesus declares over the shared cup, "This is my blood of the covenant, which is poured out for many so that their sins may be forgiven" (Matt 26:28). In this context, we should remind ourselves that divine forgiveness was central to the restoration of God's people in Second Temple

Jewish thought. To proclaim "forgiveness of sins" was to speak of God's acting to restore Israel as his people.

In Luke and Acts, forgiveness is so important that it serves as a virtual stand-in for the message of salvation. Peter promises to those who repent that their sins may be "wiped away" (Acts 3:19). The blessings of salvation come into focus in the forgiveness that is available through Jesus (Acts 5:31; 13:43). It is important, therefore, that we grasp the obviously social dimension of forgiveness. Inasmuch as forgiveness was the means by which persons who had excluded themselves or been excluded from the community of God's people might (re)gain entry into the community, the promise of forgiveness can never be reduced to talk about an individual's relationship to Yahweh.

In Jesus' teaching, divine forgiveness is correlated with the forgiveness we extend to one another: "Forgive us our sins, for we also forgive everyone who has wronged us" (Luke 11:4; see also Matt 6:15). In Matthew's Gospel, Jesus goes so far as to contrast the forgiveness of a colossal debt extended by a master to a servant with that servant's failure to forgive the puny debt of one of his comrades. Discovering this, the master said, "You wicked servant! I forgave you all that debt because you appealed to me. Shouldn't you also have mercy on your fellow servant, just as I had mercy on you?" Jesus continues, "His master was furious and handed him over to the guard responsible for punishing prisoners, until he had paid the whole debt. My heavenly Father will also do the same to you if you don't forgive your brother or sister from your heart" (Matt 18:23-35). Jesus does not thereby establish a relationship of *quid pro quo* between divine and human forgiveness, as though God's extending forgiveness were dependent on human activity. In Luke's Gospel, for example, such a view would be flatly denied by Jesus' request that God forgive those responsible for his crucifixion (Luke 23:34). Rather, Jesus grounds the disciples' request for divine forgiveness in their own practices of forgiveness. Jesus draws out the implications for human behavior from God's own activity. As he says elsewhere, "Be compassionate just as your Father is compassionate" (Luke 6:36). Hence, the embodiment of forgiveness in the practices of Jesus' followers is nothing less than an expression and imitation of God's own character.

Justification

If "reconciliation" is a concept borrowed from the world of interpersonal relations, justification finds its first home in the courtroom, so to speak. This has led to a widespread misconstrual of "justification," as though it referred to salvation as little more than the abstract work of God in declaring someone "not guilty." As with healing, so with justification, a lot depends on how a concept is framed. In this case, the question is what legal frame best makes sense of justification as a term for salvation.

In the world of Israel's scriptures, justification is a profoundly relational term, signifying faithfulness to the covenant. "Justification" can be used with reference to God, then, on account of God's determined faithfulness to the covenant. In this case, the terminology of justification is typically translated in scripture with reference to God's righteousness. But God's righteousness is not measured in terms of God's adherence to a legal code that demands divine retribution for those to break the law; rather, it is measured in terms of God's covenant faithfulness, which, for Paul in Romans 3, is revealed in the faithfulness of Jesus Christ. In the same way, justification in relation to humanity would refer to practices of unwavering faithfulness to the covenant made with God in Jesus' death, the ultimate expression of God's covenant faithfulness. "Righteousness" is thus both a guarantor of God's promises and a call on humanity to keep covenant with Yahweh. "To be justified," in this reading, is to be included within covenant relationship with Yahweh. Accordingly, God restores to a covenantal relationship those whose sin has led to their exile, and even extends the lines of God's family to include all who believe. Remembering that human identity and health are developed in essentially relational terms, we can easily grasp how the image of justification overlaps with the notion of salvation-as-healing.

In the Old Testament, a riveting example of justification is found in the person of Tamar, who plays the role of a prostitute, tricks Judah into fathering her sons, and yet is pronounced "more righteous" than he. This is because she has maintained the terms of the covenant while he has defaulted on his covenant obligations (Gen 38:1-26; see Deut 25:5-10). We find a parallel notion in the Sermon on the Mount, wherein Jesus demands that the righteousness of his followers surpass that of the Pharisees and legal experts, that is, that their faithfulness to the covenant with Yahweh be more enduring than theirs (Matt 5:20). Tracing this motif into the letter of James, we find that the passive verb "to be justified" might more helpfully be translated, "to show to be righteous," since James' concern is that faith must express itself in faithfulness (Jas 2:21, 24, 25: "shown to be righteous"[13]). Paul's overall concern in his letter to the Romans is twofold, both having to do with justification: (1) Was God right to extend covenant relations to people who are outside of the law? (2) If not by means of Torah, how might persons be placed in covenant relation to God? The answer on both accounts is centered on the cross of Christ. God is shown to be "just" in Jesus' faithfulness, and especially his death, just as sinners are brought into covenantal relationship with God through Jesus' faithfulness, and especially his death. How this is so is the concern of chapter 4.

Peace

Salvation as "healing" is also related to the biblical concept of peace, which moves far beyond the absence of war or conflict to denote the cosmos in a state of tranquility: the orderly creation in order, lacking nothing, dwelling in happiness and harmony, all under the canopy of God's gracious rule. It is no wonder, then, that the Israelite greeting is a wish for peace: *Shalom!* (e.g., 1 Sam 25:6; Luke 10:5; Rom 1:7). Peace is of God (see Judg 6:24; Rom 16:20), and comes from God: "I will create reason for praise: utter prosperity [i.e., "peace, peace," or "unmitigated peace"] to those far and near, and I will heal them, says the LORD" (Isa 57:19). In the later parts of the Old Testament, peace is the focus of Israel's hope. Embracing the notions of security, justice, truth, and righteousness, peace is the divine blessing that will be poured on God's people, with his purpose restored and completed. At the beginning of Luke's Gospel the angels announce at Jesus' birth, "Glory to God in heaven, and on earth peace among those whom he favors" (Luke 2:14); similarly salvation (in its most comprehensive sense) can be pronounced in Jesus' words to those forgiven and healed, "Go in peace" (Mark 5:34; Luke 7:50). For Paul, peace refers to overcoming the breach separating God and humanity as well as the inauguration of new relations with God, together with the blessings that accompany life with God (e.g., Rom 5:1-2). The apostle can write, "The peace of Christ must control your hearts—a peace into which you were called in one body" (Col 3:15), this text that clearly points to the inner dimensions of the experience of peace. This way of putting things can be deceptive, however, as inner peace can never be segregated from peaceful relations with God, with the community of God's people, and from a commitment to and hope for God's gift of everlasting peace for all of creation.

Sanctification

Salvation understood as sanctification refers to the holiness of Christ's followers, that is, to their "being made holy." For example, Peter characterizes his audience in relation to God's call to holiness: "As obedient children, you must be holy in every aspect of your lives, just as the one who called you is holy. It is written, *You will be holy, because I am holy*" (1 Pet 1:14-16). As he sketches the believer's comportment vis-à-vis the world, Peter neither condemns the world around them nor urges believers to separate themselves from it. He explains the vocation of the faithful in constructive terms, not negative ones. Accordingly, if we find that Christ-followers are not participating in the goings-on of the world (Peter lists activities like "unrestrained immorality and lust," "drunkenness," "excessive feasting," "wild parties," and idolatry [1 Pet 4:3]), this is not because they renounced the world but rather because they embraced the call to be like God (which, as a by-product, entailed their leaving behind them their past ways). The central question is how one is formed: sculpted according to former desires or modeled after God? Peter goes so far as to say that, in Christ's death, Christ liberated us from "the empty lifestyle" inherited from our ancestors (1 Pet 1:18-21). He thus calls on people not to live their lives "in ways determined by human desires but in ways determined by God's will" (1 Pet 4:2). Peter chooses to speak of becoming holy in terms that we might identify with moral formation.

The road Peter maps draws its lines from God's call on Israel: "I am the LORD, who brought you up from the land of Egypt to be your God. You must be holy, because I am holy" (Lev 11:45). As Leviticus 19 has it, all of these commitments and practices are embraced in the call to holiness. In order for Israel to fulfill its mission of being Yahweh's priesthood in the midst of the nations (Exod 19:6), God's people were to be "holy," that is, "different," or "distinctive." This was not at root a call for segregation, but a model of engagement. To make a difference in the world of nations, Israel was to be different—in the words of Christopher Wright, "recognizably, visibly, and substantively different, as the people belonging uniquely to Yahweh and therefore representing his character and ways."[14]

The Old Testament thus portrays holiness both as a reality of life (God calls out a people, making them distinctive) and a command (God calls that people to a particular way of life). God's people should be what they are; their doing should reflect their being as they live out their identity as God's people. Notice how Paul begins his letter to the troubled believers at Corinth: "to God's church at Corinth, to those *who have been sanctified* in Christ Jesus, *called to be sanctified*" (1 Cor 1:2, my translation).[15] He uses the verb and noun forms of the language of holiness, or sanctification, to speak to the reality within which believers live and into which believers grow. At one and the same time, they have been made holy and they need to live into their call to holiness. This perspective is developed in a different way in Romans 6:19–23 (see also 1 Thess 3–4), where we are told that it is impossible to be a slave both of sin and of righteousness. Rather, having been freed from sin and enslaved to God, believers are placed on the path that leads to sanctification—"a holy life," the outcome of which is "eternal life" (Rom 6:23). "Being holy," then, has an eschatological dimension (insofar as it will be realized fully in the eschaton), but it is already a present experience and calling on account of God's grace at work through the Holy Spirit. "Sanctification" reminds us that salvation is ongoing, that "human health" is not a momentary affair but a gift and way of life.

Hebrews observes that Jesus was holy, blameless, pure (Heb 7:26)—tempted, but without sin (Heb 4:15). The perspective of Hebrews is that the Old Testament is incomplete in itself, and that the Old Testament actually points beyond itself, warning its readers not to make themselves too much at home there. One of its inadequacies is that its prescribed means for dealing with sin, the priesthood and sacrifice, were incapable of leading persons on to the desired goal of perfection. This is overcome in Jesus in two ways. First, he is both the perfect priest and the perfect sacrifice so that his self-offering can deal with human sinfulness once and for all. Second, and more to the point for our concerns here, he is the trailblazer or pioneer of human salvation, who opens up the path of perfect faithfulness. What sense does "perfect" have here? Clearly, moral goodness is part of the picture, but "perfection" cannot be limited to moral goodness in Hebrews. This is because Jesus, though "holy, innocent, incorrupt, separate from sinners, and raised high above the heavens" (Heb 7:26), had still to become perfect (Heb 2:10; 5:7-9; 7:28). Accordingly, "perfect" has to do with Jesus' character, dispositions, allegiances, and behavior, *and* with his becoming fully qualified for the task before him. On the one hand, Hebrews emphasizes that Jesus, the pioneer of salvation, was in every respect like other humans, including the full experience of suffering and temptation, and yet walked faithfully the path of obedience to God. On the other, this book presents Jesus as the one who opened up the road of holy living so that others might follow (Heb 12:1-2).

Epilogue

We have seen in this chapter what a marvelously supple concept salvation is, in biblical perspective. This is not because "salvation" is hard to understand or difficult to tie down in a meaningful way. Rather, it is because salvation speaks to the wide diversity of life experiences, all of them, all of us. It resists reductionisms of every kind—to one "aspect" or "part" of the human person, or even to one person at a time. The terms we have explored, those related to healing and health, shine an array of lights both on people nested in all sorts of relations: with God, with God's people, with the whole of the human community, and with God's good creation, as well as on personal integrity and wholeness. Healing impulses and agents bring all sin and all of sin's effects into the realm of healing, brokenness of all kinds under the careful attentiveness and succor of the Healer.

Thinking of salvation in this way presses against our sensibilities, at least for many of us. We have grown accustomed to thinking of ourselves in isolated ways (my need, my treatment, my health) and in ways more segregated (spiritual versus physical, relational versus genetic, private versus public). It is precisely here that scripture's witness holds out its promise and challenge. Rather than begging to be "applied" to our lives, seeking for its message to be molded to the contours of our needs, the scriptures yearn to reshape and reconstitute the categories by which we comprehend our lives, our worlds, even our greatest needs. We find in scripture who we are and what we might become. Reading scripture, we enter into its evaluation of our condition, but also encounter its promise of restoration, its hope of health.

The biblical motif of healing locates God at center stage. Before there can be talk of salvation, first there is talk of God. God-talk leads to salvation-talk. Theology pours forth as a curative, as a healing regimen, as soteriology. This is the God of the Old and New Testaments, whose work of restoration is displayed in exodus, promised in the prophets, expressed definitively in Jesus, and even now is moving toward its completion in the end. New creation, forgiveness, reconciliation, peace, justification—these motifs and others besides are used in scripture to sketch the expansive grace of God at work in restoring us to health.

There is no escaping the human side of the equation, though, nor those forces that transcend the acts of human beings in their hapless pursuit of malady, disorder, death. Those who know they are ill may desire a return to health, may welcome the gift of healing with arms open wide, but one of the tragedies of prolonged and pervasive illness is its ability to refashion itself as health, to mask infirmity as wellness, to blind us both to the possibility of more and to our need for restoration. Having lost the capacity to reflect critically on our own lives, a loss that is itself symptomatic of our disease, we may not recognize our ill health or perceive how close the pathway we carelessly traverse is to the abyss of death. Alternatively, our disease may cause us to turn on ourselves, and others, to pull away from or actively resist the gracious gift and work of healing.

Those who are ill and seek wellness know that the return to health often involves struggle and cost. Images of warfare come to mind: battling a virus, in the grip of a fever. Luke's Gospel typically sees healing as a defeat of diabolic power, as release from malevolent shackles. And we have noted in the case of Jesus' own healing ministry that wellness-work is not always welcome. So it is not enough to speak of Yahweh the healer and salvation as healing. The biblical story is written with other chapters, illustrated with different images, especially those that congregate around the portrait of the Divine Warrior, Yahweh the Liberator.

chapter three

Yahweh, the Liberator

"With all my heart I glorify the Lord!
   In the depths of who I am I rejoice in God my savior.
He has looked with favor on the low status of his servant.
   Look! From now on, everyone will consider me highly favored
      because the mighty one has done great things for me.
Holy is his name.
He shows mercy to everyone,
   from one generation to the next,
   who honors him as God.
He has shown strength with his arm.
  He has scattered those with arrogant thoughts and proud inclinations.
  He has pulled the powerful down from their thrones
      and lifted up the lowly.
He has filled the hungry with good things
   and sent the rich away empty-handed.
He has come to the aid of his servant Israel,
   remembering his mercy,
   just as he promised to our ancestors,
      to Abraham and to Abraham's descendants forever." (Luke 1:46-55)

These words from Luke's Gospel comprise Mary's Song, known also as the
Magnificat, in which God's mercy and covenant faithfulness are set side by
side with Mary's portrait of God as the Divine Warrior whose incomparable
power is on display in divine deliverance. God is the "mighty one" who ac-

complishes "great things," exhibits "strength" and scatters the arrogant, brings down the powerful from their thrones, and sends the rich away with nothing. This is the God who battles on behalf of his people, who performs dynamic acts in the service of his will.

These words invite serious reflection as we begin this examination of the biblical presentation of God the Liberator who triumphs over those who oppose God and his project. This is because Christians too often relegate the portrait of God the Warrior to the Old Testament, sometimes even drawing a contrast between the God of the Old Testament and the God of the New, warrior versus friend, warmonger versus peacemaker, wrath versus compassion and grace. But here, in a passage that epitomizes the nature of the good news according to Luke's Gospel, we find this vivid presentation of Yahweh as the champion of his people who saves Israel from those who would oppress them. Mary paints a portrait with hues resplendent already in the Old Testament, evoking long and deep reminiscences of God's mighty act of deliverance in the exodus from Egypt and of the divine promises in the prophets of the coming deliverance.[1]

Of course, the image of God at war is obvious in the Old Testament in a way that it is not in the New Testament. This is true especially in Deuteronomy and the historical books. Old Testament scholar Tremper Longman has identified a pattern woven into this theological tapestry. First, Yahweh reveals to Israel that war is pending and discloses when and with whom they were to engage in battle. In other words, Israel is to enter war not on its own initiative, but according to God's behest. Joshua 5:13-15, for example, narrates a divine visitation in which the Warrior God outlines for Joshua the strategy by which he is to defeat Jericho. Later, in Joshua 9, Joshua displeases God by his decision not to proceed with battle. The sacred character of warfare is signaled in these narratives by divine initiative, and also by the rituals that accompany preparation—sacrificial offerings, for example (1 Sam 13:1-15).

Second, Israel ensures God's presence in the midst of battle, signified by the presence of the ark of the covenant with Israel's armies (CEB: "covenant chest" and "chest containing the covenant"). If Yahweh is present, then Israel need not (and must not) depend on its possession of more potent weapons, more stalwart defenses, or superior numbers. Indeed, the Lord informs Gideon that the warriors under his command are too numerous: "You have too many people on your side. If I were to hand Midian over to them, the Israelites might claim credit for themselves rather than for me, thinking, We saved ourselves" (Judg 7:2). Accordingly, Gideon's numbers were reduced from 32,000 to 10,000, and from 10,000 to a mere 300 (Judg 7:3-8). Similarly, though Goliath had a bronze helmet, wore a coat of mail (that weighed 125 pounds!), wore bronze plates to cover his shins, carried a huge spear and a bronze sword with a curved blade (CEB: "scimitar"), and was attended by a shield-bearer, David refused all armor and weaponry, save the staff befitting a shepherd, five smooth stones, and a sling (1 Sam 17). According to the psalmist, "Kings aren't saved by the strength of their armies; warriors aren't rescued by how much power they have. A warhorse is a bad bet for victory; it can't save despite its great strength" (Ps 33:16-17). In the face of battle, says Israel, "Some people trust in chariots, others in horses; but we praise the LORD's name" (Ps 20:7). Finally, after the battle has been engaged, praise is given to Yahweh. Israel, when obedient, wins the war because of Yahweh's power.[2]

The prominence of warfare, and of the portrait of God as Liberator, in the Old Testament, should not mask the presence of these images in the New Testament.[3] Jesus himself engages in warfare (e.g., Matt 12:25-30), for example, the Christian life is sometimes cast in militaristic terms (e.g., 2 Cor 10:3-5; Eph 6:11-12; 1 Tim 6:12; 2 Tim 4:17; Jude 3), and the book of Revelation envisions a great and final battle leading to the defeat of God's enemies. If the nature of this warfare is understood in different ways, if the enemies wear different masks and the weapons used against them derive from a different armory, this does not detract from the potency of the theme of Yahweh the Liberator in New Testament soteriology. The opponents of God and God's purpose and actions are many and powerful, and these cannot be placated or simply fooled but must be defeated if God's creation is to enjoy salvation in all of its fullness.

In this chapter, then, we turn our attention to images of Yahweh the Liberator in scripture. The focus will be on Scripture's definitive and paradigmatic act of liberation, the exodus from Egypt, together with the hopes for deliverance this event activated in Israel's imagination. This will take us to traditions related to the expectation of New Exodus in the latter pages of the Old Testament, as well as the announcement of the actualization of God's promises in the advent of Jesus Christ. This discussion will raise several pressing questions: Given that the exodus from Egypt seems clearly focused on the liberation of a people, what of the liberation of the cosmos? What can "liberation" mean in the context of the Roman Empire? And, in what sense can we speak of God's people "at war"? Throughout this chapter we will see how such related motifs as redemption and ransom, deliverance and rescue, are woven together in scripture.

Exodus as a Paradigm of Israel's Salvation

The fresco of Israel's scriptures is splattered with images of exodus, with scores of unambiguous references to and hundreds of echoes of this foundational event in the life of God's people. References, whether explicit or implicit, to the exodus from Egypt are found in all of the Old Testament's subsections: law, historical narrative, writings, and prophets. Exodus is alive in the memory of God's people, not only as a historic event but also as the lens through which to make sense of present experience and as the matrix within which to shape future hopes. Clearly, the identity of Israel as a people—indeed, as God's people—comes into focus in the exodus: in Israel's deliverance from Egypt, the journey through the wilderness and reception of the law at Sinai, and entry into the land of promise. It is not only God's people who gain an identity here, however. God first reveals his own identity in this story: "I Am Who I Am" (Exod 3:14); and from the exodus onward, this God is known as "the LORD your God who brought you out of Egypt, out of the house of slavery" (Exod 20:2).[4]

The story is anticipated already in Genesis, where God predicted to Abram, "Have no doubt that your descendants will live as immigrants in a land that isn't their own, where they will be oppressed slaves for four hundred years. But after I punish the nation they serve, they will leave it with great wealth" (Gen 15:13-14). However macabre this turn of events might have seemed in prospect (in the case of Abraham) or in reality (in the case of Abraham's descendants), it is precisely through this means that God would accomplish his covenant promises to Abraham, to make of him a great and mighty nation, many in number and occupying a vast expanse of land (Gen 12:2, 7; 13:14-17; 15:5, 18; 18:18). Here is a microcosm of how God would establish a new humanity, provide Israel with a land fit for the gods, and live among them: "I'll take you as my people, and I'll be your God. You will know that I, the LORD, am your God, who has freed you from Egyptian forced labor" (Exod 6:7). Through this sequence of events, God demonstrates both the inclination of his ear to the distressed cries of the oppressed and the nature of his intervention not only to alleviate that distress but also to form among the marginal a people called to embody his own character (see Deut 26:5-10).[5]

The opening chapter of the book of Exodus orients us. Interestingly, it is Pharaoh himself who first declares of this ragtag confederation of clans that they are a "people," "larger in number and stronger than we are" (Exod 1:9). Pharaoh ironically gives voice to God's own perspective and plan, ironic since his intent and actions are set in defiance of God's words. Having labeled the

Hebrew people as a "people," Pharaoh pronounces an official ideology capable of justifying their enslavement—not first as a means of deploying them in his colossal building programs, as we might have anticipated, but, more importantly, as a means of social control: "'Come on, let's be smart and deal with them. Otherwise, they will only grow in number. And if war breaks out, they will join our enemies, fight against us, and then escape from the land.' As a result, the Egyptians put foremen of forced work gangs over the Israelites to harass them with hard work" (Exod 1:10-11). In a series of moves, Pharaoh first enslaves the Hebrews, then tries secretly to slaughter their sons, and finally decrees publicly, "Throw every baby boy born to the Hebrews into the Nile River, but you can let all the girls live" (Exod 1:22). The circumstances sketched here are heinous by any human measure, and it is no wonder that the Israelites are said to groan and cry out (Exod 2:23).

For our purposes, it is crucial that we place the perhaps more obvious suffering and oppression of Israel side by side with the concomitant reality that, in adopting his solution to the problem of the bourgeoning of Abraham's descendants, Pharaoh has usurped God's role and contravened God's promise of blessing. Over and over in these opening chapters of Exodus, Egypt's head is referred to as "king" (Exod 1:8, 15, 18; 2:23; 3:18, 19; 5:4; 6:11, 13, 27, 29; 14:5, 8), a characterization that contrasts sharply with the words that Moses and the Israelites sang after crossing the Reed Sea: "The LORD will rule forever and always" (Exod 15:18). The Song of Moses in Exodus 15 thus celebrates how, through mighty acts, God dethroned Pharaoh, Egypt's king. "The LORD is my strength and my power; he has become my salvation. This is my God, whom I will praise, the God of my ancestors, whom I will acclaim. The LORD is a warrior; the LORD is his name" (Exod 15:2-3). Indeed, in Deuteronomy's retelling of the story, we recognize that God liberates Israel so as to transform their status from a people who serve Egyptian taskmasters to a people who may serve him alone: "Now in light of all that, Israel, what does the LORD your God ask of you? Only this: to revere the LORD your God by walking in all his ways, by loving him, by serving the LORD your God with all your heart and being" (Deut 10:12).[6] This transformation would entail the deconstruction of Egyptian idolatry, the humiliation of Egypt and its gods through the ten plagues visited upon Egypt through God's mighty hand and outstretched arm, as well as the destruction of Egypt's army: "Horse and rider he threw into the sea!" (Exod 15:1).

Biblical theologian Walter Brueggemann has identified a series of verbs used in Israel's testimony to "Yahweh, the God Who Delivers": Yahweh *brings out, delivers, redeems, and brings up.*[7]

63

- Yahweh *brings out*—that is, the movement of Israel is geographical, from one location to another (e.g., Exod 6:6; 13:3). This movement entails liberation, however, and not simply resettlement. It is the consequence of God's initiative, not Israel's. God is the agent who propels his people out of the land of oppression. This decisive act on God's part did not come by means of God's working within the borders of Egypt to cause a redistribution of goods and services, for example, but through the re-creative act of forming a people from among those who were not a people (Hos 1:9; 2:23; cf. 1 Pet 2:10). The Out-of-Egypt-Bringing God has established a Not-Like-Egypt People.

- Yahweh *delivers*—that is, God acts powerfully, forcefully, to rescue Israel from danger (e.g., Exod 3:8; 14:30). This signals the divine struggle with those powers that threaten the well-being of God's people, powers that Israel itself was impotent to counter.

- Yahweh *redeems*—that is, God takes on himself the role of kinsperson to the marginal, intervening on their behalf to forestall the downward spiral of violence against oppressed Israel (e.g., Exod 6:6; 13:15; 15:13). This is not the redemption of slaves through purchase, as one might expect from the economic connotations of the term "redeem," but the emancipation of the enslaved and their restoration to wholeness in relation to him.

- Yahweh *brings up*—that is, when God leads Israel from one place to another, from the land of slavery to the land of promise, he also reverses their status (e.g., Exod 3:8, 17). Human refuse, dregs of the social order—such are those whom God raises up, exalting them. To note an example from later in Israel's history, even if Daniel hardly seems to fit the description of "refuse" or "dregs," he is looked on by the elite as a misfit and threat. God's rescuing him from the lion pit constituted for him a status reversal. A fatality of political intrigue, thrown to the lions, but protected by God, Daniel was lifted up out of the pit even as his enemies were thrown into it. Afterward, "Daniel was made prosperous during the rule of Darius and during the rule of Cyrus the Persian" (Dan 6:28). As Mary would later celebrate, "He has pulled the powerful down from their thrones and lifted up the lowly" (Luke 1:52).

In all of these ways, and more, Israel testifies to the exodus as God's act, and thus to their own existence and character as a nation purposed and established by Yahweh the Liberator.

It is this act that is celebrated in the Song of Moses, and of Miriam:

> I will sing to the LORD, for an overflowing victory!
>> Horse and rider he threw into the sea!
>
> The LORD is my strength and my power;
>> he has become my salvation.
>
> This is my God, whom I will praise,
>> the God of my ancestors, whom I will acclaim.
>
> The LORD is a warrior;
>> the LORD is his name.
>
> Pharaoh's chariots and his army he hurled into the sea;
>> his elite captains were sunk in the Reed Sea.
>
> The deep sea covered them;
>> they sank into the deep waters like a stone.
>
> Your strong hand, LORD, is dominant in power;
>> your strong hand, LORD, shatters the enemy!
>
> With your great surge you overthrow your opponents;
>> you send out your hot anger; it burns them up like straw.
>
> With the breath of your nostrils
>> the waters swelled up,
>> the floods surged up in a great wave;
>> the deep waters foamed in the depths of the sea.
>
> The enemy said, "I'll pursue, I'll overtake, I'll divide the spoils of war.
>> I'll be overfilled with them.
>> I'll draw my sword; my hand will destroy them."
>
> You blew with your wind; the sea covered over them.
>> They sank like lead in the towering waters.
>
> Who is like you among the gods, LORD?
>> Who is like you, foremost in holiness,
>> worthy of highest praise, doing awesome deeds?
>
> You raised your strong hand; earth swallowed them up . . .

The LORD will rule forever and always. (Exod 15:1-18)

This song invites lengthy reflection and rumination, but here I will draw attention to only two observations. First, unlike songs of this type, that is, ancient victory songs, this one is emphatic in its singular focus on God's work. No king, no deliverer, no human being at all occupies central stage. Not even Moses, agent of deliverance, comes in for recognition. We find no hint of self-congratulation on Israel's part. Salvation belongs to God.

Second, this celebration of the exodus from Egypt borrows terms and images from the story of creation. With its affirmations of divine action, the spreading of the waters, the divine breath, and more, the creation story is reprised in this story of intervention and exodus. "In a trembling moment, the world is brought back to the chaotic situation 'in the beginning,' when an act of divine creation is needed to overcome chaos."[8] Deliverance recapitulates creation, so that liberation is cast as new creation.

New Exodus: Hope in Memory

It is difficult to overestimate the influence of the exodus story in Israel's ongoing life and identity. Recent work in neuroscience has brought to our attention how central meaning-making is to our day-to-day experience, and to what lengths we will go to shape and share stories that provide a context for understanding and interpreting our perceived realities. Apparently, one of the distinguishing characteristics of the human family, when compared with Earth's other inhabitants, is this capacity for and drive toward making sense, *storied* sense, of our experienced world.[9] Clearly, one of the ways we do this is through history-telling and history-writing, forms of memory-making that serve generally to make sense of the present in relation to the past and in this way form identity and shape expectations.[10] A perusal of Israel's scriptures with an ear tuned to the resonances of exodus suggests how this event has guided the meaning-making activity of God's people, how profoundly the exodus story has been imprinted on Israel's collective thought patterns. Life rarely comes to us with built-in structures and meaning. By situating the story of our lives within a larger narrative, we find both structure and meaning, and this is precisely the creative and hermeneutical effect of exodus.

The exodus story is captured in liturgy:

> My father was a starving Aramean. He went down to Egypt, living as an immigrant there with few family members, but that is where he became a great nation, mighty and numerous. The Egyptians treated us terribly, oppressing us and forcing hard labor on us. So we cried out for help to the LORD, our ancestors' God. The LORD heard our call. God saw our misery, our trouble, and our oppression. The LORD brought us out of Egypt with a strong hand and an outstretched arm, with awesome power, and with signs and wonders. He brought us to this place and gave us this land—a land full of milk and honey. (Deut 26:5-9)

In the future, God's people are told, children will wonder about the meaning of the laws, regulations, and case laws given by God. Parents are to respond by relating the exodus story: "We were Pharaoh's slaves in Egypt. But the LORD brought us out of Egypt with a mighty hand" (Deut 6:21; see 6:20-25). The ritualized retelling of this story was no mere exercise in memorization and recitation, nor was it motivated by antiquarian interests. Clearly, Passover did not happen to "people way back then." It happened to *us*, to *our* people: "*my* father," "the Egyptians treated *us* terribly, oppressing us and forcing hard labor on us," "we cried out," and so on. The exodus story *is* our story. Successive generations would thus write themselves into this story of Israel's origins, when God created a "people," rescuing them from genocidal slavery and, taking their enemies as his own, proved himself the undeniable and relentless opponent of human oppression. And in thus inscribing themselves into their ancestors' narrative, they would give meaning to their own, contemporary lives.

In Israel's scriptures, this process of community formation around the exodus had two significant effects. The first is the ongoing formation of a people whose imagination is determined by God's liberating initiative and leadership. The second is the exodus-shaped hope that would emerge, guiding Israel into its future and playing so central a role in the pages of the New Testament. By *imagination*, I refer to what theologians call "the power of taking something as something by means of meaningful forms, which are rooted in our history and have the power to disclose truths about life in the world."[11] If "imagination" seems too fanciful, too romantic a term, we could just as easily refer to exodus as formative of certain *conceptual patterns*—the patterns of thinking, feeling, and believing by which we conceive the world (conceptual), which we share with our people (communal), and which guide our behaviors (conative). *Imagination* or *conceptual patterns* work like invisible eyeglasses through which we perceive and construct a unified sense of ourselves, our interactions with others, and, indeed, with the cosmos. Here are the categories by which we construe and experience life, conceive of its unity, and reckon its form and integration. Generally, these conceptual patterns are not systematically articulated, but operate at the unacknowledged level of day-to-day life. To speak of the importance of exodus for Israel's imagination, then, is to signal how Israel's experience of the God who liberated them from the iron grip of Pharaoh and who led them through the wilderness to Sinai and on to "a land flowing with milk and honey" has provided the structures by which Israel comprehends God and life in the world in relation to God. Formed around this experience and image of God, God's people see themselves not as one nation among many, but as occupying a special place of responsibility within the grand narrative of the outworking of God's purpose from creation to new creation.

As a result, the exodus story is not an artifact to be located or discovered among the mothballs of bygone days. Rather, the language of exodus seems always on the tip of the tongue, images of exodus seem always on the horizons of the field of vision, and memories of exodus provide the categories for interpreting life, past, present, and future. The exodus story plays this hermeneutical role for Israel, but not Israel alone. God's people understand that God's mighty deeds, definitively expressed in exodus, lie too at the forefront of God's own declarative memory and are a transparent window into God's own character. And why not? Exodus is God's own signature, after all. Exodus is celebrated annually in the Passover Festival. Exodus is the ground and warrant of Torah, and the giving of Torah at Sinai marks nothing less than the creation of a people whose corporate life was to reflect God's own purpose and character.

The images are everywhere. The story of exodus is fused with the story of the conquest of Canaan (Joshua), with Joshua portrayed as a new Moses. Joshua 3–4 reports the rise of Joshua as Israel's leader, the crossing of the Jordan by Israel in a scene filled with reverberations of the Reed Sea crossing, and the branding of Israel's deliverance on the landscape of Israel's corporate memory. The building of the temple under Solomon is dated from the exodus (1 Kgs 6:1), and the coming of God's glory on the temple at its dedication is portrayed as the culmination of the exodus (1 Kgs 8). Moral decay in Israel under Solomon and Rehoboam is reminiscent of Egypt, and Jeroboam's return from Egypt to deliver his people echoes the story of Moses and Aaron (1 Kgs 11–12). In Psalms, hymns of praise celebrate exodus (e.g., Pss 66, 68, 105), psalms of lament appeal to God's mighty act of deliverance (e.g., Pss 74, 77, 80), and numerous texts draw on the memory of exodus to contrast God's powerful deeds and faithful mercy with the people's faithlessness. Amos, Hosea, and Micah, to mention only three of God's prophetic spokespersons, paint Israel's infidelity with patterns taken either from Egypt or from Israel's rebellion in the wilderness, while portraying Yahweh as the faithful, liberating God who would restore Israel. In these and countless other texts, the scriptures weave the story of Israel's life with strands of yarn spun out of exodus.[12]

Efforts at casting Israel's hope in the well-formed patterns of exodus reach their zenith in Isaiah, and especially Isaiah 40–66. Israel is now in exile on account of its drawing back from its life as a people formed by exodus, its having withdrawn from covenant partnership with God. What hope remains? Just as God had warred against Egypt so as to deliver Israel, God clashed with Israel when Israel patterned its life after oppressive Egypt. Even so, God's judgment against Israel would not be the final word. Importantly, the promise of restoration is formed in the mold of exodus. The book of Isaiah reaches a turning point with chapter 40, insisting that the age of restoration remains a future hope but declaring the certainty of that hope nonetheless. In exodus, God delivered the Hebrew people from Egyptian subjugation, forming them into his own people, and leading them to the land of promise. In New Exodus, God would deliver his people from exile, restoring them as his people. *Apparently, the only way to characterize Israel's reformation and restoration as God's people would require evoking the story that belongs to the founding moment of Israel's life, the exodus story.* This shows, however, that, the exodus story was not to be found on display in a glass cabinet in some gallery of Israel's past but was vibrant and dynamic in the people's ongoing life and self-understanding. And at the center of this story was God: "The LORD is a warrior" (Exod 15:3). "The LORD will go out like a soldier; like a warrior God will stir up rage. God will shout, will roar; over enemies he will prevail" (Isa 42:13).

In the hands of Isaiah, the exodus story is transformed for its role in the service of New Exodus hope.[13] First, the pattern of exodus is reformulated as a future event predicated on the merciful, powerful act of God in Israel's past. Second, taking up threads already evidenced in the Song of Moses (Exod 15), Isaiah recasts the exodus pattern in ways that meld the restoration of Israel with the restoration of the cosmos itself. New Exodus thus merges into New Creation. Third, the identity of God's people is expanded in a way that recalls the promise to Abraham, who was to be the father of many nations (Gen 17:4-5) and not only of Israel. Says the Lord:

> It is not enough, since you are my servant, to raise up the tribes of Jacob and to bring back the survivors of Israel. Hence, I will also appoint you as light to the nations so that my salvation may reach to the end of the earth. (Isa 49:6)

This demonstrates the importance of the exodus story for the past, present, and future work of sorting out the identity of God's people. Integral to this universalistic emphasis is a further, central concern, namely, the claim that Yahweh alone is God and the concomitant rejection of idolatry in all of its forms. Indeed, God's sovereign power is manifest in his liberating, restorative acts, a claim that could never be made on behalf of the idols of the nations (see Isa 40:12-31; 41:1-10; 44:9-20; 46:1-13). Finally, the Isaianic vision of

New Exodus identifies the performative word of God as the instrument by which God would deliver and restore his people. Anthropomorphic images of the Lord's mighty hand and outstretched arm are eclipsed by the word as the means by which God's liberating purpose is actualized. God's word will stand forever (Isa 40:9).

> Just as the rain and the snow come down from the sky and don't return there without watering the earth, making it conceive and yield plants and providing seed to the sower and food to the eater, so is my word that comes from my mouth; it does not return to me empty. Instead, it does what I want, and accomplishes what I intend. (Isa 55:10-11)

This word is a "solemn pledge; a word has left my mouth; it is reliable and won't fail. Surely every knee will bow and every tongue will confess" (Isa 45:23; cf. Phil 2:6-11).

Each in its own way, the opening books of the New Testament pick up and continue the story of Israel, as do other New Testament witnesses. To give one example from among the Gospels, Matthew provides for Jesus an ancestral record structured around exile and anticipating restoration (Matt 1:1-18), then moves into an account of Jesus birth' that recalls Moses' story. At the forefront of this parallelism is the attempt of a malevolent ruler to murder the future liberator of God's people, a scheme that is disappointed even though it leads to the execution of other children. In both accounts, Egypt figures centrally, and a period of exile leads finally to the deliverer's return to his own people where he engages in a divine vocation of bringing salvation to Israel (Matt 2). Even more important than these hints of Jesus' status as the New Moses (cf. Deut 18:15-18), however, is the evidence Matthew provides that Jesus embraces the role of True Israel, together with the many echoes to Israel's Scriptures urging the view that, with Jesus' advent, the hoped-for New Exodus has begun. For example, with regard to Jesus' exile in Egypt, Matthew declares that the child is replicating the historic journey of Israel. Citing Hosea 11:1, a text that speaks of Israel's escape from its oppressors in the ancient past, Matthew writes, "This fulfilled what the Lord had spoken through the prophet: I have called my son out of Egypt" (Matt 2:15). Again, after his baptism, Jesus' responses to the devil's wilderness temptations are each drawn from Israel's experience en route from Egypt to the promised land. Whereas Israel's testing in the wilderness led again and again to failure, Jesus proves himself to be faithful. Indeed, he is the authentic son of God, True Israel (Matt 4:1-10; Deut 8:3; 6:16, 13). The message of the kingdom of heaven is articulated by John the Baptist in relation to Isaiah's prophecy of

New Exodus (Matt 3:1-3; Isa 40:3), and liberation is secured by the Isaianic Servant (Matt 20:28; Isa 53:6-12). The presence of five major discourses of Jesus in Matthew's Gospel suggests that the evangelist portrays Jesus as the New Moses. Matthew also makes explicit the relation of Jesus' ministry of healing to his role as the Isaianic servant in concert with Isaiah's New Exodus (Matt 8:17; 11:5; Isa 35:5-6; 53:4; 61:1-2).

Within Matthew's Gospel, this emphasis on the New Exodus is not first and foremost a matter of Christological interest, as though the evangelist's primary purpose had to do simply with identifying the character of Jesus for his audience. Rather, Matthew's agenda is pointedly ecclesiological, concerned with the nature of the church and its relation to God's purpose and activity among God's people. Just as the events surrounding the exodus were concerned with the calling out and formation of a people through liberation and instruction, so Jesus comes to "save his people from their sins" (Matt 1:21) *and*, in doing so, to form a people who gather in allegiance and submission to him and who carry out the mission that takes its direction and authority from Jesus himself (Matt 28:18-20). As God had promised to Abraham, and as anticipated in images of the New Exodus found in Isaiah, according to Matthew God's renewed people would include "many nations" (cf. Matt 8:5-13; 21:43). And just as God had been present to Israel—in the pillar of fire and cloud—on the exodus journey, so God is "with us" in the advent and ongoing presence of Jesus (Matt 1:23; 28:20; cf. 18:20).

Similar threads are woven into the cloth of 1 Peter, a letter in which the historical distinction between Israel of old and the author's own audience is collapsed in the service of theological identity. Images of exodus and exile, both drawn from Israel's past, form the warp and woof of Peter's portrayal of his audience. They are people on a journey, sojourners, aliens—metaphors that speak to the oppression experienced (yet again) by God's people, the temporary nature of the experience of diaspora in which the people of God are depicted as a journeying people (e.g., 1 Pet 1:3-12) who face the possibility and threat of assimilation and defection. In a wonderful patchwork of images borrowed from Israel's journey, Peter emphasizes the character and hope of his audience as God's people: "But you are a chosen race, a royal priesthood, a holy nation, a people who are God's own possession. You have become this people so that you may speak of the wonderful acts of the one who called you out of darkness into his amazing light. Once you weren't a people, but now you are God's people. Once you hadn't received mercy, but now you have received mercy" (1 Pet 2:9-10). Here are strong reverberations of Exodus 19:1-6 and Isaiah 43:20-21, exodus account and New Exodus promise, through which Israel gained its particular self-awareness, centered in its status as a community liberated, gathered, and led by Yahweh.

The honorable status of God's people, Peter's audience, could hardly more profoundly be highlighted. At the same time, the membership of these people within the community of God's people could hardly stand in more stark contrast with their location on the social fringe of the world-at-large. In their cities across the Anatolian Peninsula, modern-day Turkey, they did not belong, they had no real home, and they suffered the indignities of alienation, dislocation, and venomous ostracism. Abhorred among the nations, these Gentile Christ-followers now share in the elect and precious status of God's covenantal people. As Isaiah had written of the coming New Exodus, "The LORD, redeemer of Israel and its holy one, says to one despised, rejected by nations, to the slave of rulers: Kings will see and stand up; commanders will bow down on account of the LORD, who is faithful, the holy one of Israel, who has chosen you" (Isa 49:7).

Matthew's Gospel and 1 Peter are only two of many New Testament witnesses to the pervasiveness of the theme of New Exodus in early Christianity. The identification of Jesus as "our Passover lamb" (1 Cor 5:7), images of the journeying people of exodus as a model for the Corinthian community (1 Cor 10:1-4), the roots of the language of redemption (e.g., Luke 2:38; Rom 3:24) deep in the soil of exodus reflection (e.g., Deut 7:8; 9:26; Pss 25:22; 26:11) and New Exodus promise (e.g., Isa 41:14; 43:1), these and myriad other texts point to the ongoing significance of understanding salvation in terms of exodus and of the biblical portrayal of Yahweh as Liberator.

The Depth and Breadth of Liberation

Two questions are raised by this emphasis on the liberation motif. First, how does God's work to deliver the oppressed figure in God's concern for the welfare of the whole of creation? Does God's salvation, understood as liberation, reach as far as the cosmos? Second, if Jesus came to restore Israel, and if early Christians proclaimed the actualization of New Exodus in the coming of Jesus and the outpouring of the Spirit, what are we to make of the status of God's people in the Roman Empire? If God's kingdom has drawn near, why does the empire still stand? Both questions are important as we make our way through the witness of scripture on salvation. They also have immediate repercussions for how we understand the place of God's people in the world, not least in a world occupied by kingdoms and governments whose laws and practices do not align themselves with the ancient purposes of God.

What about the Cosmos?

Is proclamation of Yahweh the Liberator good news not only for human beings but also for the cosmos? That such a question could even be raised is evidence already that something has gone wrong. As we have seen in chapter 1, the witness of scripture is that one of the first words that must be spoken over humanity concerns its inseparable, nonnegotiable relation to the world within which the human family has been created and which it inhabits. This suggests already that there are no glad tidings for the human creature that are not also good news for all of creation.

Such categories of thought do not come easily, however. At least, they do not come easily to people who for millennia have understood the world above all in relation to themselves, and especially to people in the United States who have long parsed the human race even further with biases toward individual dignity and responsibility. In their classic account of the American middle class, *Habits of the Heart*, Robert Bellah and his research team identified "autonomous individualism" as the defining quality of American life. Their account of American life would accord privilege to definitions of salvation that have to do with "finding yourself," with gaining independence, with "pulling myself up by my own bootstraps" or, as they put it, by freedom through mobility and detachment from social obligation.[14] What room does this leave for talk of God's saving a people? What room does this leave for God's liberating the whole world? If Bellah's conclusions from the 1980s seem dated in our increasingly postmodern world, a recent study of books published in the United States between 1960 and 2008 suggests otherwise. Over this period, the use of first-person plural pronouns ("we," "our," us") decreased by 10 percent and first-person singular pronouns ("I," "me") increased 42 percent, supporting the researchers' hypothesis concerning increased individualism and decreased collectivism in the United States.[15]

Of course, the conclusions Bellah and his research team reached attracted immediate criticism for giving insufficient attention to minority traditions within the United States—African American and Hispanic communities, for example, or the influences of feminism.[16] And it is true that minority movements have brought to the American table community-valuing interests and practices; however, it is not clear that those commitments have always been embraced and there is plenty of evidence that those commitments have been and continue to be in danger of being overrun by the majority culture. For example, reflecting on the women's movement at the end of the twentieth century, Suzanne Gordon lamented the degree to which women's commitments to relationships, interdependence, collaboration, and community had gone the way of individualism and hierarchy. "Transformative feminism" was too often eclipsed by the "economic woman," characterized by competition and self-interest. "We have entered the male kingdom," she writes, "and yet we have been forced to play by the king's rules."[17] Paralleling these developments is the tragic fragmentation of African American communities, and it is surely of interest that, in a highly significant and justly celebrated collection of essays written by leading African American biblical scholars on the role of African American experience in biblical interpretation, the importance of the location of biblical study within the church as the community of God's people for the reframing and refashioning of biblical interpretation was not a characteristic concern.[18] A counter-example is found in Justo González's *Santa Biblia: The Bible through Hispanic Eyes,* which locates biblical interpretation squarely and profoundly in the Latino/Latina community as a hermeneutical presupposition;[19] the question nonetheless remains whether the American church will learn anew from its Hispanic brothers and sisters something of its own birthright and mandate as the community of God's people.

Still, with the rise of postmodernism, has the autonomous individualism of the mid- and late-twentieth century not given way to new emphases on community? If we took seriously how significant our social interactions are in the formation of our "selves," right down to the formation of processes involved in the cooperative interactions within our brain systems,[20] we would not be surprised that the autonomous individualism espoused and embodied in the dominant American culture has spread and continues to spread like a virus. We come to embody the influences nearest to us. Some might point to portrayals of community and friendship on popularly rated television programs as evidence that the tide is turning; after all, these media products arguably both express and shape the imagination and practices of their viewers. Still others might point to heightened interest among Americans in the small group movement, which in 1994 was reported to involve some 40 percent of the population. Although they underscore the human yearning for community, these phenomena do not signal a radical departure from earlier decades. Rather, like counting Facebook friends or Twitter followers or additions to Google+ circles, the "community" they represent is often characterized better by its breadth than its depth. Such "community" places few demands on its "members," who are more likely to control their sense and experience of community than to subject themselves to related commitments and obligations; and movement from friend to friend, group to group—friending and unfriending, following or unfollowing—comes with relative ease, in the service of a self-serve, do-it-yourself "community life."[21]

To be clear, I am not denying the reality or importance of these emerging forms of "community" as much as recognizing how they stretch the concept of "community" itself. My point is that these forms of social interaction actually do little to undermine the conclusions Bellah and his team reached. Notions of community in scripture typically refer to life together in daily interaction, communal meals, common allegiances, even shared resources; living proximately and with lives intertwined, secrets are hard to keep, emoticons are unnecessary, and working toward agreement is not only a theological but a practical necessity.

And, of course, the real point is that it is difficult to think of good news for the redemption of the cosmos when life is defined in terms so fully human and individual. Again, however, this admission is less a commentary on the biblical portrait of salvation and more a commentary on human proclivities on this side of Eden. Without neglecting the importance of an emphasis on the *personal* aspects of God's liberating power, then, we must push further by recognizing, on the one hand, that human beings are embedded in the human family and the human family is embedded in the whole cosmos and, on the other, that the forces of evil that must be overcome in salvation have targeted the whole of God's good creation and not only individual human beings.

Already latent in the exodus tradition is ancient testimony in Israel's scriptures that God's people have long been aware of those larger forces requiring Yahweh's attention. The God of Israel is portrayed in the exodus story as sovereign over the world's powerful structures, and as seeking and shaping new structures within which his aims and character are to be embodied. As interpreted elsewhere in the scriptures, Genesis 3 already testifies to the presence of a most potent enemy against God and his purposes. This is the snake, whose introduction into the story disrupts creation harmony and leads to enmity within the human family and conflict in the cosmos (Gen 3:1-15). By the writing of the Christian Bible's last book, Revelation, this snake has become unmistakably identified as the devil, Satan, whose unqualified defeat is set within the framework of the coming of the day of salvation:

> Then there was war in heaven: Michael and his angels fought the dragon. The dragon and his angels fought back, but they did not prevail, and there was no longer any place for them in heaven. So the great dragon was thrown down. The old snake, who is called the devil and Satan, the deceiver of the whole world, was thrown down to the earth; and his angels were thrown down with him. Then I heard a loud voice in heaven say, "Now the salvation and power and

kingdom of our God, and the authority of his Christ have come. The accuser of our brothers and sisters, who accuses them day and night before our God, has been thrown down." (Rev 12:7-10)

In general terms, this interpretation is not a New Testament novelty, but is anticipated in Isaiah's vision of the new creation, with its echo of God's curse on the snake in Genesis 3:14: "Wolf and lamb will graze together, and the lion will eat straw like the ox, but the snake—its food will be dust. They won't hurt or destroy at any place on my holy mountain, says the LORD" (Isa 65:25). In another Isaianic text, the demise of the snake is correlated with an important motif from the exodus story, namely, Yahweh's authority over the sea as an image of the conquest of evil. In the book of Exodus, Israel's enemies "sank like lead in the towering waters" (Exod 15:10), whereas in Isaiah the prophet declares of the coming day of salvation, "On that day, the LORD will take a great sword, harsh and mighty, and will punish Leviathan the fleeing serpent, Leviathan the writhing serpent, and will kill the dragon that is in the sea" (Isa 27:1).

The conflict between Yahweh and the sea, and between Yahweh and sea monsters, is an often-repeated motif in Israel's scriptures. Yahweh overcomes the sea's potency through his rebuke (Nah 1:4), sits in conquest over the flood (Ps 29:10), and has crushed the heads of Leviathan (Ps 74:12-17; cf. Isa 27:1). It is little wonder that John the Seer writes of the coming of the new creation and final conquest of evil with these words: "Then I saw a new heaven and a new earth, for the former heaven and the former earth had passed away, *and the sea was no more*" (Rev 21:1, emphasis added).

This provides the frame we need if we are to grasp the significance of other stories in scripture, such as the Gospel accounts of Jesus walking on the water. For example, in Mark 6:45-51, we read:

Right then, Jesus made his disciples get into a boat and go ahead to the other side of the lake, toward Bethsaida, while he dismissed the crowd. After saying good-bye to them, Jesus went up onto a mountain to pray. Evening came and the boat was in the middle of the lake, but he was alone on the land. He saw his disciples struggling. They were trying to row forward, but the wind was blowing against them. Very early in the morning, he came to them, walking on the lake. He intended to pass by them. When they saw him walking on the lake, they thought he was a ghost and they screamed. Seeing him was terrifying to all of them. Just then he spoke to them, "Be encouraged! It's me. Don't be afraid." He got into the boat, and the wind settled down.

If our patterns of thought were not shaped by Israel's scriptures, we might label this story a "nature miracle" or otherwise wonder at this strange report of the seemingly impossible. Note, however, echoes from the exodus story:

- the explicit time element ("very early in the morning"), an allusion to the morning's approach in Exodus 14:24, which marked the onset of Israel's crossing of the Sea

- the parallel description of the crossing of the Sea in Psalm 77:16-20, which describes the waters as trembling at the sight of God and God's leading Israel by his taking a path on the mighty waters ("But your footprints left no trace!" [Ps 77:19])

- the analogy of Jesus' intention to "pass by them" with God's passing in front of Moses (Exod 34:6)

- Jesus' self-identification with the words, "I am" (ἐγώ εἰμι, *egō eimi*; CEB: "It's me"), echoing the "I Am" of Yahweh's self-disclosure to Moses at the burning bush (ἐγώ εἰμι, *egō eimi*; Exod 3:14)

Note too the scriptural testimony to Yahweh's power over chaos, his unqualified sovereignty, expressed by his control of the waters, walking on the waters, trampling the waves, overcoming its fury, and his rescuing people from the sea (e.g., Gen 1:2, 6-9; 8:1-3; Job 9:8; Hab 3:15; Pss 18:16; 77:19; 107:23-32; Isa 43:16; 51:9-10; Jonah 1). In short, reports of Jesus walking on the water present Jesus in the role of liberator from the chaos of evil and as the one through whom new creation is being actualized.

The portrait of Jesus in battle against the powers of evil extends further in the Gospels, especially to his engagement with Satan and demons. Stories of Jesus' temptation in the wilderness and accounts of exorcism are found in the Gospels of Matthew, Mark, and Luke.[22] An important window into their significance is provided by the controversy over Jesus' association with Beelzebul in Luke 11:17-22. Having been accused of expelling demons by the power of the ruler of demons, Jesus responds:

> Every kingdom involved in civil war becomes a wasteland, and a house torn apart by divisions will collapse. If Satan is at war with himself, how will his kingdom endure? I ask this because you say that I throw out demons by the authority of Beelzebul. If I throw out demons by the authority of Beelzebul, then by whose authority do your followers throw them out? Therefore, they will be your judges. But if I throw out demons by the power of God, then God's

kingdom has already overtaken you. When a strong man, fully armed, guards his own palace, his possessions are secure. But as soon as a stronger one attacks and overpowers him, the stronger one takes away the armor he had trusted and divides the stolen goods.

What is at stake in this exchange is the source of Jesus' authority. The charge brought against him, "He throws out demons with the authority of Beelzebul, the ruler of demons" (Luke 11:15), acknowledges Jesus' success as an exorcist, but attempts to marginalize Jesus' influence among the people by casting him in the role of a magician or witch, that is, as a social and religious deviant who should not be taken seriously. Jesus' response presumes that the names "Beelzebul" ("Lord of the Flies") and "Satan" refer to the same entity; that Satan is the head of a household or kingdom; that Satan exercises command over demons, who serve his aim; and that Satan's dominion is unified. Consequently, if Jesus were to wield Satan's authority, this would signal Satan's countenancing civil war within his own domain, an absurdity. Instead, Jesus insists, his exorcisms bring to tangible expression a stronger power than that brandished by the Lord of the Flies. They are manifestations of God's own power, the sovereignty of God breaking into the world by means of Jesus' ministry. In v. 20, Jesus refers to his casting out demons "by the finger of God" (CEB: "power of God"), an idiom found in the struggle between God's rule and Pharaoh's in the exodus story. Faced with the plagues brought against Egypt, Pharaoh's magicians exclaim, "This is the finger of God!" (Exod 8:19; CEB: "This is something only God could do!"). In the Synoptic Gospels, Jesus' ministry serves as the flash point for a clash of kingdoms; read against this backdrop, Jesus' exorcisms are manifestations of the power of the liberating God, who sets free those whom Satan has bound (cf. Luke 13:10-17). If, as Jesus' ministry of exorcism portends, "God's kingdom has already overtaken you," then Satan's dominion is already being repealed.

Turning from the Gospels to Paul, we move from this sort of direct engagement with diabolic power to numerous references to "principalities and powers," a phrase Paul uses to refer to powers aligned against God's purpose and, thus, against Christ and his church. Actually, Paul deploys a range of related terms: "rulers," "authorities," "powers," "thrones," "angels," and "forces of cosmic darkness," to name the more prominent (Rom 8:38; Eph 3:10; 6:12; Col 1:16; 2:15).[23] What these terms denote is not always certain, though in Pauline usage they typically refer to spiritual forces that come to expression in sociopolitical realities. Only rarely, if ever, can one attribute to Paul a concern with spiritual forces of evil devoid of their expression in human institutions; similarly, it is hard to find in Paul a theology of human institutions aligned against God that does not account for the animation of those institutions with diabolic breath. In Paul's world, popular religion, associated with magic, mystery, and astrology, conjured a world inhabited by spirits capable of being manipulated to achieve ends both good and evil. Spiritual powers were often regarded as malevolent, to be feared and, whenever possible, appeased. Paul does not deny the existence of "thrones or powers," but he does put them in their place (see especially Col 1–2). First, they should not be regarded as eternal. Since they were created through Christ, they were inhabitants of a created cosmos over which God could pronounce the verdict, "It is good." Second, though the details of the narrative are missing in Paul, it is clear nonetheless that these powers had failed to exercise their assigned role in the cosmos and had become hostile to God, his purposes, and his people. Third, nevertheless, he affirms, in the cross of Christ, the powers had been unmasked in their pretensions to royal authority and grandeur. Stripped of the garments of their dominion, the powers were not annihilated but restored to their purpose in creation. Having been conquered in Jesus' death, they had been reconciled to Christ. Borrowing language from the exodus story, Paul sketches this process of reconciliation in terms of deliverance: "He rescued us from the control of darkness and transferred us into the kingdom of the Son he loves. He set us free through the Son and forgave our sins" (Col 1:13-14). Indeed, images tumble over each other in this text so that salvation is represented as divine rescue both from the shackles of an evil dominion aligned against God and from the dire consequences of our sinful acts, and as the anticipation of the restoration of creation.

Without in any way wanting to undermine the concrete realities of the liberation Paul has sketched, I also want to underscore how Paul understands liberation as having hermeneutical value. That is, God's people are those who have passed from one way of construing the cosmos to another so that they are able to see with the eyes of faith the astounding presence of God at work in the world and to reconsider the value they place on the constituents of that world. For example, in Galatians 4:3, 9, Paul uses a much-contested phrase, "the elements of the cosmos" (my translation; CEB: "this world's system" and "world system"). If we take this phrase in its most simple sense, it refers to the basic elements of the world—air, earth, fire, and water—and then, in the philosophical thought of his day, to the fourfold opposition of air/earth, fire/water, cold/hot, wet/dry. In the socioreligious world defined in this letter to the Galatians, these basic oppositions would be Jew/Gentile, slave/free, male/female (Gal 3:28). Here, then, is an instance of transformation, not only in the referent of "elements of the cosmos," but, more crucially, with regard to the basic way the world is defined.[24] With the advent of Christ, and with the appropriation of the work of Christ in Christian baptism, the elements of social and religious distinction are reinterpreted. "There is neither Jew nor Greek; there is neither slave nor free; nor is there male and female, for you are all one in Christ Jesus" (Gal 3:28). Similarly, Paul writes to the Corinthians, "So then, from this point on we won't recognize people by human standards. Even though we used to know Christ by human standards, that isn't how we know him now" (2 Cor 5:16).

What about Rome?

For some, words about liberation and rescue in the New Testament may sound rather hollow, since when they were first spoken or written in the first century, they appear not to have found expression in proactive resistance against Rome. How could those first Christians speak of divine deliverance without dealing immediately and forcefully with Rome, whose imperial life stood in conspicuous opposition to the aims of God and the commitments of God's people? If exodus from Egyptian oppression provides the paradigm for God's intervention, what does it mean to proclaim New Exodus, if not deliverance, from Roman oppression? These are important questions that invite serious reflection. Let me mention three considerations that might guide those reflections.

A Problem of Category: First, we need simply to set aside those past approaches to this problem that reflected too much of the modern Western world and too little of the ancient Mediterranean world. Previous studies of "church and state" (as they were often labeled) were troublesome in two respects. First, as the pair "church and state" already implies, those studies tended to assume ideas about "separation of church and state" (or religion and politics) more at home in our world than in the first century. Consequently, readers of the New Testament tended to highlight Jesus' (or Paul's) "spiritual" message while assuming his apathy on political matters.

To take one particularly grievous example, I heard repeatedly in my teen years the story Matthew reports concerning the final judgment (Matt 25:31-46), retold in ways that stripped Jesus' words of any social, economic, or political concern. In Matthew's Gospel, king Jesus speaks of those of whom it could be said, "I was hungry and you gave me food to eat. I was thirsty and you gave me a drink. I was a stranger and you welcomed me. I was naked and you gave me clothes to wear. I was sick and you took care of me. I was in prison and you visited me" (Matt 25:35-36). In the retelling so familiar to me, king Jesus rewarded those who shared with people who were hungry for the meat of God's word (cf. 1 Cor 3:1-2) and thirsty for the living water of eternal life (cf. John 4:10, 14), who shared the gospel with those who were strangers to God, who helped people who were spiritually naked to put on God's armor (cf. Eph 6:13-17), and who prayed for those who were sickened or imprisoned by sin. The message I heard in my youth spiritualized Jesus' words in ways that ensured that the measure of faithfulness among God's people could be taken without reference to the day-to-day challenges of the needy. A few years later, as a college student, I was impressed to take Jesus' words at face value, with the result that I talked the local jailers into letting me come to the city and county prisons each week.

Today, we recognize more and more that politics and religion, economics and religion, social life and religion were inextricably interwoven in the ancient Mediterranean world. The compartmentalization of life many of us take for granted would never have even been considered as an option in Greco-Roman antiquity.

A second error in previous study had to do with what we allow to count as evidence for political interest in the New Testament. A message about Rome could be regarded as political if and only if it called for outright resistance, even rebellion. This resulted in two basic options. Either Jesus and the early church were apolitical or Jesus and the early church should be numbered among first-century freedom fighters. Since they were obviously not freedom fighters,[25] then they must have been apolitical.

If we dismantle these anachronistic categories and inquire into how marginal groups worked to maintain and cultivate their identities in the midst of empire, as well as how they display their true allegiances through unconventional practices (notice the use of Jewish names and the choice of a traditional diet in Dan 1), then we can begin to think differently about the political ramifications of the coming of Christ. Indeed, we can begin to examine afresh those implicit and unspoken scripts in Jesus' words and actions, and the words and actions of his followers, which actually demonstrate their freedom from and challenge to imperial demands.[26]

Who Are My Enemies (and What Is My Responsibility to Them)? Second, we must recognize how the terms of the exodus have been transformed. Previously, the line between Israel and its enemies seems to have been more easily drawn: the Hebrew people on the one side, their Egyptian oppressors on the other. The tenets of Torah complicated this somewhat, by extending Yahweh's care and compassion and, therefore, Israel's, also to the immigrant living among God's people. Stories in Israel's scriptures demonstrate further how God's mercy and healing extended beyond the borders of Israel, to Naaman the Syrian leper, for example, or to the Sidonian widow, stories that provide a pattern for Jesus' ministry in Luke's Gospel (1 Kgs 17:8-24; 2 Kgs 5:1-19; Luke 4:16-30). The tale of Jonah illustrates how easily, and erroneously, those outside Israel's boundaries might be regarded as the enemy. Indeed, God must go to extraordinary ends to convince Jonah of the reach of his compassion and of the capacity of those beyond the boundaries of God's people to hear God's word and respond appropriately: "Can't I pity Nineveh, that great city, in which there are more than one hundred twenty thousand people who can't tell their right hand from their left, and also many animals?" (Jonah 4:11). In the dim light of only the most unadorned of prophetic warnings—"Just forty days more and Nineveh will be overthrown!" (Jonah 3:4)—both humans and animals mourn and repent (Jonah 3:6-10). The irony of Nineveh's response is not lost on Jesus, who declares to God's own people, Israel: "The people of Nineveh will rise up at the judgment with this generation and condemn it, because they changed their hearts and lives in response to Jonah's preaching—and one greater than Jonah is here" (Luke 11:32).

"Who is my neighbor?" the legal expert asks of Jesus, in the midst of their exchange on the implications of Leviticus 19:18: "You must love your neighbor as yourself." Who could have anticipated that neighborly compassion would (must!) extend to Jew-Samaritan relations? And yet this is the position Jesus takes in the parable of the Compassionate Samaritan (Luke 10:25-37), a position that he regards as fully congruent with Torah. Similarly, Paul recognizes that Gentiles could no longer be cast as enemies, pure and simple, since Christ's death had obliterated the old dividing walls and opened the way for a single human family in Christ (e.g., Gal 3:10-14; cf. Col 1:21; Eph 2:17). The heavenly gathering of God's people, John reports, includes persons "from every nation, tribe, people, and language" (Rev 7:9-11). How does one think about the political ramifications of the good news when, central to that good news, is an anointed king, Jesus, who speaks of loving one's enemies (e.g., Matt 5:43-48; Luke 6:27-36)? Clearly, the line between "us" and "them" has become more difficult to manage or maintain, or even draw.

Perhaps even more far-reaching is the depersonalization of the concept of "enemy." The true enemy of God's people could not be identified with the people of Rome, but rather with the forces and powers that found expression in Roman rule. An important consequence is a shift of battleground, from flesh-and-blood hostility to a confrontation over what values, what allegiances, what interpretations of the world would govern the commitments and behaviors of God's people.

Rewriting Political Scripts: Third, we must take seriously the multitudinous ways in which the pages of the New Testament are subversive of the Roman Empire, of Roman rule, of Roman religion, of Roman ideology. Because the New Testament writers do not call for outright revolutionary resistance, they have sometimes been thought to promote a pro-Roman stance. Nothing could be further from the truth,[27] as these four examples will suggest:

- The birth of Jesus as narrated by Luke contrasts two ways of peace, two kingdoms (Luke 2:1-20).[28] On the one hand is Roman peace—celebrated as "good news," lodged in worldwide recognition of Emperor Augustus as Rome's savior and lord of all civilized peoples, expressed by and enforced in the business of census-taking, itself the necessary precursor to exacting yearly taxes from a subjugated people. On the other hand is Jesus, "Savior" and "Lord," whose birth is celebrated as the "good news" that signals the advent of peace that comes from God. In the context of imperial Rome, Mary's Song in Luke 1:46-55 takes on a more threatening and revolutionary tone: "He has pulled the powerful down from their thrones and lifted up the lowly. He has filled the hungry with good things and sent the rich away empty-handed."

- For Paul, the lordship of Christ is an enormously significant political statement. In a world in which Gentile kings "lord it over" their subjects, Paul's Christology has special poignancy. In Philippians, for example, Jesus' lordship is universal (so that even lord Nero would bow, confessing that Jesus Christ is Lord) and grounded in his humility and death, indeed, in the ignominy of his death by crucifixion (Phil 2:6-11). On this basis, Paul can argue throughout his letter that the Philippians are to take their standards for comportment in the empire from Lord Jesus and not from lord emperor (e.g., Phil 1:27-30).

- In an apparently innocuous list of prescribed attitudes, Peter writes, "Honor everyone. Love the family of believers. Have respectful fear of God. Honor the emperor" (1 Pet 2:17). In a world determined by Roman hegemony, the last admonition, "Honor the emperor," is expected, a reflection of the increasingly pervasive influence of the worship of the emperor as though he were a god. Juxtaposing this admonition with the universal counsel, "Honor everyone," undercuts the cult of the emperor by leveling the playing field, however. The emperor is to be honored not as a deity nor even as the elitist of all people, as though he were separate from and above everyone else, but simply because, like everyone else, he is a member of the human family.

- One last example: John divulges the contents of a Rome-bound seafaring cargo in order to portray the center of the empire as a mistress-prostitute who maintains her luxurious lifestyle at the expense of her lovers, the conquered peoples of the Roman Empire. John thus exposes a network of economic interests, including kings, merchants, and mariners (those who have most to gain from Roman economic dominance), as well as common people, exploited but bedazzled by Roman opulence and propaganda. John copies into his account an ancient bill of lading: "gold, silver, jewels, and pearls; fine linen, purple, silk, and scarlet; all those things made of scented wood, ivory, fine wood, bronze, iron, and marble; cinnamon, incense, fragrant ointment, and frankincense; wine, oil, fine flour, and wheat; cattle, sheep, horses, and carriages; and slaves, even human lives" (Rev 18:12-13). Where the CEB reads "slaves, even human lives," we could translate "bodies, that is, human lives." On ancient cargo lists, one might find a reference to "bodies," a term from a Roman slave trade that reduced human beings, slaves, to their bodies. John corrects this view, however: slaves are not bodies, but human beings. With only a few strokes of the pen, then, he presses hard against Roman ideology. Slaves are more than their physicality; they are human beings wrongly cataloged as mere meat, like so many carcasses, alongside cattle and sheep.

These are subtle, but real illustrations of the way the gospel would erode the seemingly impregnable strongholds of Roman ideology. Read through lens provided by the biblical witness to Yahweh as Liberator, such texts remind us that the message of exodus continues into and beyond the New Testament.

Epilogue

Many of the threads of this discussion come together in Revelation, the Bible's last book. This may be expected, since in so many ways the books of Genesis and Revelation form a matching set of bookends to the Christian scriptures, with New Creation embracing and extending Creation. In the New Testament, our interest in Yahweh the Liberator comes into particular focus in Revelation, with its major development of the motifs of war and conquest. It is not too much to say that Revelation is the Bible's most violent book, with images of combat, battle, and conquest splashed across almost every page. At the conclusion of this discussion of salvation as liberation for the whole cosmos, including the people of God, it will be helpful to explore these images briefly, not least given the role this prophetic book gives to the people of God in the Last Battle.

The importance of the cosmos to the revolutionary message of salvation of Revelation is signaled in several ways. First, in the opening scene of John's vision, located in heaven's great throne room, God is celebrated as Creator:

> You are worthy, our Lord and God,
>> to receive glory and honor and power,
>>> because you created all things.
>> It is by your will that they existed
>>> and were created. (Rev 4:11)

God's saving purpose and intervention are set within the larger framework of the whole of creation and his prior work as Creator. This is fully congruent with Israel's expectation that the time of restoration would not be concentrated narrowly on the salvation of individuals, nor even on humanity alone; Israel's hope was for the restoration of the whole of God's creation.

This is in fact the reality to which John's vision would finally point: "Then I saw a new heaven and a new earth, for the former heaven and the former earth had passed away, and the sea was no more" (Rev 21:1). Continuity between the present and future is guaranteed by the dual mention of heaven and earth. Discontinuity is indicated by the repetition of the adjective "new," which here, as in Second Temple Jewish literature more generally, might better be translated as "renewed." It is "new" in the sense that cosmic restoration requires the fresh, creative work of God, but not in the sense that the old is discarded so as to be replaced by an altogether different creation. "Look!" the Creator proclaims, "I'm making all things new" (Rev 21:5), using words that echo the promise of renewal in Isaiah 65:17 and that cast the work of salvation on a mural of the grandest of proportions: the whole cosmos.

Second, and perhaps more noticeable, is how John has portrayed the character of evil in Revelation. At times, it may appear that Rome is the axis of evil in the world John paints, but it is significant that Rome, also known as Babylon, is not the primary target of divine warfare. God's people are to abandon Rome, but they are not called to work for its destruction (Rev 18:4). God's principal enemy, the enemy that must be defeated, is that diabolic triad: the dragon or snake, the deceiver of the world, the devil, or Satan (Rev 12:9; 20:2); the sea-beast, which exercises the dragon's dominion (Rev 13:1-

10); and the earth-beast, which causes people to worship the sea-beast (Rev 13:11-18). Within the world John portrays, the sea-beast is none other than Rome's imperial dominion, which exerts itself over against God's purposes and claims for itself the possession and exercise of exalted, absolute power. Given our earlier comments on the association of the sea with chaos and evil, it is no wonder that John envisions the dragon as calling this beast out of the sea, nor that Rome has extended its power in large part through its control of the Mediterranean. Through sea travel Rome would have first made its presence and power known to the lands of the east, including the territories to which John has addressed his book. Similarly, the earth-beast would refer to those varied means by which the worship of Rome and Rome's leader would have spread throughout the empire. In other words, the battle between good and evil does not pit Christians against nonbelievers. The confrontation of which John writes is cosmic in scale, with divine authority and energies arrayed against the powers lurking behind and guiding the human faces of this world's empires.

For John, a chief symbol of salvation is the exodus, with Jesus himself presented as the Passover Lamb through whom the forces of evil are overcome and God's people are ransomed and gathered together as "a kingdom and priests to our God" (Rev 5; cf. Exod 19:5-6). Combining references to the exodus and to Isaiah's New Exodus, John shows that the liberating roles of Passover Lamb and Suffering Servant of Isaiah converge in the sacrificial death of Jesus. Other images from exodus abound: Christian martyrs who have experienced the New Exodus, crossed the heavenly Sea, and stand at its banks singing the Song of Moses (Rev 15:1-5), for example; and the series of plagues by which God judges those who oppose his will (Rev 15-16).

What is the role of God's people in the battle? John attributes victory to the Lion and the Lamb, both references to Christ, in Revelation 5:5 and 17:14. More pervasive, however, is the designation of God's faithful as those who conquer (e.g., Rev 2:7, 11, 17, 26; 15:2; 21:7). Clearly, they are engaged in the conflict, not passive or disinterested onlookers. On the one hand, this means that quiet acquiescence and withdrawal are not among the options available to God's people as they seek a faithful response to the presence of evil in the world. On the other, it presses the importance of identifying clearly and exercising faithfully their implements of war. As we interact with Revelation, seemingly overrun with images of violence, this is all the more crucial. How do God's people join the battle? Revelation 12:11 is thematic in this respect: "They gained the victory over him on account of the blood of the Lamb and the word of their witness. Love for their own lives didn't make them

86

afraid to die." God's people are called to overcome the enemy, but not with artillery provided them by any earthly military machine. Instead, the weapons of their conquest are patient endurance, faithfulness, the Lamb's death, and the word of their witness (see Rev 2:3, 7, 10, 11, 25, 26; 3:5, 12; 12:11; 13:10; 14:12; 15:2; 19:10). That is, the divine war against evil is engaged and won through adopting the way of the Lamb, through active participation as witnesses to the truth of God, even at the cost of one's own life. "To be faithful to the true God even to the point of death is not to become a victim of the beast, but to take the field against him and win."[29]

John thus underscores for us the radical character of evil, together with the even more vital power of God. Conquering is costly and demands a rebirth of images that will allow us to imagine that faithful witness in life and death has unrivaled and irrepressible potency in the face of evil. The chorus sung to the Lamb of God draws on exodus-memory to remind us of the topsy-turvy way Yahweh the Liberator actualizes his purpose:

> You are worthy to take the scroll
> and open its seals,
>> because you were slain,
>> and by your blood you purchased for God
>>> persons from every tribe, language,
>>> people, and nation.
> You made them a kingdom and priests
> to our God,
>> and they will rule on earth. (Rev 5:9-10)

chapter four

How Can We Be Saved?

S ave yourselves from this perverse generation!" These words summarize Peter's prophetic address to those gathered at Pentecost, as Luke
narrates the story (Acts 2:40, my translation). We find in this demand both
puzzle and perplexity.

The puzzle lies in the apparent assertion that people in Peter's audience
ought "to save" themselves—that is, that they should do something to be
saved, that they might be the agents of their own deliverance. It is possible to
translate the verb differently, as a passive, so that it reads, "Be saved" (CEB).
It is precisely as we try to navigate these two options that we are confounded,
however, since throughout scripture these two are held in tandem: the identification of God alone as Savior and God's invitation for partners in the way of
salvation. We find in scripture requests made to God that he save (e.g., 1 Sam
7:8; 2 Kgs 19:9; 1 Chron 16:35), as well as ample evidence that people can
serve as God's agents to bring salvation to others (e.g., 1 Sam 24–26), though
even these texts make clear that salvation belongs to the Lord. Salvation is not
ours to accomplish. Salvation has as its consistent subject God, yet this does
not relegate human beings to the sidelines, passive with regard to their own
liberation.

Since human beings cannot adopt a passive role in the face of God's work
of salvation, human response must be necessary. In fact, Peter's prophetic

warning at Pentecost presumes that the divine work of salvation can be embraced as well as resisted. Moreover, his reference to "this perverse generation" presumes that God's saving work actually will be resisted, at least by some. Salvation is clearly available, but the announcement of good news doubles as a word about a pending division within Israel (see Luke 2:34-35). As was the case in the past with Israel in the exodus story, so is the case now with New Exodus, people can and will respond to God's saving initiative perversely, rebelliously (Exod 32:9; 33:3; Deut 10:16; 32:5; cf. Luke 11:29-32; 50-51; 17:25; Acts 7:51-53). Accordingly, from this perspective, salvation involves disassociating ourselves from those perverse grumblers who resist God's ways, and we do this through responses of faith, a change of heart and life, and baptism (Acts 2:38).

In chapters 2 and 3, we gained an overview of the identification of God as the subject of the work and initiator of salvation. We can extend this emphasis a bit further by noting the background in Israel's scriptures of the central Christian concern with the "gospel." Since the days of Justin Martyr (ca. 100–165 CE), Christians have known the first four books of the New Testament as "Gospels" and so have learned to associate the term with narratives of the ministry, death, and resurrection of Jesus. For Paul, and in Christian proclamation more generally, however, the "gospel" is "the true message" (Col 1:5), the "message of reconciliation" (2 Cor 5:19), the "good news of your salvation" (Eph 1:13), the "message of the cross" (1 Cor 1:18), the transforming word, which has Jesus Christ as its object and source. The New Testament authors also know this "gospel" as "God's good news,"[1] the background of which is found in announcements of glad tidings in Israel's scriptures. There, and especially in Isaiah, this gospel is the good news of God's restoration of Israel, which signals the end-time salvation marked by Yahweh's presence. "Strengthen the weak hands, and support the unsteady knees. Say to those who are panicking: 'Be strong! Don't fear! Here's your God, coming with vengeance; with divine retribution God will come to save you" (Isa 35:3-4). This is the wilderness cry of Isaiah's messenger of comfort and compassion: "Here is your God!" (Isa 40:9). "How beautiful upon the mountains are the feet of a messenger who proclaims peace, who brings good news, who proclaims salvation, who says to Zion, 'Your God rules!'" (Isa 52:7-8). The Lord's advent inaugurates the regathering and restoration of God's people from their exile among the nations. When he comes, he will lead them through the waters and the fire as once he led them through the sea; he will shepherd and provision them, and they will see his glory.[2] The coming of Yahweh entails salvation. Without his return, apart from his presence, there is no salvation.

If the biblical witness is clear in its identification of Yahweh as the source and author of salvation, the question remains how salvation is mediated to and embraced by human beings. This is the concern of this chapter. Taking as our point of departure scripture's witness that Yahweh draws near to save, we will first explore three "moments" in the life of Israel where the saving presence of God is exhibited. This agenda will turn our focus first, and briefly, to exodus—briefly because the exodus was so central to our interests in chapter 3; and then to the role of the temple (and temple sacrifices) in the life of God's people; and finally to the advent of Jesus the Savior. Following this, we will examine the sort of question asked of John the Baptist early in the Gospel of Luke and of Peter in the context of his Pentecost address: What should we do? (Luke 3:10, 12, 14; Acts 2:37). Here we will explore the notion of "conversion" as response to God's gift of salvation.

God Draws Near to Save

The terms of the exodus are thematic for reflection on how salvation is mediated: Israel in need, God drawing near to save, God as a traveling companion, and the concomitant need for God's people to comport themselves as God's people. "Do these things because the LORD your God travels with you, right in the middle of your camp, ready to save you and to hand your enemies over to you. For this reason your camp must be holy" (Deut 23:14). God's presence distinguishes these people as God's elect, secures their liberation, and calls for these people to align themselves with his instruction. The exodus account of Moses's commission is suggestive in this regard (Exod 3:1–4:17). Called by God to serve as God's instrument to deliver the Israelites from Egyptian slavery, Moses constructs one excuse after another, and each is answered with reference to God's assurance, promise, and sign. God promises: "Now go! I'll help you speak, and I'll teach you what you should say" (Exod 4:12). "I'll help you," "I'll teach you." These promises are themselves grounded in God's assurance: "I'll be with you" (Exod 3:12).

The exodus journey itself is replete with reminders of the divine presence: "The LORD went in front of them during the day in a column of cloud to guide them and at night in a column of lightning to give them light. This way they could travel during the day and at night" (Exod 13:21). God is present, both as leader and protector (cf. Exod 14:19, 24). God's glorious presence is such that God is guarded by a dense cloud (Exod 19:9, 16). En route to the promised land, Israel proved itself a stubborn people so that the divine presence had to be located outside the camp. There Moses pitched the "meeting tent," and "the column of cloud would come down and stand at the tent's entrance while the LORD talked with Moses" (Exod 33:3-7, 9). When materials for the "meeting tent dwelling" were gathered (Exod 25–31), instructions were given for its construction; when it was finished, "the cloud covered the meeting tent and the LORD's glorious presence filled the dwelling" (Exod 40:34). This was "the LORD's cloud," which determined the daily journeying of the exodus people. Here was the observable assurance of his presence among his people and the place of divine revelation (see Exod 25:22). Here too sacrifices were offered and atonement made (see Exod 29–30). Just how significant this portable sanctuary was in the life shared by God and his people is suggested by the Lord's words to David: "In fact, I haven't lived in a temple from the day I brought Israel out of Egypt until now. Instead, I have been traveling around in a tent and in a dwelling" (2 Sam 7:6). This is not to say that God was shackled to this earthly tent. It is to say, rather, that his presence in this fashion was itself constitutive of Israel as a people.

God Draws Near in the Temple

In time, the theology of divine election of God's people would be extended to the choice of Zion and the city of Jerusalem as the city of God's abode. Indeed, at the Jerusalem temple's destruction in 587 BCE, the reconstruction of the temple became the centerpiece of Israel's hopes for restoration (e.g., Isa 60; Zech 6:12-13). Given the theological importance of the temple, this is not surprising.

As the religious center of Israel, the temple served as the locus of God's presence with God's people. Between them, the phrases "God's house" and "Lord's house" appear scores of times in Israel's scriptures, bearing witness to the preeminent status of the temple as God's own dwelling. When this temple was made fully ready, "the cloud filled the LORD's temple, and the priests were unable to carry out their duties due to the cloud because the LORD's glory filled the LORD's temple. Then Solomon said, 'The LORD said that he would live in a dark cloud, but I have indeed built you a lofty temple as a place where you can live forever" (1 Kgs 8:10-13). The site on which the temple was built was divinely revealed (2 Sam 24:16; 2 Chron 3:1; Ps 132:13), Zion was God's own mountain (Pss 68:17; 76:3; 78:69-70), and God's presence at the temple signified Israel's election and security. Such was the marvel of God's presence in the temple that Israel would eventually develop a self-delusional and self-defeating confidence in the protection the temple would afford. Even in the context of their unjust practices, God's people would repeat, like a mantra,

"This is the LORD's temple! The LORD's temple! The LORD's temple!" (Jer 7:4). They failed to recognize that, just as God's glorious presence had descended on the temple, so could God's glory ascend from it, in response to injustice among his people (cf. 2 Kgs 25:9; Ezek 8–10).

As with temples that formed the center of life for other peoples, so with Israel, the temple played a crucial role in constructing sacred and social life.[3] This is the meeting place between humanity and God, a site imbued with reminiscences of the Garden of Eden (cf. Ezek 47). In its very architecture, God's abode represented the cosmos. God's presence was accessed here, making this the center of divine illumination and revelation, of sacrifice and prayer, and so, of worship. As one moved closer to God's dwelling place, within the temple's courts and within the sanctuary itself, one moved closer to the presence of his holiness. For God's people, this called for increasing attention to purity, to religious sanctity.

The characteristic act of worship for Israel in relation to the temple was the offering of sacrifice; in fact, in Israel's scriptures, "worship is tantamount to sacrificing."[4] God's people not only rendered service to their God in this way but they also declared their humility before and dependence on God. The variety of sacrifices—burned offering, grain offering, communal sacrifice of well-being, purification offering, compensation offering—and general regulations for how to perform them are found in Leviticus 1–7, though related rituals are found throughout the Pentateuch. More central to our purposes than sketching these matters of detail is our need to understand the significance of sacrifice, especially in terms of their efficacy in returning the people to right relationship with God. In large part, this is due to the way New Testament authors were drawn to Israel's sacrificial cult as they contemplated the meaning of Jesus' death.

For our purposes, then, the most important of the sacrifices are the "purification offering" (Lev 4:1–6:7; 6:24–7:10) and the sacrifice offered annually on *Yom Kippur*, the Day of Atonement (Lev 16). In the former, the unblemished animal is presented to Yahweh as a purification offering, the priest lays his hand on the head of the bull before it is slaughtered, the blood is smeared or sprinkled on the altar, and the fat is removed and burned on the altar. According to the latter, once each year, the high priest presents a bull as a purification offering for himself and his kin, sprinkling the blood on the mercy seat, that is, the cover on the chest that contains the covenant. After this, he slaughters the goat of the purification offering, making atonement for the holy place, on account of the sins of Israel. Then, he presents a second goat, lays his hands on it, confesses the sins of the whole people over it, and sends it away into the wilderness. According to Leviticus 16:22, "The goat will carry on itself all their offenses to a desolate region, then the goat will be released into the wild."

Reconciliation, or atonement, refers to the restoration of relations between two parties whose relationship has been ruptured by sin and in these texts is tied to sacrifice and mediation. Here, God is the source of reconciliation, since he has provided the system through which atonement could be enacted. As Jacob Milgrom has urged, the purpose of the purification offering is to provide for the cleansing of sin's effect, that is, cultic impurity, though forgiveness is also part of the picture (e.g., Lev 4:20, 26, 31; 16:16). Milgrom understands atonement as redemption through the substitution of an animal for a human being (Lev 16), as well as purification of the sanctuary and, by extension, of the community of God's people (e.g., Lev 15:31; 16:19).[5]

How is reconciliation thus effected?[6] First, the opposition of life and death is basic to these rituals—with death a great evil to be avoided, and with everything related to death (whether the corpse itself or bloody discharge or disease) rendering people unclean and unfit to worship God. Second, the necessity of choosing unblemished animals serves as an analogy for Israel's election, the choice of this people by God, set apart for service to him. Third, in the sacrificial drama, the notion of "identification" or "representation" is basic. By laying hands on the beast's head in the ritual of sacrifice, sinners identify themselves with the beast, indicating that the beast now represents sinners in their sin. The same might be said for the rituals involving blood, the sprinkling or smearing of the animal's blood on the people on whose behalf the sacrifice is made (e.g., Exod 24:8; 29:10, 15, 19-20; Lev 3:2, 8, 13; 14:14). In this instance, the shedding of blood—regarded as the substance of life, and therefore sacred to God (cf. Lev 17:11, 14)—signifies the offering of the lives of those for whom the sacrifice is made. In God's economy, Israelites were thus to do to their animals what they were not allowed to do to their children or themselves; animal life substitutes for human life, and this brought about the restoration of right relations with God.

God Draws Near in the Advent of Jesus

Central motifs of the presentation of Jesus in the New Testament have obvious significance when read against this backdrop. According to the opening of John's Gospel, the "Word" that was "with God," "was God," and through whom "everything came into being," the "Word" that is identified with Jesus, "became flesh and made his home among us"; concerning Jesus the Word John goes on to report, "We have seen his glory" (John 1:1-14). The phrase "made his home" refers to his "pitching his tent," or "making camp," a booming echo of the exodus journey, that journey of God's people among whom God's glory was seen in the column of cloud that would descend on the meeting tent. Early on in John's Gospel, Jesus is acknowledged as "the Lamb of God who takes away the sin of the world!" (John 1:29), an identification of Jesus as the Passover sacrifice. Shortly thereafter, Jesus identifies himself with the temple—to be destroyed and, after three days, rebuilt (John 3:19-20). Already we hear in John's narrative deep resonances with scriptural accounts of God's drawing near to save.

To choose only one additional example among many, in the book of Hebrews, we find the image of Jesus as the perfect sacrificial victim positioned side by side with a portrait of Jesus as the high priest who offers the perfect sacrifice. As the perfect priest and the perfect sacrifice, Jesus obviates the need for additional sacrificial offerings (e.g., Heb 9:25-28; 10:10, 12-14). Elsewhere too the New Testament writings reflect on Jesus' life, death, and resurrection in relation to God's saving presence.

The Temple's Significance

If anything, the importance of the temple only intensified in the years surrounding Jesus' birth. Though the temple built under Solomon was leveled in 587 BCE, this edifice (or, rather, a poor facsimile of it, cf. Ezra 3:12-13) was rebuilt toward the end of the sixth century BCE. It was then renovated and significantly expanded under Herod the Great beginning in the late first century BCE. The Herodian temple to which Jesus would have been brought as an infant for dedication (Luke 2:22-38), and which would be destroyed in the Jewish War (66–70 CE), extended some thirty-seven acres (roughly the size of thirty-seven football fields) and has been called one of the wonders of the world. The words of Jesus' disciples with reference to the temple, "Teacher, look! What awesome stones and buildings!" (Mark 13:1), provide some indication of the awe the structure must have inspired, not least among small-town folk from the Galilee region who have come to Jerusalem's center. Jesus' reply, "Do you see these enormous buildings? Not even one stone will be left upon another. All will be demolished" (Mark 13:2), must therefore have been all the more stunning.

In the Second Temple period, the temple's significance reached into all areas of public life and was the focal point of profound theological reflection. In a world of religious pluralism and syncretism, Israel's one temple in Jerusalem unified Israel under one God. And the architectural plan of the temple, which segregated priest from non-priest, Jewish male from Jewish female, Jew from Gentile, clean from unclean, sanctioned the social map that determined Israel's life. That is, the temple ordered the socioreligious world of the Jewish people, correlating Jewish belief in one God (monism) with the certain privilege of Jewish election (exclusivity). The temple's basic categories of clean and contaminated extended from the temple's sacrificial altar to the customary gathering at the table in Jewish homes, determining social relations and everyday behavior in Palestine and beyond. Pivotal for this temple theology was the theology of "presence": If the temple served as God's house, then honoring the temple was tantamount to honoring God and acknowledging God's presence among his people. And honoring the temple entailed living as though its structures and values of holiness and separation actually mattered in daily routines. Even among those Jews most critical of the temple, the point at issue was typically not the temple per se but illegitimate practices that plagued temple worship, a critique already at home in the prophetic literature of the scriptures (e.g., Isa 66:3).

The ongoing significance of the temple and its sacrificial system in the time of Jesus is important to grasp because it helps us to understand the terrain of Jesus' life and ministry. Additionally, it provides a window into the temple's role in ordering Israel's life and in certifying for the Jewish people God's saving presence in their midst. Even if the prophetic critique of the temple would continue, even if visions of the new, end-time temple would infiltrate the literature of the Second Temple period, the daily din of holy activity in Jerusalem's temple nonetheless provided powerful warrant for claims of God's blessing for Israel as well as powerful sanction for the practices and teaching of the Jewish elite in Jerusalem. If Jesus were to proclaim Israel's restoration, he would have to address these powerful forces and the longings around which they were oriented.

Jesus and Israel's Restoration

To insist on the temple's importance as a tangible sign of God's blessing for Israel is not to suggest that the Jewish people of Jesus' day believed that God's promises for his people had been fulfilled. The realities of life under Roman rule kept most from thinking in such terms. For them, exilic experience was not a distant memory but a present reality. Only the names of the pagan, overlord nations had changed: from Babylon in the sixth century BCE to Rome at the turn of the era. Numerous texts of the Second Temple period interpret Israel's lot using the language of exile and oppression, and express hopes of redemption and restoration.[7] Written in the late third or early second century BCE, for example, the apocryphal book of Tobit concerns itself with the nature of faithful Jewish life. It does so in the form of a novel set in the seventh century BCE, the distant past from which it can anticipate—and, thus, interpret—impending exile and restoration. With his dying words, Tobit predicts:

> All our relatives who dwell in the land of Israel will be scattered, and they will be taken away from that good land into captivity. The entire land of Israel will be deserted. Samaria and Jerusalem will be deserted, and after a while even God's house, still in mourning, will be destroyed by fire. But God will have mercy on them again. God will bring them back to the land of Israel, and they will rebuild the house, though not like the first one, until the appointed time has been fulfilled. Afterward, they will all return from the places where they are captives and build Jerusalem in grandeur. God's house will be built in it, just as Israel's prophets have predicted about it. Then all the nations of the whole earth will turn and genuinely revere God. They will all leave behind their idols that have deceived them and led them into error. They will praise the eternal God in righteousness. All the Israelites who are delivered in those days, who are genuinely mindful of God, will be gathered together. They will come to Jerusalem and will live forever in the land of Abraham in security, and it will be given to them. Those who genuinely love God will rejoice, while those who commit sin and injustice will be wiped out entirely from the land. (Tobit 14:4-7)

Tobit thus anticipates a twofold regathering—the one (inferior) that had occurred in the sixth century and the one (superior) yet to come. This latter regathering was the end-time restoration, with its return of God's people, the rebuilding of God's house, the inclusion of Gentiles, and the repeal of sin and injustice.

Later, around the turn of the second century BCE, 2 Maccabees incorporates a letter that documents the priest Jonathan's prayer at the temple's restoration:

> Lord, Lord God, creator of all, you are fearsome, mighty, just, and merciful. You are the only king and only generous one. You are the only provider, the only just, almighty, and eternal one. You save Israel from all evil. You chose the patriarchs and made them holy. Receive this sacrifice on behalf of all your people Israel. Guard your portion and make it holy. Gather together our scattered people, free the ones enslaved among the nations, watch over those who are despised and loathed, and let the nations know that you are our God.

Punish the oppressors and those who commit arrogant acts of violence. Plant your people in your holy place, just as Moses said. (2 Macc 1:24-29)

While celebrating the return of some of the exiles and the rebuilding of the temple, Jonathan nonetheless regards those who continue to live "among the nations" as slaves and he prays that God might reverse their fortunes, punishing the oppressors and restoring God's people to their homeland.

Hence, even if in the larger Roman world, "salvation" had to do generally with the exercise of beneficent power for the provision of blessings, for Israel this concept was parsed in terms of Yahweh's coming to deliver Israel from the hands of its enemies and his providing them security as his people that they might serve him. God was to rescue his people from their oppressors, protect them from pressures to conform to alien ways, renew the covenant through forgiving Israel's unfaithfulness, and regather the people under his sovereign mercy.[8] The primary way in which these ideas are present in the Gospels of Matthew, Mark, and Luke is in Jesus' proclamation of God's kingdom. In fact, for N. T. Wright, the language of God's kingdom would have invoked in Jesus' ministry an implicit narrative: "Israel's god *[sic]* will one day become king; the establishment of this kingdom will involve the defeat of the enemy that has held Israel captive; there are clear signs that this is now happening; therefore the kingdom is indeed breaking in. YHWH really is becoming king; Israel really is being liberated."[9]

Jesus and God's Kingdom

To speak of "God's kingdom" is immediately to raise questions of language.[10] In recent decades, some have objected to the use of the word "kingdom" because it possesses inherently masculine connotations; for this reason, some have chosen to translate the Greek word βασιλεία (*basileia*) with the English term "reign" instead. This is both helpful and unfortunate. It is helpful insofar as it underscores the important insight that βασιλεία (*basileia*) often refers to God's powerful rule, God's activity in the world.[11] However, it overlooks the key observation that in the Gospels, God's kingdom has an inescapably *spatial* sense. In fact, the single most frequent action that happens with respect to God's kingdom is that it is "entered" (Matt 5:20; 7:21; 8:11; 19:23, 24; 21:31; 25:34; Mark 9:47; 10:23, 24, 25; Luke 18:17, 24, 25; John 3:5), with the corollary that people can be "in" (Matt 5:19; 11:11; 13:43; 18:1, 4; 20:21; 26:29; Mark 14:25; Luke 7:28; 13:28, 29; 14:15; 22:16; 22:30) or "out" (Matt 23:13) or "not far from" (Mark 12:34) the kingdom;

additionally, when the kingdom appears as the subject of verbs, the kingdom is said to "come," "draw near," and so on. Accordingly, "kingdom" is more than "reign," for it also includes the notion of "realm." Also problematic is the ease with which the translation of βασιλεία (*basileia*) as "reign" allows us to reduce God's work to the "life of the spirit" or to God's activity in people's hearts or to restrict the reach of God's activity as though God's rule were present and active only among those people who have submitted to God's reign. Moreover, although it is true that βασιλεία (*basileia*) possessed hierarchical and masculine connotations in Roman antiquity, this did not keep Jesus from using the term in ways that actually subverted those connotations. If "masculinity" was correlated in the Roman world with the exercise of power and self-control, for example, then Jesus' claim that "God's kingdom" belongs to little children must surely have been shocking. Similarly, if manliness were a matter of asserting and maintaining one's elite status, then Jesus' proclamation of the kingdom repeatedly and decisively militated against conventional wisdom. According to the Gospels, Jesus' use of the language of royalty and sovereignty is inescapable, but this claim must be set side by side with how Jesus reconfigured the nature and deployment of that royalty, that sovereignty.

A second question of language concerns Matthew's preferred phrase, "kingdom of heaven." The phrase appears nowhere in the other New Testament Gospels, but thirty-two times in Matthew. This is usually explained as owing to Matthew's Jewish inclination against referring to "God" directly, substituting instead "heaven" as a circumlocution for "God." This explanation draws helpful attention to the fact that the phrase "God's kingdom," which prevails in Mark and Luke, refers to the same entity as Matthew's "kingdom of heaven." With their different terms, the evangelists are certainly not trying to distinguish heavenly versus earthly realities or a present kingdom versus a future one. That Matthew can set "kingdom of heaven" in parallel with "God's kingdom" (Matt 19:23-24) and that he uses "kingdom of heaven" where the other evangelists use "God's kingdom" (e.g., Matt 4:17// Mark 1:15; Matt 5:3//Luke 6:20; Matt 8:11//Luke 13:28), is enough to show that these two phrases should not be contrasted with each other. The problem with this typical explanation is that Matthew seems actually not to have an aversion to using the word "God" (found more than fifty times in his Gospel), and, as a matter of fact, Matthew does use the phrase "God's kingdom" (Matt 6:33; 12:28; 19:24; 21:31, 43). More likely, then, is that Matthew uses the language of "kingdom of heaven" under the influence of the kingdom theology of Daniel 2–7, where God, the heavenly king, and his kingdom are contrasted with all earthly kings and kingdoms. This does not mean that the kingdom Jesus preaches in Matthew is ethereal, otherworldly, or just "spiritual." Instead, Matthew's language draws special attention to the fact that the kingdom Jesus proclaims originates and draws its character from God the Father and from the Father's domain (e.g., Matt 6:1-21).[12]

There is one more question of language. Why do Matthew, Mark, and Luke refer to God's kingdom repeatedly (altogether more than one hundred times), whereas John's Gospel uses the phrase "God's kingdom" only twice (John 3:3, 5; see, though, Jesus' references to "my kingdom" in 18:36)? The answer to this puzzle comes in John 3 where, in the interchange between Jesus and Nicodemus, the idea of seeing God's kingdom is clarified in terms of eternal life and salvation (John 3:15-16). Thereafter in John's Gospel, "life" and "eternal life" are used where, in the Synoptic Gospels, we might have expected the language of God's kingdom.

What, then, of the nature of the kingdom proclaimed in the Gospels? One of the most important observations to report may be that, in their preaching the kingdom, John the Baptist, Jesus, and Jesus' followers introduced very little that could be described as novel. Even though the phrase "God's kingdom" does not pepper Israel's scriptures, the concept is everywhere, for example in references to Yahweh the king, to Yahweh's rule and throne, and to Yahweh's command over the heavenly forces. Particularly with the rise of the prophets Amos and Hosea in the eighth century BCE, Israel turned its eyes to the future activity of God in history. For them, hope focused on the coming of the Lord in history as king. Later, Isaiah would describe the triumph of God as Deliverer and Sovereign in anticipation of the glorious reign of God (e.g., Isa 24:23; 30:33; 32:1; 33:17, 20-22). This portrait of God is not restricted to the prophets, however. The concept of God as king is present in the earliest history of the nation, as God serves as deliverer, leader, and lawgiver in Israel's experience of exodus from Egypt and settlement in the promised land. Not surprisingly, the language of kingship surfaces most clearly in the period of the monarchy; irrespective of what human king sat on Israel's throne, the true king was God, and it was God who then defined faithful kingship. Then, in the prophets, God's coming reign was announced as a symbol of Israel's renewal. In Isaiah's words, the good news is focused in this proclamation, "Your God rules!" (Isa 52:7).

Second Temple Jewish literature likewise affirmed God's continuing rule at the same time that it looked forward to the day when God's already-present dominion would be universally disclosed, signaling God's intervention to vindicate his people and to establish justice and peace throughout the cosmos. In this respect, a text from the *Psalms of Solomon* (first century BCE) is especially interesting:

Lord, you are our king forevermore,
> for in you, O God, does our soul take pride.
How long is the time of a person's life on earth?
> As is his time, so also is his hope in him.
But we hope in God our savior,
> for the strength of our God is forever over the nations in judgment.
Lord, you chose David to be king over Israel,
> and swore to him about his descendants forever,
> that his kingdom should not fail before you.

See, Lord, and raise up for them their king,
> the son of David, to rule over their servant Israel
> in the time known to you, O God.

Undergird him with the strength to destroy the unrighteous rulers,
> to purge Jerusalem from Gentiles
> who trample her to destruction;
> in wisdom and in righteousness
> to drive out the sinners from the inheritance. . . .
> (*Pss. Sol.* 17:1-4, 21-22)[13]

According to this passage, God continues to rule even when evidence of his sovereignty is hard to discern and even when his people fail to live faithfully under his rule. Moreover, this text anticipates the coming of a "son of David" in whom God's rule will be actualized in the saving of God's people and the destruction of Israel's foreign overlords.

How might Jesus' contemporaries have understood "God's kingdom"? Granted that, as in most other areas, Second Temple Judaism had room for a variety of views concerning the kingdom,[14] we can nonetheless summarize four central features. First, to speak of God's kingdom is to speak of God's activity—creating, providing, leading, sending, calling, liberating, judging, conquering, caring—and God's domain, inclusive of the whole cosmos, though centered on Israel. If God's kingdom was understood as a reality of present existence, then eschatological hope would center on the future, cosmological revelation of God's already-present reign. Second, God's kingdom entailed a vision of God's universal, peaceable rule. God's rule spells justice, the triumph of righteousness and establishment of peace in the world, *shalom.* Accordingly, many would have heard in references to God's kingdom an eschatological hope focused on God's coming in power to restore and vindicate God's people. Third, the disclosure of God's kingdom necessarily evokes response from God's subjects, responses cast either as allegiance or rebellion, responses that provide the basis for royal judgment. Fourth, and finally, the Gospels situate Jesus within those currents of Second Temple Judaism that tied the actualization of God's kingdom to a hope in God's raising up an anointed king, the Messiah.

What is the relationship of these expectations to Jesus' ministry? Are these hopes actualized in Jesus' coming? The only possible answer is equivocal: Yes *and* No. We must say yes because this is precisely what the Gospels broadcast, that Jesus not only shares these expectations but actually regards them as being actualized in his ministry. They present Jesus as the Christ, anointed king, who announces and enacts the kingdom. Wherever Jesus is engaged in ministry, there God's kingdom is on display. We must answer no because Jesus did not perform in the expected way. According to the Gospels of Matthew and Luke, even John the Baptist was baffled by the direction of Jesus' mission: Where is the anticipated fiery judgment on Israel's enemies (Matt 3:11-12; 11:2-3; Luke 3:16-17; 7:18-20)?

If we follow the Gospels, then, we realize that Jesus interpreted his mission from within Israel's story against the backdrop of the Roman Empire. Jesus' advent as God's anointed king, then, marks the decisive disclosure of God's royal rule, together with the consequent unmasking of all rules, all authorities, all powers that would compete with God's sovereignty. The time of restoration was at hand, evil was being exposed and rolled back, peace with justice was being established throughout the world, and God was present to rule: all in Jesus' ministry. For the Gospels, this is true even if Jesus does not perform in the ways commonly expected or articulated among his contemporaries. But this is because Jesus is king and, as king, he is the one who decisively demonstrates the nature of the kingdom. That is, his kingship exhibits and defines the nature of royal power. This royal authority and power was not like what we see among "those who rule the Gentiles" or "their high-ranking officials" who "show off their authority" and "order them around" (Matt 20:25; cf. Mark 10:42; Luke 22:24-27). Rather, Jesus demonstrates through his ministry that royal power is defined by its orientation to the marginal, to the least, and to the lost. The nature of God's kingdom is exhibited through the character of Jesus the king's engagement with people. For him, disclosure of God's will means standing at the threshold of fresh ways of conceiving God's work and stepping across it. The New Exodus was underway, the new era was breaking in upon the old, and all of this was manifest in Jesus' person and work.

Consider the "heading" of Mark's Gospel, which succinctly summarizes Jesus' message throughout the Gospel: "After John was arrested, Jesus came into Galilee announcing God's good news, saying, 'Now is the time! Here comes God's kingdom! Change your hearts and lives, and trust this good news'" (Mark 1:14-15). David Wenham captures well the significance of this summary: "The longed-for revolution is now underway."[15] With this startling image, Wenham draws attention to expectations for peace and justice among the Old Testament prophets, the restoration of a people and a world out of step with their God, and God's kingship over the whole earth. If Jesus decisively unveils the presence and character of God's kingship, then the call to believe and to change hearts and lives is nothing less than an invitation, as it were, "to join the revolution."

Mark has structured the opening of his Gospel with matching references to the "good news"—the "good news about Jesus Christ, God's Son" and "God's good news" (Mark 1:1, 14-15)—and with strong resonances of Isaiah's expectation of New Exodus:

- The *beginning* of the good news about Jesus can be traced back to Isaiah (compare Mark 1:1-3 with Isaiah 40; cf. Exod 23:20; Mal 3:1)

- John's coming (compare Mark 1:4-8 with Isaiah 40)

- Jesus' baptism (compare Mark 1:9-11 with Isa 42:1; 61:1)

- Jesus in the wilderness (compare Mark 1:12-13 with Isaiah 40, 65)

- Jesus' proclamation of God's good news (compare Mark 1:14-15 with Isa 40:9; 52:7)

That is, as Mark draws particular attention to Isaiah and constructs his preface with repeated echoes of Isaiah 40–66, so his understanding of God's kingdom plainly builds on the Isaianic portrait of God's restoration of Israel from exile, the New Exodus, the eschatological disclosure of God's reign.[16] This means that the times have changed, and the structure of the universe must now be gauged through a fresh lens. Jesus is the true king and the king is on the move.

Mark's programmatic summary of Jesus' message in Mark 1:14-15 is important in two additional and interrelated ways: It certifies that the kingdom is God's and it clarifies that human activity with respect to the kingdom is human response to God's prior work. God's kingdom does not depend for its existence on human activity. Humans do not create, build, construct, extend, or render present the kingdom. The kingdom originates with God, it draws its character from God, and it precedes any human response to it, even though its presence invites (or demands) human response. The calling of the first disciples in Mark 1:16-20 demonstrates the appropriate response: setting aside one's way of life (cf. Mark 8:34), means of livelihood, even family obligations in order to follow Jesus and participate in his mission. Even proper responses like these do not bring the kingdom nearer, help to build the kingdom, or advance the kingdom, however. As Jesus will go on to instruct, the kingdom grows quite apart from human contributions (Mark 4:26-29: "by itself" [αὐτόματος, *automatos;* Mark 4:28]); even grasping the message of the kingdom and entering the kingdom are quite impossible apart from divine initiative (Mark 4:11; 10:23-27). The activity of God is prevenient: People are to respond *because* the ancient project of God has been initiated in Jesus' ministry and not *in order that* God's work might be established.

For more than a century, discussion about God's kingdom has focused preeminently on the *timing* of the kingdom. Is it now? Is it future? Is it both? Simply put, this is the wrong question. God's kingdom, as we have already seen, is not restricted by time and neither is it restrained by spatial boundaries. Accordingly, questions like when and where have little relevance. In Jesus' proclamation, the central question lies elsewhere: To serve or not to serve? That is, Jesus' message of the kingdom is realized in the call to change one's heart and life and thus to align oneself with God's rule, to engage in the practices of the kingdom, and to serve as recruits who through word and deed participate in the mission of making evident what is otherwise unclear or hidden from view, namely, God's royal rule, and in this way unmasking those powers that compete with God's rule. Through conversion, a change of heart and life, people find that they are no longer working at cross-purposes with God's ancient purpose but are living in sync with God's own aims and are actively serving God's redemptive project.

Jesus' Mission

The emerging portrait of Jesus' mission to save can be expanded further by exploring briefly three representative texts that set out Jesus' aims. We find the first in Mark's Gospel:

> Jesus went out beside the lake again. The whole crowd came to him, and
> he began to teach them. As he continued along, he saw Levi, Alphaeus' son,

sitting at a kiosk for collecting taxes. Jesus said to him, "Follow me." Levi got up and followed him.

Jesus sat down to eat at Levi's house. Many tax collectors and sinners were eating with Jesus and his disciples. Indeed, many of them had become his followers. When some of the legal experts from among the Pharisees saw that he was eating with sinners and tax collectors, they asked his disciples, "Why is he eating with sinners and tax collectors?" When Jesus heard it, he said to them, "Healthy people don't need a doctor, but sick people do. I didn't come to call righteous people, but sinners." (Mark 2:13-17)

In these two paragraphs, Jesus crosses social and religious boundaries to include in his circle of disciples and friends people who make their homes at the periphery of acceptable society.

Our reading of this episode is enhanced if we grasp three aspects of Jesus' social world. The first is the importance of meals. What one ate and with whom one ate have to do with the satiation of hunger, of course, but they also signaled important social and religious messages in the ancient world. Table fellowship had to do with intimacy; to share a meal with others involved including them as extended family, so to speak. For many Jews, Pharisees especially, the table was the focus of issues of clean and contaminated, acceptable and unacceptable. Second, among the range of possible occupations in first-century Palestine, collecting tolls was one of the least reputable. Toll collectors were the entrepreneurs of Roman antiquity, but they paid a heavy price for the wealth they were able to accumulate. This is because, among the social elite, what mattered was "old money" or "landed wealth"; those like toll collectors, who had to earn their money, had no place in society's upper echelons. People like Levi, who staffed a toll kiosk day after day, would not have been enjoying much wealth anyway; in this ancient private enterprise tax system, much of their collections would have been passed up the line to those who hired them and those who hired them. In popular opinion, moreover, toll collectors were regarded as small-brained snoops and social drivel. Third, "sinners" were not necessarily doers of great evil, nor were they simply people who failed to measure up to the requirements of the Jewish law. Rather, the term "sinner" had become in first-century Judaism a label for those who failed to follow God in the way prescribed by one or another group within Judaism. That is, persons belonging to one Jewish group might refer to those of another group as "sinners," regarding them as little better than Gentiles.

Mark's portrait of Jesus is a stark one, then, and it is little wonder that the legal experts question Jesus' behavior and attempt to influence his disciples to join them in criticizing him. He has extended table intimacy to society's throwaways. In doing so, though, Jesus interprets his behavior within a health care model: toll collectors and sinners are sick, but he is a doctor. Crossing boundaries between the well and the sick is precisely what doctors do, and this justifies Jesus' behavior. Jesus thus draws on biblical notions of the Lord as healer and of divine redemption as healing, where healing is defined as restoration to relationship with the Lord and his people—that is, as forgiveness.[17]

A second text, actually a string of texts, is drawn from Luke's Gospel. Luke includes the episode of the calling of Levi and the banquet that follows (Luke 5:27-32). He develops this portrait of Jesus at the table even further, though, by underscoring the hostility Jesus attracted because of his table practices and meal partners (e.g., Luke 14; 15:1-2), and telling the story of Zacchaeus (Luke 19:1-10), with its close parallels to the story of Levi.[18] These accounts reveal the low status of toll collectors, categorize toll collectors with sinners, document appropriate responses to Jesus (involving possessions and extending hospitality to Jesus), and generalize from Jesus' encounters to summarize the nature of Jesus' mission: "I didn't come to call righteous people but sinners to change their hearts and lives" (Luke 5:32) and "The Human One came to seek and save the lost" (Luke 19:10).

Zacchaeus is a strange character within Luke's narrative. He is introduced to us as rich and as a ruler (or chief) among toll collectors, two descriptions that go together since the ancient system of collecting tolls from traveling merchants held the promise of wealth not so much for the toll collectors themselves but for those who hired their services. Note, though, that Zacchaeus is thus called a rich ruler in a Gospel where the wealthy and rulers typically appear in opposition toward Jesus.[19] Yet, he is a ruler of despised toll collectors, and he is regarded by the crowd as a sinner, and this in a Gospel where persons referred to as "sinners" habitually welcome Jesus and are welcomed by him.[20] Zacchaeus is not an easy person to classify, at least not according to the labels used elsewhere in Luke's Gospel. By the end of the account, though, Jesus has named Zacchaeus as a "son of Abraham," a status that is evidenced in Zacchaeus's behavior with his money: He gives half of what he has to the poor and makes fourfold restitution to any who are cheated under his watch (cf. Luke 3:10-14). Additionally, Jesus regards Zacchaeus as someone who has been "lost," but is now restored. From Luke's account, it is obvious that Zacchaeus is looked upon within his own community as an outsider ("a sinner," Luke 19:7), but Jesus restores him to full status among God's people.

What Luke portrays in the encounter between Jesus and Zacchaeus is consistent with his larger presentation of Jesus' mission and message. In Luke

4:18-19, borrowing words from Isaiah 61, Jesus announces that his mission is "to preach good news to the poor," a mission that is defined in three ways. First, it is a mission to "the poor," who in Luke's Gospel are identified above all as those who live at or beyond the frontiers of larger society. "Poor" is for Luke an expansive category of persons that includes the economically dispossessed as well as those who belong to the margins of their own communities on account of gender, family heritage, disease, religious purity, ethnicity, and so on. Second, Jesus' mission is one of "release," which in Luke's Gospel is developed along different lines with regard to restoration to human wholeness, including socioeconomic relations, forgiveness, and liberty from the shackles of evil.[21] Third, Jesus goes on in his sermon to develop his mission in relation to the prophets Elijah and Elisha (Luke 4:16-30). Elijah, he points out, was sent by God to a woman, a non-Jew, a widow, while Elisha was sent to a non-Jew whose disease, leprosy, symbolized his distance from Israel's God (see Lev 13–14). Drawing on these examples, Jesus emphasizes that "good news to the poor" embraces the widow, the unclean, the Gentile, and all others whom society regards as misfits and outcasts. Of course, Isaiah envisions the restoration of Israel in the words Jesus has borrowed, and Luke's Gospel envisions the same now underway. As Jesus asserts, "Today, this scripture has been fulfilled just as you heard it" (Luke 4:21). However, in a way that is consistent with the cosmic scope of Isaiah's vision, God's saving initiative in Israel's restoration has a domino effect, extending salvation in all of its fullness to all people.

Taken together, these three statements of ministry (Luke 4:16-30; 5:27-32; 19:1-10) point to Jesus' mission as opening the way for the inclusion of people in God's kingdom, for salvation, who otherwise have no apparent claim on God. They are "the poor" to whom Jesus proclaims "good news," and this is basic to the identity of his messianic mission.

We turn to the Gospel of John for a final example. Commenting on the exchange between Jesus and Nicodemus (see John 3:1-21), the evangelist observes, "God didn't send his Son into the world to judge the world, but that the world might be saved through him" (John 3:17). The significance of this pronouncement is set in relief by two observations. First, it was customary in Jewish end-time hope that the coming of God's kingdom would involve God's judgment on God's enemies. Second, this way of thinking presumed an obvious distance or distinction between Israel and Israel's enemies. John's commentary mitigates this emphasis on judgment in two ways. On the one hand, salvation is not for Israel only but for "the world." As John 3:16 has it, God's love and so Jesus' saving mission are oriented to "the world," extending beyond boundaries drawn by race or culture or nationality. Second, the coming of salvation does not preclude the possibility of belief, but actually invites and enables belief. Jesus' advent does not mark the pronouncement of the final verdict, then, but provides for further opportunity for positive response.

As John 3:1-15 makes clear, further opportunity is important, since (1) the condition for entering life with God is belief and (2) the response of faith is unavailable to darkened minds and unyielding hearts, apart from divine intervention. Nicodemus, a Pharisee and legal expert, representative of the Jewish elite, is a case in point. In spite of his status and expertise in handling Torah, he seems incapable of understanding Jesus' message. A complete reversal is needed. What we have called *a conversion of the imagination* is required. For Jesus, this entails being "born anew." Nicodemus's failure to grasp Jesus' words illustrates his present alienation from divine ways of thinking. Jesus' response to Nicodemus is therefore plastered with irony: "You are a teacher of Israel and you don't know these things?" (John 3:10).

The good news is that it is precisely to effect this reversal, to enable this belief, that Jesus has come, and this belief is available in the very presence of doubt (John 20:19-29). From John's perspective, his own narrative of Jesus' wondrous signs can serve to bring persons into a faith-full encounter with the Messiah (see John 20:30-31). Using exodus imagery, John draws again the analogy from Israel of old to New Exodus, in order to declare the basis of human salvation: "Just as Moses lifted up the snake in the wilderness, so must the Human One be lifted up so that everyone who believes in him will have eternal life" (John 3:14-15). The "lifting up" of Jesus refers in the Gospel of John to his suffering and death on the cross.[22] Just as gazing at the serpent was God's provision for restored health in Numbers 21, so Jesus, in his suffering and death, embodies God's will to give eternal life (see John 14:1-11).

The Atoning Death of Jesus

A further mission statement occupies a prominent place in the Gospels of Matthew and Mark. I refer to Jesus' words, "The Human One didn't come to be served but rather to serve and to give his life to liberate many people" (Matt 20:28; Mark 10:45). This declaration functions both to confirm the other-oriented ethic Jesus proposed in his ministry and to provide Jesus' self-disclosure of the life goal given him by God. λύτρον (*lytron*, "ransom" or "the cost of release"; CEB: "to liberate") invites reflection on two images. One is borrowed from the Roman slave trade, where a ransom might serve as the price of emancipation, after which the one freed belonged to the one who paid the price. In terms of understanding the significance of Jesus' death or what it accomplishes, this image does not help us much. This is because Mark and Matthew provide no hint that, in Jesus' crucifixion, God (or Jesus) "paid" anyone or anything to win our liberation. The second image is of greater importance. It derives from Israel's own past: God "ransomed" Israel, delivering the people from Egyptian slavery in Egypt (Exod 6:6; 16:13—both using the verbal form of the noun found in Matthew and Mark: λυτρόομαι, *lytroomai*, "to liberate"). With this image, Matthew and Mark provide no particular insight into the mechanics of how Jesus' death liberates. Rather, in their respective accounts, Jesus both instructs his followers to give their lives in the service of others and reveals the purpose of his own other-oriented life, even to the point that he will embrace death on behalf of others. And they show that Jesus' death brings about the liberation at the heart of New Exodus hope while calling on Jesus' followers to incarnate an ethic of service to others.

Widening our perspective in relation to other writers in the New Testament, we encounter an extensive menu of ways to understand Jesus' death. In fact, the New Testament writers seem never to tire of generating fresh models for communicating the saving importance of the cross. Taken as a whole, however, these images congregate around five spheres of Roman public life: the legal system (e.g., justification), the business world (e.g., redemption), personal relationships (e.g., reconciliation), worship (e.g., sacrifice), and the battleground (e.g., triumph over evil). This variety is necessary in part because of the need to articulate the significance of the cross in relation to the particular needs of the mission and Christian communities. It is also due to the fact that Jesus' death is an event of such pivotal importance to the plan of God that its significance can never be fully measured.[23] This variety might appropriately lead us to the conclusion that our understanding of the meaning of Jesus' death could never be reduced to a single concept or theory or metaphor. Paul himself can write of substitution, representation, sacrifice, justification, forgiveness, reconciliation, triumph over the powers, redemption, and more. For Hebrews, the notion of sacrifice is paramount, with Jesus presented as both the perfect high priest and the perfect sacrificial victim. First Peter speaks of Jesus' death as a ransom and sacrifice, while the book of Revelation presents Jesus' death in terms of military triumph and redemption. And this is only the beginning.

Because of the centrality of sacrifice to Israel's worshiping life and to early Christian approaches to Jesus' death, we might pause for a moment to reflect on the image of Jesus' death as a sacrifice. Actually, we would need immediately to expand our reflection to include images (plural), since Jesus' death is interpreted as a covenant sacrifice (e.g., Mark 14:24; 1 Cor 11:25; Heb 7:22; 8:6; 9:15), a Passover sacrifice (e.g., John 19:14; 1 Cor 5:7-8), the sin offering (Rom 8:3; 2 Cor 5:21), the offering of first fruits (1 Cor 15:20, 23), the ritual of the Day of Reconciliation (Heb 9–10, traditionally translated as "Day of Atonement"), and an offering like that of Isaac by Abraham (e.g., Rom 8:32). Ephesians summarizes: "He was a sacrificial offering that smelled sweet to God" (Eph 5:2). This reminds us, as we saw earlier in this chapter, that Israel knew many types of sacrifices, and to those earlier ruminations we can add the further observation that, in Second Temple Judaism, we find precursors to the interpretation of Jesus' death as a sacrifice in accounts of faithful martyrs (cf. 1 Macc 2:7-38; 2 Macc 6:18–7:42; 4 Macc 6:24-30). These texts interpret martyr-deaths as means of resisting evil and of calling on God to vindicate God's people and as atoning for one's sins or Israel's sins.

We find something of this mishmash of images in 1 Peter 1:18-19: "Live in this way, knowing that you were not liberated by perishable things like silver or gold from the empty lifestyle you inherited from your ancestors. Instead, you were liberated by the precious blood of Christ, like that of a flawless, spotless lamb." Peter blends three Old Testament images: "liberation" or "ransom," "lamb," and the combination of "blood" and "a flawless, spotless lamb." The result is an atonement theology that is part exodus (e.g., Exod 6:6; 15:13; Deut 7:8; Isa 43:1), part Passover sacrifice (Exod 12), and part purification offering (e.g., Lev 4:1–6:7; 6:24-7:10). In this way, Peter portrays Jesus' honorable death as effective in wiping away sin and its effects. For Peter, the problem Jesus' death addresses is not God's anger or even an abstract notion of human sinfulness, but "the empty lifestyle you inherited from your ancestors."

It may be helpful to highlight one further text, Romans 5:1-11, where we find that Christ's death is the ultimate expression of God's love: "But God shows his love for us, because while we were still sinners Christ died for us" (v. 8). Paul's message here highlights four important points. First, God's love for humanity is immeasurable, since there are no human parallels by which to comprehend it. Second, God's love is prevenient; it precedes and does not depend on human activity or response. Third, Paul's audience can be certain that their suffering has significance because Christ's suffering has proven so meaningful. Through his death "we have been *made righteous*," "we will be *saved*," and "*we have been reconciled to God.*" In the midst of our impotence, Christ took on the measure of our powerlessness and died in our place. As a result of his death, we share in his life, and we find that our own suffering has significance in relation to his. Fourth, we are told that *God* demonstrates

God's love by means of what *Christ* did. We might have anticipated that God's love would be revealed in God's own deed, and this would certainly have been the case were Paul sketching an atonement theology oriented toward divine recrimination. Paul's way of putting things shows instead the oneness of the purpose and activity of God and God's Son in the cross.

As the apostle puts it elsewhere, "God was reconciling the world to himself through Christ" (2 Cor 5:19). In another passage where descriptive terms for the saving effects of Jesus' death congregate (2 Cor 5:14–6:12: substitution, representation, sacrifice, justification, forgiveness, and new creation), Paul carefully shows how the work of God and of Christ are one. What is more, Paul does not speak of the need for mutual reconciliation. "The world" is estranged from God and needs to be brought back into relationship with God, but God is not estranged from "the world." For this reason, Paul has no need to show how God can be appeased, or how God might be coaxed into extending his love again. Rather, Paul affirms that God's love always has the upper hand in divine-human relations, and that the work of Christ had as its effect the bringing of "the world" back to God.

What Must I Do to Be Saved?

How are humans to respond to God's drawing near to save? Luke's account of the encounter of Paul and Silas with the Philippian jailer and his family in Acts 16:23-40 can orient our thinking. After Paul and Silas's miraculous release from prison by an earthquake, the jailer gives voice to our question, "Honorable masters, what must I do to be rescued?" (Acts 16:30).

The introduction of the jailer is abrupt. Told to confine Paul and Silas securely (Acts 16:23), "he threw them into the innermost cell and secured their feet in stocks" (Acts 16:24), as though they were "dangerous low class felons."[24] Thinking that those under his charge have escaped in the aftermath of the earthquake, he apparently fears his own death (cf. Acts 12:18-19) and opts for the honor of suicide over the shame of execution (Acts 16:27). How should we read his question to Paul and Silas? The problem revolves around the first word, κύριοι *(kyrioi),* translated here by the CEB as "honorable masters," but often translated as "lords." Parallel questions appear in Luke 3:10-14 and Acts 2:37, but it seems doubtful that we should hear in the jailer's voice a request for salvation in the full, Christian sense as this is developed in the Lukan narrative. I also wonder whether the jailer's address to Paul and Silas as κύριοι is simply a matter of polite address (e.g., "sirs," as in the NRSV and NIV); after all, only a few hours ago these men were humiliated, beaten prisoners, not honorable guests. Clearly, the jailer has had to reconsider his evaluation of them on account of their incredible escape from prison. Either he fears them, as though they were more than human, or he sees in them a power capable of rescuing him from his certain fate in the service of the emperor. Thus, he addresses them with a term, "lords," that was prominent in references to the emperor and in emperor worship. The message he receives, which Luke characterizes as *"the Lord's* word" (Acts 16:32), names Jesus as *Lord* (Acts 16:31). In other words, Paul and Silas deflect the honor given them by the jailer and call attention instead to Jesus. They unambiguously name Jesus as the source both of the power behind these spectacular events and of authentic deliverance.

The result is that an enemy—who because of his own oppressed status must fear for his life even though he has made a livelihood as the instrument of oppression for others—and his whole household, are transformed. Paul and Silas call on the jailer and his household to "believe in the Lord Jesus" (Acts 16:31). Their response is comprehensive: They believe, they rejoice, they extend hospitality to Paul and Silas, and they are baptized. The true Lord is named and this household comes under the lordship of Jesus rather than that of Caesar.[25] We would like to know the rest of the story perhaps, for example, what shape "repentance" might take in the everyday life of this jailer (see Luke 3:10-14), but this is not the story Luke has chosen to tell. The focus falls instead on the validation of their faith and the accompanying practices of this jailer and his household. Baptism in this case thus signifies God's acceptance of this household, authenticates their faith and hospitable practices as markers of the new order over which Jesus is Lord, and signals the ongoing progress of the Christian mission.

Luke's account of the jailer first illustrates, even in a single book like Acts, that there is no one single way to describe the appropriate response to the gospel. Second, it exposes the dichotomy we sometimes place between "faith" and "life" as a false one.

What of the variety of responses to the good news? True, throughout Acts, the call for a radically different understanding of the world calls for response, but the narrative presents different ways of portraying a change of heart and life. In Acts 26:17-18, Paul recounts his commission from Jesus, who sends him "to open their eyes. Then they can turn from darkness to light and from the power of Satan to God." Here, Luke draws on the familiar language of religious conversion, but interprets God's salvation and human response in terms of the cosmic battle, one kingdom giving way to the other. Elsewhere the Christian mission can be represented as one of debate and dialogue—a battle of interpretation, as it were (e.g., Acts 13:16, 38, 41; 17:3; 19:8-10). Among Greek audiences, Paul calls for people to leave the way of idolatry and turn to "the living God" (Acts 14:15-16). Although Luke is concerned with movement from one form of life to another, he outlines no "typical" way of understanding conversion. He does not provide a "technology" for changed hearts and lives. The "order of salvation" that runs through these accounts is this: God initiates → people hear the message of salvation → people respond. In fact, this is the heart of Peter's defense of the inclusion of Gentiles in the community of God's people in Acts 15:7-11: "God chose me from among you" → "as the one through whom the Gentiles would hear the word of the gospel" → "and come to believe" (v. 7).

To deny that Luke presents a technology of response is not to deny the possibility of our making a few generalizations. (1) Baptism in the name of Jesus is a normal response, as suggested by the Ethiopian's question, "Look! Water! What would keep me from being baptized?" (Acts 8:36; cf. 2:41; 8:12; 9:18; 10:47-48; 16:15; et al.). Within the Lukan narrative, baptism takes its meaning in part from John's ministry, where it is both "gift" and "response" (Luke 3:1-20). Baptism expresses a desire to embrace God's purpose anew and to be embraced within the community of those oriented around God's ways. (2) Repentance (or "turning to God"), a change of heart and life, is mentioned explicitly and repeatedly as an appropriate response to God's salvific work (cf. Acts 2:38; 3:19; 5:31; 11:18; 17:30; 20:21; 26:20). Again, Luke's portrayal of this response is rooted in his account of John's ministry (especially Luke 3:1-14), where a change of heart and life is marked by behavior that grows out of and demonstrates that one has indeed committed oneself to service in God's purpose (e.g., Luke 3:10-14; Acts 26:20). (3) That Christians are sometimes called "believers" signals the importance of faith in Luke's understanding of salvation (cf. Acts 2:44; 3:16; 11:17; 13:39; 14:9; 15:7; 16:30-31; 18:8).

Let me turn now to the second issue, the false distinction between "faith" and "life" with regard to human responses to the gift of salvation. Here I refer to a variety of dualisms by which we have learned to make sense of our lives: inner self versus outer self, "being" versus "doing," right faith versus right actions, and the like. These ways of phrasing things belong more to our world than to the world in which the New Testament was written. As noted in chapter 1, Charles Taylor has observed how personal identity has come to be shaped by such assumptions as these: human dignity lies in self-sufficiency and self-determination; identity is grasped in self-referential terms: I am who I am; persons have an inner self, which is the authentic self; and basic to authentic personhood are self-autonomy and self-legislation. Biblical anthropology, by way of contrast, places a premium on the construction of the self as deeply embedded in social relationships, on the integrity of the community and thus the contribution of individuals to that integrity, and on the assumption that a person *is* one's behavior; that is, one's dispositions are on display in one's practices. If we took seriously the implications of this change in viewpoint, we would see that transformation in the arena of one's essential beliefs, commitments, and allegiances is unavoidably on display in one's behavior and practices in the world. Conversion, then, really is a change of heart *and* life. Put simply, the call to salvation is the call to live according to another world order, faith is entrusting ourselves to God's view of things (even when the evidence before us seems contrary), and this faith is irrepressibly on display in faithfulness.

Seen from this vantage point, conversion entails *autobiographical reconstruction*. As Peter Berger and Thomas Luckmann put it in a classic study, "Everything preceding the alternation is now apprehended as leading toward it . . . everything following it as flowing from its new reality. This involves a reinterpretation of past biography *in toto*, following the formula 'Then I *thought* . . . now I *know*.'"[26] Conversion shatters one's past and reassembles it in accordance with the new life of the converted; former understandings of one's self and one's experiences are regarded as erroneous and are provided new meaning (cf. Luke 9:23). In his own classic statement, Paul revels, "From this point on we won't recognize people by human standards. Even though we used to know Christ by human standards, that isn't how we know him now. So then, if anyone is in Christ, that person is part of the new creation. The old things have gone away, and look, new things have arrived!" (2 Cor 5:16-17).

More pervasive in the New Testament are those instances where one's reshaped allegiances and dispositions are expressed in terms that reflect a fresh grasp of God's character as well as fresh ways of understanding the nature of God's people. This generally comes through understanding one's place within the history of God's purpose, or writing oneself into the ancient story of God's work with Abraham and Sarah, Moses, and Ruth. Stephen and Paul, for example, prove themselves to be adept at retelling Israel's history (e.g., Acts 7; 13:16-41). Acts makes clear that, for Paul, this comes after his own extensive formation in Israel's scriptures (see Acts 22:3) has been recast through his encounter with Jesus as the risen Lord (Acts 9:1-19). The whole of Israel's history and self-understanding is now reevaluated for presentation in light of the newly found understanding of God's purpose resident in Jesus' crucifixion and exaltation. Conversion is thus the process of *embracing a new life-world,* a conversion of the imagination, now on display in the Christian community.

Interestingly, these new conceptual patterns come to expression most fully in the context of one of the characteristic practices of the Christian community. This is prayer, which provides the opportunity for the disclosure of God's salvific purpose especially at pivotal points in the mission. The book of Acts portrays prayer as a community-defining practice that invariably leads to the expansion of the community. This is because the habits of prayer counseled by Jesus serve as an ongoing catalyst for the conformation of the community around the capacious mercy of God (cf. Luke 6:35-36; 11:1-13). Prayer of this sort allows for the infusion of a worldview centered on the gracious God, on dependence on God, on the imitation of God, and on the disclosure of God's purpose for humanity, all understood against an eschatological horizon in which the coming of God in sovereignty and salvation figures prominently.

This means too that a change of heart and life marks one's *incorporation into a new community,* which includes adopting the rituals and behaviors peculiar to or definitive of that new community. In the Lukan narrative, this is evident immediately in Acts 2:42-47: "The believers devoted themselves to the apostles' teaching, to the community, to their shared meals, and to their prayers," and so on. The generalizations about the community of Jesus' followers—economic sharing, daily meals, and more—sketched here amplify the response urged by Peter in 2:38, "Change your hearts and lives." Incorporation into the community is marked through baptism, the medium by which repentance comes to expression as well as the sign that forgiveness has been granted.[27] To put it differently, baptism serves a community-defining role, communicating on the part of the baptized an unswerving loyalty to the Lord and on the part of the church the full acceptance of the baptized into the community. Baptism in Acts has as its consequence, among other things, unity and simplicity (e.g., 2:41-47) and the extension of hospitality (e.g., Acts 10:47-48; 16:14-15, 28-34)—behaviors, then, that must be included under the heading of "fruit that shows you have changed your hearts and lives" (Luke 3:7-14).

All of this is to say, then, that "conversion" is a many-sided affair. It is first the story of God's prevenience, God's gracious visitation that precedes and opens the way for human responses of changed hearts and lives. This conversion reaches the whole of life and cannot be reduced to one's inner being; in fact, conversion is intertwined with baptism, that most bodily experience of washing, and it entails conversional practices that flow out of and signal covenant renewal. It is difficult to tie to a single moment the idea of "appropriate response" to God's saving activity. Even if one can point to its beginning, conversion is more of a journey in which people receive and participate in God's saving activity; joining the revolution, so to speak, they share in the ministry of disclosing through word and deed the nature of God's kingdom.

Epilogue

One way to get at the issues addressed in this chapter is by rephrasing the question this way: *What does it mean "to perform" salvation?* God is actualizing his purpose to save, and in doing so throughout Israel's history has set out ways in which his blessings might be mediated to his people. Chief among these blessings is the gift of covenant and particularly restored relationship or covenant renewal with God, out of which unfolds the way of life for which we were created and liberated. God acts out, or performs, his will, and the consequence is that the way of salvation is opened to us. Importantly, this "us" knows no boundaries, but includes all who are willing to embrace and act on the grace of seeing what could not otherwise be seen, to stand at the threshold of fresh ways of conceiving God's work and to step across.

The "performance" of salvation requires more than one actor, however. If God's is the aim we are to serve, it is nonetheless true that God's drawing near to save forces a crisis among people. A decision is necessary: to resist or to embrace, to serve or not to serve. This is precisely the Y-junction that Jesus' advent represents: turn this way or that way. Of course, the coming of Jesus opens the way of salvation and enables faith. His ministry, death, and resurrection signal the expression of God's good news in the plainest way possible. With God's self-disclosure in Jesus Christ, the way is open, but it is a way that must be taken. The community of the saved are those who elect no longer to work at cross-purposes with God, and who thus find themselves in sync with God's own aims and active in God's redemptive project. Faith and faithfulness cannot be distinguished in the lives of those so thoroughly transformed. Those who perceive God in Christ ultimately revealing himself in the world behave in that world as new persons. This is because they are, indeed, new persons, whose allegiances are given over to the reality breaking into the world.

chapter five

The End of Salvation

The Bible tells a grand story. It is true that, within its pages, we find numerous side stories, episodes that seem to take us along strange paths or corridors not easily integrated into the whole. For this reason, each reading of scripture invites a different emphasis, since each new reading allows one or another motif more prominence than in the last reading.

Even so, the canon of scripture places limits on the variety of "tellings" that the Bible can support. Thus far we have named two primary points in the grand narrative of scripture, points that provide clear, if minimal structure and shape to the whole. It is simply inconceivable that we could plot the biblical narrative without reference to the beginning of the narrative and to its middle. The beginning concerns God's purpose and action in creation, whereas the middle concerns redemption, which must be comprehended in two "movements": exodus and New Exodus, God's saving work in delivering Israel from Egypt and God's saving work in the advent of Jesus Christ. In other words, if we take seriously scripture's own narrative, there is no bypassing creation or Israel or Jesus.

Since Aristotle, a narrative has been characterized as possessing not only a beginning and middle but also an end (*Poetics* 1450[b]). In this chapter, we turn, then, to the climax toward which the biblical story is heading. We recognize that, strictly speaking, God's story is not open-ended. This is true of every story, of course, since a beginning already sets out the contours within which the narrative can progress. Every storyteller is constrained by earlier

117

chapters already completed. To say that God's story is not open-ended is to say more than this, though. This is because we already have in scripture images of the end as it has been determined by God. God has already given glimpses of this story's finale. In general terms, God's good future is a given that determines the range of possible plotlines and the significance of events leading up to it. And God's good future, because it is already revealed to us in its essentials, casts its shadow backward and determines how we today might grasp the character of God's project. As we find our places in that narrative, it pulls us forward into its vision of the way things ought to be.

With many narratives we read, novels, for example, we press on to discover what will happen: Who did it? How will they escape or get caught? Why did she take this road and not that one? What are the ripple effects of that decision? Will all of this make sense in the end? We are pulled forward as we await resolution and denouement. Good writers cultivate our interest and motivate us to keep reading by weaving tension into the plotline, by leaving multiple possible conclusions. This is not the way of the scriptural narrative. The New Testament leaves no doubt about the nature of its climax. God will be God. Evil will be shattered. God's people will enjoy life forever and always with God in a restored cosmos. This is not in doubt. But there is tension nonetheless, since throughout the New Testament we find people struggling, as we ourselves struggle, with the wait and even with evidence that seems to counter the claim that God will be God and evil will be shattered. The story to which these pages in scripture bear witness is not like a suspense novel. It is a formative one. It does not want to tease or entertain us; it wants to shape us. Given what God has done, is doing, and will do, what kind of people are we and what will we become? How might we cultivate the senses necessary to see God at work in what seems at times to be a godless world? And as we see God's handiwork in the universe, this too might cause us to wonder, as it did the psalmist, what are human beings (Ps 8:3-4)? What does it mean to let this story tell us who we are? What does it mean to live lives determined by this grand story of salvation?

Our aim in this concluding chapter, then, is twofold. The first is to set out a vision of where this story is heading. In traditional terms, this is *eschatology*, our understanding of the last things (from the combination of two Greek terms: ἔσχατος, *eschatos*, "end" + λόγος, *logos*, "understanding"). Because our primary interest is in the biblical witness to salvation, our principal question is, What will it mean, in the end, to be saved? What we will discover is that end-time thinking, if it is genuinely to be biblical, cannot be lost in speculation or shallow optimism. Rather, it must be fully integrated into our contemporary existence and sense of vocation. If we know where we are going—indeed, if we are committed to a particular destination—we can and ought to orient our lives toward that destination. Second, we will explore how end-time thinking is for us intertwined with our understanding and experience of, and commitment to, the church. What is the nature of this salvation, which must be understood always as a process moving toward an end just beyond the horizon? What of the community, the church, in which salvation is embodied and lived and sought? Not surprisingly, questions like these are interwoven with many others, about the nature of Christ, for example, or the work of the Holy Spirit, with the result that our exploration will press us to reflect on a wide array of concerns.

Salvation and Its "Ends"

The message of scripture is clear: This is not all there is. The importance of this affirmation is evident already in accounts of Jesus' interaction with his detractors. He announced the coming of God to save, yet Rome still exercised its power and human tragedy still made the headlines. As Luke records, people in Jesus' day might speak of "the Galileans whom Pilate had killed while they were offering sacrifices," or those eighteen people "who were killed when the tower of Siloam fell on them" (Luke 13:1-4). How do such occurrences square with "good news"? Jesus' response was twofold. First, he pressed his audience to see what could not be seen with eyes unaided by faith. The Gospels' witness to Jesus' extending recovery of sight to the blind (e.g., Luke 7:21-22; John 9) is as much about illumination as it is about ophthalmology. Just as Elisha once prayed regarding his fearful servant, "LORD, please open his eyes that he may see" those divine resources arrayed against the enemy (2 Kgs 6:1-17 [v. 17]), so Jesus pressed for and enabled people to expand their conceptual patterns, their imaginations, to account for the sometimes less obvious and overshadowed work of God among them. Second, Jesus assured his listeners that the actualization of God's kingdom was a process, that God's work as yet remained unfinished, and that God would yet consummate his saving design. "Consider a mustard seed. When scattered on the ground, it's the smallest of all the seeds on the earth; but when it's planted, it grows and becomes the largest of all vegetable plants. It produces such large branches that the birds in the sky are able to nest in its shade" (Mark 4:31-32).

Feasting in God's Kingdom

These two emphases can be illustrated with reference to Jesus' story of a wealthy householder and his invitation list (Luke 14:15-24), a story that is susceptible to two quite different readings.

> When one of the dinner guests heard Jesus' remarks, he said to Jesus, "Happy are those who will feast in God's kingdom."
>
> Jesus replied, "A certain man hosted a large dinner and invited many people. When it was time for the dinner to begin, he sent his servant to tell the invited guests, 'Come! The dinner is now ready.' One by one, they all began to make excuses. The first one told him, 'I bought a farm and must go and see it. Please excuse me.' Another said, 'I bought five teams of oxen, and I'm going to check on them. Please excuse me.' Another said, 'I just got married, so I can't come.' When he returned, the servant reported these excuses to his master.
>
> The master of the house became angry and said to his servant, 'Go quickly to the city's streets, the busy ones and the side streets, and bring the poor, crippled, blind, and lame.' The servant said, 'Master, your instructions have been followed and there is still room.' The master said to the servant, 'Go to the highways and back alleys and urge people to come in so that my house will be filled. I tell you, not one of those who were invited will taste my dinner.'"

The first, and the more well-known, interpretation has it that this is a parable of the end-time banquet. On this reading, the master of the house is God himself. God invited some who refused to attend, leading to his extending the invitation to include others, especially the marginalized and the Gentile. Typically in this reading, recipients of the first invitation are regarded as the Jews, or perhaps the Jewish leadership, whose relationship to the master is marred by their silly excuses for their refusal to take their places at the banquet. According to this reading, this is a parable of warning and hope—warning to those already on that list, lest they refuse to accept the places reserved for them at the table, and hope to those on the periphery of acceptable society that they too will be included on the end-time invitation list.

Although this is the usual reading, I find it troubling for its suggestion that God's invitation to the dispossessed comes as an afterthought, as though God originally invited to the end-time banquet only those capable of purchasing a farm, buying a team of oxen, or marrying, unlike the poor, crippled, blind, and lame. After all, when God rescued Israel from Egyptian slavery, were they not more like the impoverished of this parable—that is, people who actually needed a good meal?

An alternative reading would prioritize the location of this story within its context in Luke 14, where Jesus has just instructed his table companions regarding their own table practices. In this instance, the question, Who will enjoy God's hospitality at the end-time banquet? is answered with reference to a second question: Who is now enjoying the hospitality of your table? That is, one's place at the kingdom feast is determined by one's behavior in the present, particularly with regard to the poor and dispossessed. Jesus counsels, "When you give a banquet, invite the poor, crippled, lame, and blind. And you will be blessed because they can't repay you. Instead, you will be repaid when the just are resurrected" (Luke 14:13-14). On this reading, the central message is this: Will those who hear Jesus' teaching actually include the outcast among their table intimates, without concern for payback and self-promotion? According to this reading of the Lukan story, Jesus provides in his parable an exemplar of someone, a wealthy householder, who heard his message well and put it into practice.

What holds these two interpretations together is the one exclamation of the anonymous guest, "Happy are those who will feast in God's kingdom" (Luke 14:15). According to the first reading, Jesus responds to this dinner companion by highlighting the character of the end-time banquet. The second has Jesus reflecting on the end-time image of the kingdom feast in a way designed to show the importance of the future for how one lives in the present. A portrait of the future thus calls for transformed dispositions and practices in the present.[1]

The End in Fantastic Images

Broadening our vision, we may observe the variety of, and often fantastic, ways in which the end is portrayed in the Bible. In an essay with the rather foreboding title "Scientific Accounts of Ultimate Catastrophes in Our Life-Bearing Universe," William Stoeger speaks matter-of-factly about the certainty of the ultimate demise of life on this planet and, indeed, of the universe. Speaking only of Earth, he discusses the possibilities of destruction through impact with a massive asteroid or comet, the eventual decline and death of our sun, and the explosion of a supernova in a neighboring system. Turning to consider the cosmos as a whole, he forecasts the eventuality that the universe will gradually fade or perhaps collapse upon itself.[2] The biblical writers sometimes speak of the same prospects, but with more surreal language, drawing on the imagination to portray coming realities that can scarcely be imagined. For them, the language of choice is apocalyptic, the language of word pictures, often fantastic. "The sun became black as funeral clothing, and the entire moon turned red as blood. The stars of the sky fell to the earth as a fig tree drops its fruit when shaken by a strong wind. The sky disappeared like a scroll being rolled up, and every mountain and island was moved from its place" (Rev 6:12-14).

The emergence of the dreadful images that we find in selected biblical writings, most prominently in Daniel and Revelation but also in Zechariah, Joel, Mark's Gospel, and others, can be credited to the environment within which apocalyptic was born and nurtured. Apocalyptic was grounded in the social experience of powerlessness, marginalization, and the conviction that Israel's destiny would never be fulfilled within this world; it would come in the next, as a consequence of God's direct intervention. As Paul Hanson puts it, "The ancient Jewish apocalyptic writings grew out of the courage to stare into the abyss on the edge of which an entire civilization tottered, and a willingness to describe what the fantasy of faith enabled the human eye to glimpse beyond tragedy."[3] The ambiguities of present history would make sense when portrayed on the greater mural of God's dealings in history and beyond history, on the earth and in the world of the supernatural.

Apocalyptic images of the future in the Bible congregate around a relatively stable series of motifs: (1) the immediacy of the end, (2) the cataclysmic character of the end, (3) the transformation of the cosmos, and (4) divine provision in the new era of salvation; and these grow out of two pervasive affirmations, concerning (5) the malignant ubiquity of evil and (6) the sovereign triumph of God.

(1) The Immediacy of the End: In the New Testament, the immediacy of the end is conveyed in a variety of images, including the thief who comes during the night (e.g., Matt 24:43; 1 Thess 5:2, 4; 2 Pet 3:10; Rev 16:15), the master who returns unannounced after a long journey (e.g., Mark 13:34-36; Luke 12:35-38, 42-48), and the bridegroom who arrives in the middle of the night (Matt 25:1-13). Lists of events or historical records could serve this purpose too. In Daniel, for example, as in Revelation, many of the events that were to have happened before the end had already occurred when the book was first written. Similarly, in Mark 13, the events that would precede the end are plainly characteristic of just about every age. If these are signs of the end-times, then their identification as such insinuates strongly that the end is always near. But this is because "immediacy" in scripture is not always a reference to "soon." Sometimes the New Testament writers communicate that "the end is soon" by emphasizing that "the end could come at any time, unexpectedly."

(2) The Cataclysmic Character of the End: Most apocalyptic texts that warn of the end of the world do so with reference to a conventional list of catastrophes expected to precede the final judgment. These include famine, earthquakes, wars, betrayal, signs in the heavens, and so on (cf., e.g., Joel 2; Mark 13; Revelation). The apocalyptic discourse in Mark 13 also speaks of the destruction of the Jerusalem temple as a sign of the end, due no doubt to the centrality of the temple in defining Israel's world. Some writings also speak of the coming of a time of great distress (e.g., Dan 12:1; Mark 13:24; Rev 7:14), an unprecedented time of hardship numbered among the many woes that accompany the end. Second Peter 3:10 summarizes this idea: "But the day of the Lord will come like a thief. On that day the heavens will pass away with a dreadful noise, the elements will be consumed by fire, and the earth and all the works done on it will be exposed." Importantly, these texts do more than describe the coming horror; they also put it in perspective. Suffering and hardship are interpreted as "woes" that accompany the birth of God's kingdom into present life. Repeatedly, the suffering of the faithful is folded into the work of the Messiah, by which God's redemptive work is brought to consummation. Paul puts it this way: "Now I'm happy to be suffering for you. I'm completing what is missing from Christ's sufferings with my own body. I'm doing this for the sake of his body, which is the church" (Col 1:24). As such, this suffering is defined as both necessary (and therefore not without significance in the divine plan) and temporary.

(3) The Transformation of the Cosmos: Second Peter also summarizes well the apocalyptic vision of reversal at the end: "But according to his promise we are waiting for a new heaven and a new earth, where righteousness is at home" (2 Pet 3:13). John uses similar symbolism (Rev 21), drawing attention to the absence of death, mourning, crying, and pain, "for the former things have passed away" (Rev 21:4; cf. Isa 33:24; 65:20). Nor, John adds, will the new earth include any "sea," a reference to the final triumph over evil, symbolized by the powers of chaos represented in the sea and the sea monster: the dragon (Job 7:12; Ps 74:13), Leviathan (Job 40:15-24; Pss 74:13-14; 104:26; Isa 27:1), Rahab (Job 9:13; Ps 89:10; Isa 51:9-11), and the snake (Job 26:13; Isa 27:1).

The scenario painted in scripture thus shares with the natural sciences catastrophic expectations concerning the world's end, but scripture looks beyond calamity to new creation. Contemporary cosmology looks at the future only with pessimism, envisioning in the far-distant future a cold universe composed of nothing more than dead stars and black holes. A theology that takes its beginning from God and God's assessment of the goodness of creation, that recognizes the role of God's Son in creation and new creation, that finds in Jesus' resurrection a way of thinking about the character of life in this world and in the world to come, such a theology is not stymied by the prospect of accelerated heat death but invigorated by the prospect of God's transformation of the cosmos.[4]

Paul uses apocalyptic imagery to draw attention to the transformation already overtaking creation "in Christ," when he writes of participating in God's "new creation" (2 Cor 5:17). Elsewhere, he observes: "The whole creation waits breathless with anticipation for the revelation of God's sons and daughters. Creation was subjected to frustration, not by its own choice—it was the choice of the one who subjected it—but in the hope that the creation itself will be set free from slavery to decay and brought into the glorious freedom of God's children" (Rom 8:19-21). A more serious counter to the human tendency to regard ourselves as our own makers or to regard ourselves and our destinies apart from the whole of creation could hardly be articulated. The final "revealing" (that is, the end-time unveiling of God's salvation) locates a restored humanity within a restored cosmos. Peaceful, harmonious relations, characteristic of life in Eden, but contorted by human sin, are restored in God's kingdom, introduced in the advent of Jesus.

(4) Divine Provision in the New Epoch of Salvation: Apocalyptic visions are not all doom and gloom. It is true that apocalyptic writers express little hope in the recovery of the world in its present form, but this does not keep them from believing that God will bring "a season of relief" (Acts 3:20) or that God is working in the present world to bring his purposes to completion. Irrespective of present evidence to the contrary, God is God. And God will provide for his people, though how that provision is imagined is often context-specific. To people experiencing economic oppression or deprivation, portraits of God's provision might take the form of a city with a golden main street, "transparent as glass" (Rev 21:21). To the hungry or to those who long for restored fellowship with God, the heavenly feast, with a table set and hosted by God, is an apt symbol of restoration (e.g., Isa 25:6; Luke 14:15; Rev 19:9).

(5) The Malignant Ubiquity of Evil: One of the primary concerns to which apocalyptic addresses itself is the problem of suffering in the world, particularly the suffering of the righteous. A crucial response is provided in heightened emphasis on the authority of the devil and the demonic world, that is, the malevolent power aligned against God's aims and the lives of God's people. For these apocalyptic visionaries, evil could never be reduced to an individual's bad choices, but was a cosmic reality. This does not mean

that evil can simply be personified in the devil, however; especially in Daniel and the book of Revelation, evil is embodied in social structures, political entities, and governmental institutions and is all-pervasive. Evil must be taken seriously. So powerful and widespread is evil that it would not disappear or be overcome by human efforts alone, however loving and good. Divine intervention would be needed, and this is precisely what these writers promise.

(6) The Sovereign Triumph of God: End-time images are often accompanied by end-time timetables—for example, "for one set time, two set times, and half a set time" (Dan 12:7; cf. Rev 12:14) or "it was given authority to act for forty-two months" (Rev 13:5). Timetables like these are not easily converted into dates on our calendars, and for centuries this has frustrated those who are mesmerized by efforts at reading the signs of the end-times in order to fix the date of the world's end. But those who write apocalyptic timetables are not interested in calendar-making; this is not their purpose. Rather, apocalyptic lists of events that must happen in preparation for the end serve first to indicate that the suffering and woe that accompany these days are temporary and limited. Suffering is not the whole story nor the story's end. Second, these sufferings come as no surprise to God. The God of Israel knew of them beforehand, and has incorporated them into the means by which he will bring final restoration. Third, they serve to remind us that, despite appearances to the contrary, God is in control.

The book of Revelation underscores these points in profound ways. Revelation begins and ends with God's self-declaration, "I am the Alpha and the Omega" (Rev 1:8; 21:6; cf. 1:17; 22:13), which uses the first and last letters of the Greek alphabet to affirm God's status as the beginning and the end, the first and the last, the one who was, is, and is to come (Rev 1:4, 8; 4:8; 11:17; 16:5). Moreover, the single most pervasive portrait of God in Revelation has God sitting on the true throne. The word itself, "throne" (θρόνος, *thronos*), appears more than forty times in the book, almost always of God in his glory and sovereignty. Honor and power belong to the one on the throne; God is the sovereign actor who brings history to its determined end, who brings salvation, who pronounces judgment, who makes all things new.[5] Satan's power is false, a poor imitation of genuine authority, and his throne will be crushed. God will still be God when current turmoil has ended.

The Future Is for the Present

For what purpose are all of these words concerning the future the end? In the hands of the New Testament writers, talk about the end times actually serves multiple purposes, especially (1) to encourage faithful life in the present, (2) to disclose the nature of reality from the perspective of the end, and (3) to remind its readers that salvation is a journey.

Eschatology and Ethics

In some instances in scripture, end-time talk provides warnings and promises that should serve as motivation for the present. One New Testament writer seems to have this in mind when he writes, "But according to his promise we are waiting for a new heaven and a new earth, where righteousness is at home. Therefore, dear friends, while you are waiting for these things to happen, make every effort to be found by him in peace—pure and faultless" (2 Pet 3:13-14; see 3:1-18). With these words, the author of 2 Peter works to counter false teachers who have denied final judgment and have thus pulled the rug out from under accountability for life in the present. Within this setting, eschatology and ethics go hand in hand.[6]

From time to time, both in the larger New Testament world and in the New Testament itself, instruction about the afterlife is tethered to the need to rebalance the scales of justice on the other side of death. We find a striking example of this concern in the story Jesus tells concerning an exorbitantly rich man and the destitute Lazarus. After death, their respective roles in the life to come are the mirror opposite of their former situations. As Abraham says to the rich man, "Child, remember that during your lifetime you received good things, whereas Lazarus received terrible things. Now Lazarus is being comforted and you are in great pain" (Luke 16:25). This interest in balancing the scales is another expression of the relationship between eschatology and ethics. Clearly, the wealthy man's plight serves as a not-so-subtle reminder to the Pharisees within the narrative but also to readers of Luke's Gospel of the importance of listening to Moses and the Prophets when it comes to caring for the needy at one's own front door (Luke 16:19-31).

Of course, this concern with rewards and punishments is not without its surprising twists, a point made especially strong in Matthew's Gospel. "The children of the kingdom will be thrown outside into the darkness" while people from around the world, Gentiles among them, join Abraham, Isaac, and Jacob in the end-time banquet (Matt 8:11-12). Those who claim to be Jesus' followers are likewise vulnerable (cf. Matt 18:6-14; 25:1-30), since only in the final judgment will it become clear who are "followers of the kingdom" and who are "followers of the evil one" (Matt 13:36-43, 47-50). Most astonishing of all, in the scene Jesus paints in Matthew 25:31-46, both the blessed and the cursed seem baffled by the basis of final judgment: "When did we see you . . . ?"

What Is Really Real

Although talk of the future can serve to motivate ethical comportment in the present, it is more often the case that attempts to speak of the end are ways of presenting "how things ought to be" and "how things will be." That is, end-time images are designed as an antidote to the myopia that threatens us, those of us whose horizons of meaning are so easily determined by a fallen world.

This need for a change of perspective could hardly be emphasized more dramatically than what we find in the book of Revelation. In chapters 4 and 5, an angel leads John the Seer into God's throne room in order to acquire a refreshed, heavenly perspective from which to view and comprehend what is real. We might say that he is ushered into history's backstage, behind the curtains, as it were, so that he can see what is really going on in his world and in the world of his audience. In time, he will also be given a vision of the end so that he can see the present from the perspective of God's ultimate purpose for the cosmos. All along the way, his categories for making sense of things are exploded; in turn, the visions he records in the book of Revelation are nothing less than an assault on his readers' everyday conceptual patterns, their theological imaginations. His eyes are opened and through his book their sights will be opened to the world beyond the world, that is, to the transcendent, to God's unseen work. He is exposed and now he exposes them to an alternative portrait of the world. The effect is the juxtaposition of two competing visions: reality from God's perspective and reality from the viewpoint propagated by imperial Rome. Suddenly, the almighty power of Rome is unmasked as deceitful and anemic, capable of being resisted.

> In heaven and from the perspective of heaven John sees what is ultimately the truth of reality: who God really is, what God's purpose for his whole creation is, and how God is accomplishing that purpose through Jesus, the Spirit, and the church. From a merely earthly perspective, the military and political might of imperial Rome (the beast) and the economic dominance of the city of Rome (Babylon) seem irresistible, even divine. But from the perspective of heaven the ultimacy Roman propaganda claimed for Rome is seen to be illusory. The reign of the evil powers who appear to contest God's sovereignty on earth so success-fully is neither ultimate (in heaven God reigns over all) nor eternal (God's rule must come on earth as it already is in heaven).[7]

In short, Revelation is concerned with a conversion of the imagination.

End-time thinking more generally in scripture has this primary focus, namely, to readjust the boundaries of what is real and what is possible. As Paul Ricoeur has described it, imagination has to do with what we allow to count as real so that to transform the imagination is to transform human existence. Thus, "if you want to change a people's obedience, you must change their imagination."[8] Expanded horizons have as their corollary fresh allegiances and practices in the world. Those who adopt Revelation's perspective on the cosmos will be transformed in their dispositions and will behave in ways appropriate to the world as God has thus revealed it to be. In the case of Revelation, this means that evil is neither to be feared nor served, but resisted and destroyed. God's kingdom will be actualized through the victory of the Lion-Lamb (Rev 5), whose faithful witness to the point of sacrificial death stands as the measure of the faithfulness of those who would serve God's dominion. In this way, end-time thinking serves as a call to march according to the drumbeat of a distant, future drummer. It is to begin the performance of a script that is clear in its basic parts but still in the process of being written and which actually belongs to a future time and place. It is to live "as if" God's kingdom were fully present, and so to see with the eyes of faith those things not otherwise seen (cf. Heb 11:1).

What is the alternative? For many today, we might say, the alternative is a modern form of the ancient philosophy of Epicureanism: find happiness in the present, for the present is all we have. "Take it easy! Eat, drink, and enjoy yourself," said the rich fool (Luke 12:19). Another response might be despair, as if this were all there is, as if there were no divine ending to the story, as if God were not even now pulling us toward his good future. Robert Jenson identifies this response as the sin of "acting as if I were not delivered over to the future, as if in what I already am I were my proper self."[9] Despair might take the form of a horrifying illusion that Christian hope has as its object nothing more than life in the present, as if this were the destination for which we began the journey of salvation, as if the present were our true home. Alternatively, despair might take the form of abandoning hope in the face of wrong. Either option overlooks the fact that Christian life in the present has the form of exile. The one imagines that Babylon is our home while the other imagines that it belongs to Babylon to determine our reality. The first assumes that courageous resistance in the world is not necessary while the second assumes that courageous resistance in the world is useless. Paul's words to the Corinthians come to mind: "If we have a hope in Christ only in this life, then we deserve to be pitied more than anyone else" (1 Cor 15:19). If the scales of justice were never to be balanced, if the violence and futility that seem to fill up so many lives were never to be overturned, if this were all there is, then despair seems warranted. It is no wonder, then, that the New Testament is peppered with reminders to press on, to remain alert, to stand firm, and to cultivate hope. This, after all, is what John encourages when he writes, "Favored are those who stay awake and clothed so that they don't go around naked and exposed to shame" (Rev 16:15).

On the Way

Finally, end-time talk serves to remind God's people that the church is a work in progress, and that salvation itself is a process. For this reason, Paul can refer to Christians as those "who are being saved" (1 Cor 1:18; 2 Cor 2:15). In a passage remarkable for its profundity and brevity, Peter can characterize salvation in three tenses—past, present, and future:

> On account of his vast mercy, he has given us new birth. You have been born anew into a living hope through the resurrection of Jesus Christ from the dead. You have a pure and enduring inheritance that cannot perish—an inheritance that is presently kept safe in heaven for you. Through his faithfulness, you are guarded by God's power so that you can receive the salvation he is ready to reveal in the last time. (1 Pet 1:3-5)

That is, the gift of the new birth rests in Christ's resurrection (past); the work of salvation is ongoing as believers are "guarded by God's power" (present); and God's work of salvation will be consummated ("reveal in the last time," future). Other New Testament texts illustrate how widespread is this way of thinking about salvation in its past, present, and future tenses: "Therefore, since we have been made righteous through his faithfulness combined with our faith, we have peace with God through our Lord Jesus Christ. We have access by faith into this grace in which we stand through him, and we boast in the hope of God's glory" (Rom 5:1-2). "Therefore, if you were raised with Christ, look for the things that are above where Christ is sitting at God's right side. Think about the things above and not things on earth. You died, and your life is hidden with Christ in God. When Christ, who is your life, is revealed, then you also will be revealed with him in glory" (Col 3:1-4). Salvation is a reality accomplished in the past, an ongoing, present experience, and an achievement still anticipated.

In chapter 4, we noted that God's grace enables and invites on the part of humans a response of conversion, that is, a realignment of one's deepest commitments and dispositions toward God's purpose. This involves a change of heart and life, and trust, but this realignment concerns more than the onset of the journey; it characterizes the journey itself. Simon Peter, James, and John may recognize their sinfulness, they may hear Jesus' call to join him in "fishing for people," and they may leave everything to follow him (Luke 5:1-11), for example, but this is only the beginning. Jesus goes on to instruct these and other disciples in the dispositions and practices appropriate to the converted life (especially Luke 6:12-49). Yet they show little understanding of the character of his mission (e.g., Luke 9) and seem very little to share in his grasp of God's purpose and work. Have they genuinely been converted? (Or are they not in the process of conversion?) In fact, just before the beginning of the lengthy journey to Jerusalem (Luke 9:51–19:48), Luke says of the disciples, "They didn't understand this statement. Its meaning was hidden from them so they couldn't grasp it" (Luke 9:45). This is not because God concealed from them Jesus' significance; after all, the disciples are those to whom the secrets of the kingdom have been revealed (Luke 8:10), and Jesus assumes that they should be able to understand his words (Luke 9:44a). Rather, in spite of a decision to follow Jesus, their experiences thus far with Jesus notwithstanding, these disciples remain still too much in the clutches of old ways of reckoning God's ways, of old allegiances, and of old values. They cannot grasp Jesus' words because they lack the necessary categories of thought. The horizons of what they regard as possible, even for God, are still too limiting. To make matters worse, even at the close of the lengthy period of instruction narrated in the central, journey section of Luke's Gospel (Luke 9:51–19:48), a journey during which the formation of the disciples is paramount, Luke records again that they "understood none of these words. The meaning of this message was hidden from them and they didn't grasp what he was saying" (Luke 18:34). Apparently, salvation is an ongoing process of illumination and reformation, of deconstruction and reconstruction. Indeed, discipleship as Luke develops it entails a renewal of one's self within a new web of relationships, a transfer of allegiances, and the embodiment of transformed dispositions and attitudes. Such a conversion requires resocialization within the community being formed around Jesus, and this is a process that continues for these disciples even beyond the Gospel narrative itself.

This is not a perspective unique to Luke, of course. Paul's recognition that the Thessalonian Christians had turned from idols to serve the living and true God (1 Thess 1:9-10) is written in deceptively simple terms. In reality, Paul thus speaks *at least* of a lengthy series of transformations: a transfer of allegiances, a relocation of social relations, a reformation of theological categories, fresh habits and behaviors, and a recalculation of one's place in the social and political world of Thessalonika. Now they inhabit a new space, "between the times"; having converted to the living God and anticipating the coming of Jesus, they now make their lives in a period of active waiting. In the interim, God's word is at work in these believers, just as Paul calls on them "to live lives worthy of the God who is calling you into his own kingdom and glory" (1 Thess 2:11-13). Growing in grace through the Holy Spirit that indwells them, they are more and more to comport themselves in the world in ways consistent with their having been set apart for service to God: "Keep living the way you already are and even do better in how you live and please God," and "you are doing loving deeds for all the brothers and sisters throughout Macedonia. Now we encourage you, brothers and sisters, to do so even more" (1 Thess 4:1, 10). Indeed, Paul's prayer is that "the God of peace himself sanctify you completely" (my translation) in order that Paul's audience "be kept intact and blameless at our Lord Jesus Christ's coming" (1 Thess 5:23).

For Paul, the present bestowal of the Spirit on believers is a sign of the coming of the end and the means by which believers are being conformed to the life of salvation. In Rom 8:23, he refers to the Spirit as "the first crop of the harvest," an agricultural image found in the Old Testament: the first of the harvest, with more certainly to come. The Spirit is also for Paul the guarantee, a kind of down payment providing assurance of the consummation of God's redemptive work (2 Cor 1:22; 5:5; cf. Eph 1:14). The Christian life as a whole is described as walking "in" or "based on" the Spirit (Rom 8:4, 9), and the indwelling Spirit produces in the lives of believers the characteristic dispositions and behaviors of Christians: love, joy, peace, patience, and the rest (Gal 5:22-23).

The motif of progress in salvation can be traced endlessly in scripture. Paul's confidence among the Philippians is that "the one who started a good work in you will stay with you to complete the job by the day of Christ Jesus" (Phil 1:6). Metaphors drawn from the building trade, athletic competition, journeying, human development, and agriculture are all put into play in the service of encouraging Christian growth. "Like a newborn baby, desire the pure milk of the word. Nourished by it, you will grow into salvation" (1 Pet 2:2). "Let's not get tired of doing good, because in time we'll have a harvest if we don't give up" (Gal 6:9). "So, whether someone builds on top of the foundation with gold, silver, precious stones, wood, grass, or hay, each one's work will be clearly shown. The day will make it clear, because it will be revealed with fire—the fire will test the quality of each one's work" (1 Cor 3:12-13). For Luke, the community of Jesus' followers is known as "the Way" (Acts 9:2;

19:23; 22:4), a metaphor drawn from Isaiah's image of the New Exodus: "Prepare the way of the Lord!" (Isa 40:3 LXX [NETS]; Luke 3:4), signifying their commitment to the way of salvation. Paul marks the Christian life as one of progress with his favorite expression for this life, "the walk" (often translated with reference to following a way of life; e.g., Rom 6:4; 8:4; 2 Cor 5:7).

Because it holds together the whole history of God's purpose in creation, Colossians 3:9-11 is of special interest: "Take off the old human nature with its practices and put on the new nature, which is renewed in knowledge by conforming to the image of the one who created it. In this image there is neither Greek nor Jew, circumcised nor uncircumcised, barbarian, Scythian, slave nor free, but Christ is all things and in all people." The new humanity ushered in with the advent of Christ is one that rejects those distinctions that would have splintered Roman society. This vision has its foundation in creation, in God's act to make humanity, male and female, in his own image. Here, however, Paul takes the added step of noting that *the creation of humanity in God's image is an ongoing process.* This "image," in order to remain ever new, must have continuous contact with the one whose image it is, the Creator, who, in the Christology of Colossians, is none other than Christ (Col 1:15).[10] This "image" entails an obviously corporate dimension, with immediate consequences for how those who follow Christ engage in relations with other persons, and especially for how they breach those social, religious, cultural, and national barriers that segregate people from people. Those who are saved engage in an ongoing process whereby they frame their social relations and behavior in ways that nurture day-to-day renewal in their insight into and reflection of the character and purpose of God.

Just as the story of the Bible has a beginning, middle, and end, so has the story of personal salvation. From the beginning of the conversion, the end is in view, to which the letter of Ephesians refers as "the unity of faith and knowledge of God's Son," that is, maturity: "to be fully grown, measured by the standard of the fullness of Christ" (Eph 4:13). Between these two points, beginning and end, is the process of growth, walking "in newness of life" (Rom 6:4), the ongoing presentness of salvation.

The Nature of Future Salvation

Salvation is a journey with a destination. Its consummation lies in the future. Scripture provides only tantalizing glimpses of its character, but is adamant both that it is in that future that our hope lies and that our present should be worked out in relation to that future. What does this future look like? Any attempt to summarize will be selective and incomplete, but the following is suggestive.

Embodied Life

The Greco-Roman world made room for an array of views regarding the afterlife, but the two major options are easily summarized: Death is simply the end of life, after which nothing follows, or at death the soul departs the body and lives on (e.g., Cicero, *Tusculan Disputations* 1.11.23-24). Many in the Roman period were influenced by the much earlier work of Homer (perhaps from the eighth century BCE) since the *Odyssey* and *Iliad* were standard texts in Roman education. Homer portrayed the underworld as a gloomy region, the home of the wraithlike shadows of all the dead. For some, subsequent metaphysical reflection would lead to an understanding of the soul as the center of personal identity. At death, this immortal self would depart the body and live on either independently or by inhabiting another body. For Homer, death was lamentable, but for this view, death was liberation.

The primary philosophical schools of the New Testament world held different views of the afterlife. Among the Epicureans, the prospect of death gave no cause for concern since death gave way to nothingness. Numerous gravestones displayed this series of letters: "nf f ns nc"—that is, *non fui, fui, non sum, non curo* ("I wasn't, I was, I am not, I don't care"). Stoic views of the afterlife are not easy to summarize, but some apparently thought the soul could survive for a while after death, some souls indefinitely. Still others thought the ψυχή (*psychē*, "soul") was made of *aether* (the stuff of outer space, according to the ancient periodic table), so at death it did not go down to the underworld but went up into space. In general, though, Roman religion was not particularly concerned with the afterlife, and, apart from certain philosophical groups and the popular belief that a hero or emperor might through metamorphosis at death become a god or demigod (apotheosis, deification), the commonly held view was that death was followed by nothingness. "When death comes, everything will be consumed by earth and fire" (*CIL* 6.17985a).[11]

Differences of viewpoint in Roman antiquity help to explain disunity among the Christian believers at Corinth. When Paul spoke of "resurrection," some might have heard echoes of fables about the resuscitation of corpses, the stuff of popular myths. For some, talk of resurrection might have spawned images of escaping souls. Some, taught generally to degrade the body, would have found Paul's teaching about bodily resurrection incomprehensible, perhaps barbaric. Since Paul's primary objective in 1 Corinthians is to restore unity (1 Cor 1:10), his particular challenge in 1 Corinthians 15 is to represent early Christian belief in the resurrection with enough simplicity and sophistication to communicate effectively to everyone.

Paul defends belief in the future resurrection by (1) appeal to what had already become Christian tradition (1 Cor 15:1-11), (2) observing that a denial of the future resurrection was practically the same thing as denying Christ's resurrection, then moving on to an affirmation of Christ's resurrection as the guarantor of the future resurrection (1 Cor 15:12-34), and (3) sketching how one might plausibly conceive of the resurrection of the dead (1 Cor 15:35-58). Crucial for our thinking here is Paul's key affirmation of the import of the body to human existence and identity, and, then, of God's provision of a body well suited to the form of existence envisioned.

How can Paul speak of eternal, *embodied* existence, when it is self-evident that our bodies are fragile and susceptible to disease and death? By way of reply, Paul recalls what everyone in the ancient world should realize, that there are different kinds of bodies. "There are heavenly bodies and earthly bodies. The heavenly bodies have one kind of glory, and the earthly bodies have another kind of glory" (1 Cor 15:40). By way of analogy, he goes on to introduce two sorts of human bodies—one oriented toward life in this world (σῶμα ψυχικόν, *sōma psychikon*; CEB: "a physical body"), the other oriented toward life in the world to come (σῶμα πνευματικόν, *sōma pneumatikon*; CEB: "a spiritual body"; 1 Cor 15:42-49). His description of the first kind of body is drawn from Genesis 2:7, which has it that Adam was created a living being (ψυχή, *psychē*); hence, the first Adam's embodiment was appropriate for life in this world. However, this embodiment is ill suited to eternal life with God, subject as it is to death and decay on account of sin. What is needed, then, is a different embodiment, and this is provided by the last Adam, Christ, who does not simply receive life (as in the first Adam), but actually gives it. As a consequence, this second embodiment is fit for the age to come.[12]

Thus, in 1 Corinthians 15:38-58 Paul affirms the following about resurrection life:

- Continuity between present life in this world and the world to come is a given. For human beings, this continuity has to do with bodily existence. Paul cannot think in terms of a free-floating soul separate from a body.

- Present human existence is marked by frailty, deterioration, weakness, and is therefore unsuited for eternal life. Therefore, in order for Christian believers to share in eternal life, the nature of their embodiment must be transformed. Paul does not here think of "immortality of the soul," nor does he proclaim a resuscitation of dead bodies that might serve as receptacles for souls that had escaped the body in death. Instead, he sets before his audience the promise of transformation. As Paul writes in Philippians 3:21, "He will transform our humble bodies so that they are like his glorious body, by the power that also makes him able to subject all things to himself."

• For Paul, this is enormously important for grasping the nature and importance of present Christian life. This message underscores the significance of life in this world—a fact that many Christians at Corinth seem not to have been taking seriously. We should not imagine that bodily life is unimportant, then, or that what we do to our bodies or with our bodies is somehow unrelated to eternal life. Eternal life is not "escape" from our bodies, escape from embodiment, or escape from the past embodied actions. Rather, it provides the Christian with hope as well as a vision of what is important to God.

Personal, Social Life Embracing Human Diversity

Unlike the perspective of some religions, including gnostic teachings that would attract some Christians in the centuries immediately after the era of the New Testament, for biblical faith the life of the coming age is not one in which people are absorbed into God's being. People do not die only to return to some sort of primordial spirit. Nor is this future life one that obliterates human distinctiveness in favor of sameness. True, the distinction between Jew and Gentile has been overcome, so that God's people, Jew and Gentile, are united in peace (Eph 2:11-22; Gal 6:15-16). But, as John's vision of the heavenly chorus has it:

> There was a great crowd that no one could number. They were from every nation, tribe, people, and language. They were standing before the throne and before the Lamb. They wore white robes and held palm branches in their hands. They cried out with a loud voice: "Victory belongs to our God who sits on the throne, and to the Lamb." (Rev 7:9-10)

So, while the divide between Jew and Gentile has become obsolete "in Christ," and while individual rivalry has no place in the world to come, the new humanity should not be thought of as a heavenly melting pot. John's vision points to the fulfillment of God's promise to Abraham, that he would

135

have innumerable descendants, "like the dust of the earth" (Gen 13:16), as many as the stars in the sky (Gen 15:5), too many to count (Gen 16:10), "as the grains of sand on the seashore" (Gen 22:17)—a father of *many nations* and not of a single people (Gen 17:4-6).

Eternal Life

It follows that the transitory character of present life contrasts sharply with the nature of the life to come. John speaks of the blessings of salvation as eternal life, which for him begins with faith in Christ and continues beyond death into the eschaton (e.g., John 3:15-16, 36; 5:24). The seer speaks of the heavenly reign of God's people "forever and always" (Rev 22:5). For Paul, this is not because anything about the human person is immortal. Instead, he affirms in 1 Corinthians 15 and 2 Corinthians 5:1-10 that transformation and immortality are the consequence of (and not preparation for) resurrection.[13]

A Restored Cosmos

Paul actually employs the phrase "new creation" in 2 Corinthians 5:17 and Galatians 6:15, and speaks of a new person or the new nature in Ephesians 2:15; 4:23-24; and Colossians 3:9-10. These terms have roots in Second Temple Judaism, where they speak to the expectation of the restoration of the entire creation, which now exists in a state of futility on account of human sin. The fertile ground for these ideas can be found in Isaiah 56–66, with its promise of a new heaven and new earth. The end would embrace the original goodness of God's creation, but also extend beyond the original to a cosmos that would continue into eternity in its restored state. New life includes *everything* (see Rom 8:18-25; 1 Cor 15:24-28; 2 Cor 5:16-18; Phil 3:21; Col 1:15-20; Eph 1:10).

Life Ushered in by the Coming of Christ

It is clear that, as a whole, New Testament writers anticipated a decisive act of God to bring history's purpose to its close and that this end would be ushered in by the coming of Jesus Christ. Hebrews actually uses the language of a "second" coming: "Christ was also offered once to take on himself the sins of many people. He will appear a second time, not to take away sin but to save those who are eagerly waiting for him" (9:28), whereas other witnesses speak of "the revealing" of Christ (e.g., 1 Cor 1:7) or even long prayerfully for his coming: "Come, Lord!" (1 Cor 16:22); "Come, Lord Jesus!" (Rev 22:20). "You also must wait patiently, strengthening your resolve, because the coming of the Lord is near" (Jas 5:8). "The Lord is near" (Phil 4:5).

Such language can be used as motivation for ethical excellence, of course. More often than not, however, these statements of hope and anticipation are pointedly focused on putting current life in perspective, on reminding God's people that their beginning and end lie with letting God be God, and on assuring them of salvation's end as life in fellowship with God. The final vision of Revelation 21–22 has God no longer occupying his heavenly throne, but actually making his home on a renewed earth, with humanity. The language John uses to describe this apparent innovation recalls the ancient story of the wilderness journey. God "will dwell with them," the CEB translates (Rev 21:3), but we could also say that God "will pitch his tent (σκηνόω, *skēnoō*, "to pitch a tent," "to reside") among them," just as God's presence was with Israel in the tabernacle on the exodus journey and in the temple. God present with his people in his holiness and glory—in the end, this is what makes the "new heaven" and the "new earth" authentically "new," for it is God's presence that generates and nurtures new creation. As he is the Alpha and the Omega, the One "who lives forever and always" (Rev 4:9, 10; 10:6; 15:7), so the new life he gives is life in its most full sense: life in and beyond the hazards and forces that mar present existence, life in the embrace of the unmediated loving care of God, forever and always.

The Community of Salvation

What is the role of the community of God's people in the work of salvation? Simply put, the church, which owes its very existence and purpose to the coming of salvation, is that people who together embody, nurture, and propagate this good news. Just as Israel has its origins as a holy nation in the gracious election and powerful intervention of God in exodus, so the church traces its proximate beginnings to Israel's restoration in the gracious intervention of God in the birth, life, ministry, death, resurrection, and ascension of Jesus.

Salvation in Acts

In the Gospel of Luke and the Acts of the Apostles, the language of salvation is especially significant and, in narrative terms, it is easy to see that salvation is that theme around which all other elements of Luke's work are oriented.[14] In the context of Acts, salvation signifies above all else incorporation into and participation in the Christ-centered community of God's people. In this case, the term "community" must be taken in its deepest, fullest sense, as Luke repeatedly underscores the prayerful unity and concord of these persons, with their oneness vividly embodied and exhibited through their economic sharing (e.g., 1:14; 2:1, 44-45; 4:31–5:11). Their oneness is focused on their common relation to Christ, in whose name they heal (3:6, 16; 4:10, 30; 19:13), preach (4:12; 5:28, 40), and are baptized (2:38; 8:16; 10:48, 19:5); they suffer for his name (5:41; 9:16; 21:13), and are those who call on the name of the Lord Jesus (2:21, 36; 9:14, 21; 22:16).

In this narrative, baptism is both response and gift. Offering oneself to baptism is one of the prescribed ways of responding to the message of salvation, a public "turning" to God as God is revealed in the coming of Christ. But baptism is also one of salvation's blessings as it signals inclusion, belonging. As the community of God's people discerns God's acceptance of others, they incorporate those others into the community through the rite of baptism; accordingly, this rite signifies forgiveness and acceptance. Water baptism and Spirit baptism are correlated in Acts, though not in terms of simple priority of order, as though one must occur before the other. Instead, they are viewed as interrelated community and divine responses to human repentance. It is through the gift of the Spirit that God proves himself in Acts to be the savior of Jew and Gentile alike. By pouring on Gentiles the blessing of forgiveness and the gift of the Spirit, God testifies to the authenticity of their membership in the community of God's people; having "purified their deepest thoughts and desires through faith," he confirms that "he has made no distinction between us and them" (Acts 15:7-9; cf. 11:15-18). In baptism, the community of God's people recognize and affirm God's gracious work even among those regarded by many as beyond the reach of God's grace.

Luke sketches the content of salvation in terms of the forgiveness of sins and reception of the Holy Spirit too. Peter thus promises that the twofold effect of undergoing a repentance-baptism is the "forgiveness of your sins" and "the gift of the Holy Spirit" (Acts 2:38). Elsewhere in Acts, "forgiveness" can function as a virtual stand-in for the whole of salvation's blessings (see Acts 5:31; 13:26, 28; 4:10-12; 10:43; 11:14). Forgiveness marks a new/renewed relationship with God, of course, but also with God's people, and points to God's gathering together God's restored people. The same could be said of the gift of the Spirit, since the outpouring of the Spirit was promised by Joel (Joel 2:28-32) as the centerpiece of the end-time restoration of Israel from exile. That the gift of the Spirit helps to define salvation in Acts is self-evident in the narrative of Pentecost in Acts 2, but this emphasis comes to the surface again and again in the ensuing narrative (e.g., Acts 9:17; 10:43-44; 11:15-17; 15:8). Quite apart from any self-understanding or strategic thinking on the part of the community, the Spirit is poured out on those who respond to the good news, signifying both the restoration of Israel and, more to the present point, that these persons have been embraced by God as his restored people.

Christology and Preaching

For Luke, these emphases are tied together with Christology and with Christian proclamation. Central to both was news of Jesus' resurrection. For example, in the first public address recounted in Acts, Peter affirms Jesus' status as Lord and Christ with reference to his exaltation (Acts 2:36). Of course, from this perspective Jesus *becomes* nothing at the resurrection that he was not already; at his birth the angels declare that he is Savior, Messiah, and Lord (Luke 2:11). During his ministry, however, the exalted status of Jesus signified by these titles was not grasped even by his followers. Moreover, it was rejected by the Jerusalem elite who were instrumental in bringing about what must have seemed as decisive proof against Jesus' exalted status, namely, his execution on a Roman cross. Jesus' resurrection thus serves to validate the status Jesus possessed already, but which was in doubt on account of his maltreatment in Jerusalem. In Peter's Pentecost sermon, the proof of Jesus' resurrection comes in three parts: (1) David the prophet anticipated Jesus' resurrection and enthronement as Messiah (Acts 2:25-31); (2) Peter and the other apostles are themselves witnesses of Jesus' resurrection (Acts 2:32); and (3) the phenomena associated with the outpouring of the Spirit (Acts 2:1-13) are the consequence of Jesus' exaltation and reception of the promise of the Spirit (Acts 2:33). The Christology of Peter's sermon is marked by God's irrefutable vindication of Jesus' identity: Jesus is God's coregent and graciously provides the blessings of salvation.

Shortly thereafter, Peter and John are brought up on charges for this very message, that is, for "announcing that the resurrection of the dead was happening because of Jesus" (Acts 4:2). Note that their message was not simply that Jesus had been raised, but rather that in Jesus there is resurrection. This presses the question, what is "resurrection"?

The idea of resurrection is relatively scarce in the Old Testament, with hints of resurrection faith appearing in only a handful of prophetic texts. The church fathers found in Hosea 6:1-3 ("After two days he will revive us; on the third day he will raise us up, so that we may live before him" [v. 2]) a

139

prophecy of Jesus' resurrection on the third day, but in its own eighth-century BCE context, this "raising up" is more likely a metaphorical reference to the restoration of the nation. Ezekiel 37:1-14, with its dramatic image of a valley full of bones brought to life, also provides a vision of Israel's restoration. This did not keep later Jewish interpretation from finding there a graphic depiction of the resurrection, however. Note especially verses 12-13: "I'm opening your graves! I will raise you up from your graves, my people, and I will bring you to Israel's fertile land. You will know that I am the LORD, when I open your graves and raise you up from your graves, my people." In both of these texts, we find the interweaving of the promise of Israel's restoration with the re-creative work of the Lord.

Many scholars find a more direct reference to resurrection in Isaiah 26:19:

> Your dead will live,
>> their corpses will rise,
>> and those who dwell in the dust will shout for joy.
> Your shadow is a shadow of light,
>> but you will bring down the ghosts into the underworld.

Like the vision in Ezekiel 37, Isaiah's words appear in a context that proposes Israel's restoration and, indeed, exaltation among the nations. Scholars debate whether this text actually envisions the raising up of dead corpses. At the very least, though, we have here another text that relates the notion of resurrection to the activity of God by which he restores and exalts his people, and by which he pours on them the totality of his covenant blessings. The first unambiguous reference to the physical resurrection of the dead appears in Daniel 12:1-3: "Many of those who sleep in the dusty land will wake up—some to eternal life, others to shame and eternal disgrace" (v. 2). This passage marks the decisive triumph of God's people over Israel's enemies, as Daniel's concern with the vindication of God's righteous servants comes into clearest focus.

When we take these texts into account, and other Second Temple Jewish material besides, several motifs begin to take shape, and these help us to know what categories of interpretation might have been available to those with at least some exposure to Israel's scriptural traditions who first heard of Jesus' resurrection: (1) Resurrection signals Israel's restoration. (2) Resurrection signals Israel's triumph over its enemies. (3) Resurrection marks God's vindication of the righteous who have suffered unjustly. (4) Resurrection marks the decisive establishment of divine justice, where rewards and punishments are meted out in relation to the character of one's life before death. Injustice and wickedness will not have the final word, but in the resurrection will be decisively repudiated.

To return to the indictment brought against the apostles in Acts 4, then, their proclamation of "resurrection . . . because of Jesus" was simply their announcement of Israel's restoration under God's rule. For the Jewish elite, who drew their authority and stature from the status quo under Roman rule, however, this could hardly have been "good news."

Against this backdrop, the book of Acts proclaims salvation as Israel's end-time restoration, intimately correlating the resurrection and exaltation of Jesus with Jesus' role in the outpouring of the Spirit. What are the effects of this message for the life of the church? For Acts, these would include:

- The Holy Spirit creates and forms the community of God's people, so that the characteristic behaviors of Jesus' followers, as sketched in Acts 2:42-47 (e.g., prayer, worship, economic sharing, and common meals) must be regarded as the Spirit's work within and among God's people.

- The community created by the Spirit is none other than the people of Abraham, Isaac, and Jacob (e.g., Acts 3:13; 7:8, 32), signifying in a crucial sense that God's purpose is one and, therefore, God's people, across time and space, is one. Israel's story is the church's story and, then, their story is our story, because there is only one God: the God of Abraham, Isaac, and Jacob, the God who raised Jesus from the dead, the God who poured out the Pentecostal Spirit.

- The Holy Spirit empowers and directs this community for mission, moving God's people beyond long-established and taken-for-granted religious and ethnic barriers to "the end of the earth" (Acts 1:8; cf., e.g., chs. 8, 16; 10:1–11:18), so that the contours of the mission itself comprise a profound statement about the social ramifications of the message of salvation.

- The mission of the church serves to propagate the message that God's redemptive purpose is being actualized in the world. Evangelism, then, is the announcement in word and deed: The times have changed! These are the days of "resurrection"! And this changing of the eons calls for a radical reordering of life (e.g., Acts 3:12-26; 17:30-31).

- The resurrection message is realized in the life of God's people as they extend hospitality, engage in economic sharing, and otherwise ensure that "there were no needy persons among them" (Acts 4:32-35). The community of God's people embodies God's kingdom as they care for and socialize their members with respect to practices that exhibit God's concern for the needy.

- The content of preaching serves the purpose of preaching, namely, to transform the imaginations of people, to press the boundaries of what people will allow as possible, in order to grasp in fresh ways the character of God's work in the world. The story of God's history with Israel must be told and retold (e.g., Acts 7; 13:16-41), but only as interpreted faithfully in continuity with God's exaltation of Jesus and, thus, in relation to the actualization of God's purpose in Christ and through the church, then and now.

- The common life of the church, its resolve in the face of harassment, and the direction of the mission are set within the arena of worship (Acts 2:42-47; 4:24-30; 10:9, 33; 11:18; 13:2). In this sense, worship is basic, since it is precisely in relation to the worship of God that the community opens itself to a vision of reality that counters the dominant ideology of their daily experience in the Roman world. This worship is not other-worldly; it is not withdrawal from the world. Rather worship is an acknowledgment of the living God whose purpose and work in the world set the agenda for those who would serve, and not hinder, him. In worship, God's people refresh their grasp on how things ought to be, focus on God's perspective and saving project, and align themselves with God's aims.

In these and other ways, the community of God's people is the community of salvation.

Had we stepped outside of the Acts of the Apostles for this overview, we would have found similar materials, though with sometimes different emphases. For example, a closer examination of Paul would have brought to our attention the importance of the Last Supper in the definition of the church; God's people, if they take seriously the selfless, sacrificial act of Christ on the cross, will embody service and sacrifice in their common life "until he comes" (1 Cor 11:17-34). Exploration of the hymnody of the book of Revelation would have underscored for us even more the importance of worship in the projection and maintenance of a more comprehensive and integrated vision of God's work, over against those perspectives on reality inspired and publicized by the beast, in the service of the dragon. Worship, in this instance, would have served even more as an act of rehearsal in anticipation of things to come and as an act of proclaiming the world's goal and future. Already, though, we have identified important landmarks for the journey of the community of salvation.

Epilogue

The character of the message of salvation and its contemporary embodiment are inescapably determined by the end. This, at least, is the witness of scripture, however unpalatable this may seem to folks more accustomed to living for today and however distasteful it might be to those of us who have grown weary of end-time sensationalism. The message of salvation runs like a thread through the whole of scripture, from Genesis to Revelation, and participates integrally in how we understand the beginning, middle, and end of the biblical story. As with narratives more generally, so this one fails its purpose when it is reduced to one aspect of its plot or another. The end shapes the beginning and middle. Perhaps even more so, this narrative fails when we find ourselves wanting to figure it out, to contemplate it, to speculate about it, apart from personal engagement and consequences. This narrative, above all narratives, invites active participation. "Come," it beckons, as it seeks a people to indwell its story, to have their lives determined decisively by it.

What are the consequences of an engaged reading of this scripture and of our being read by it? We have highlighted several effects. First, and perhaps most profoundly, this is not all there is. Our experience of life in the world is a chapter, for us an important one, but it is not the whole book. For some, this will comes as a word of comfort and delight. This is because it urges us to place sometimes horrific images of suffering and tragedy within the larger mural of a God who can turn mourning into dancing and who wipes away tears. For others, this will come as a stunning surprise and warning, a resounding charge against the pretensions of human efforts. If consciously placed within the grand sweep of history in God's care, much of what concerns us now would pale in significance.

Second, the end casts its shadow backward on present existence, giving us perspective on what will be and, thus, what ought to be. On the one hand, this means that visions of the end serve to expand the horizons of what we allow and take to be true and important. Immersing ourselves in these biblical materials, and immersing ourselves in worship shaped by this end-time perspective, transforms our patterns of thinking and believing and, thus, refashions our allegiances and practices. On the other hand, when the end back shadows its interests into our worlds, it does so in order to generate a crisis in our lives; it calls for response. Things are not the way they are supposed to be. We serve the present age by serving the Consummation of All Things, by getting in sync with God's project and practices in bringing creation to its real purpose. In this way, as the community of God's people, we come to embody and exhibit God's salvation, as well as take on the role of agents of salvation.

Third, we come face-to-face with the reality that we, we who comprise the community of the saved, are "in process." Our past is firmly enmeshed in God's redemptive acts, in exodus, and in Christ. Our future is secured in God's sovereign purpose, guaranteed by the empowering presence of the Holy Spirit. Our present is part of God's work too. The metaphors abound: growing up in Christ, clothing ourselves in Christ, producing the Spirit's fruit, and more. These signify the imperative of pressing onward, toward Christlikeness, in the awareness that it is Christ who demonstrates for us what it means to reflect in our lives the very image of God. For this we were made and are now being remade. Like Paul, we have not yet attained the intimacy with Christ Jesus and the transformation into Christlikeness for which Christ has made us his own (Phil 3:10-14). But we press on toward this goal, which is ours in Christ.

Notes

Introduction

1. David F. Ford, *Theology: A Very Short Introduction* (Oxford: Oxford University Press, 1999), 101–19.

2. Gerald Prince, *Narrative as Theme: Studies in French Fiction* (Lincoln: University of Nebraska Press, 1992), 3.

Chapter One: Adam, What Have You Done?

1. 4 Ezra comprises chs. 3–14 of the apocryphal book 2 Esdras, which is itself a compilation of three books: (1) chs. 1–2, sometimes designated as 2 or 5 Ezra; (2) chs. 3–14, usually called 4 Ezra; and (3) chs. 15–16, sometimes designated as 5 or 6 Ezra.

2. See G. David Poznik et al., "Sequencing Y Chromosomes Resolves Discrepancy in Time to Common Ancestor of Males Versus Females," *Science* 341, no. 6415 (2013): 562–65; Paolo Francalacci et al., "Low-Pass DNA Sequencing of 1200 Sardinians Reconstructs European Y-Chromosome Phylogeny," *Science* 341, no. 6415 (2013): 565–69.

3. See, e.g., Patricia A. Williams, *Doing with Adam and Eve: Sociobiology and Original Sin* (TSc; Minneapolis: Fortress, 2001); Ian A. McFarland, *In Adam's Fall: A Meditation on the Christian Doctrine of Original Sin* (CCT; Malden, Mass.: Wiley-Blackwell, 2010).

4. Some English translations read "a little lower than the angels" (e.g., AV, NIV), on account of how the early versions (Greek, Latin, Aramaic) interpreted the Hebrew אֱלֹהִים, *ʾĕlōhîm* ("God, gods"). Other early versions

translated the Hebrew term as "God," however, and this rendering is favored by the context.

5. For a wide-ranging discussion concerned with scripture, science, and systematic theology, see David Wilkinson, *Christian Eschatology and the Physical Universe* (London: T&T Clark, 2010).

6. This list is dependent on insights garnered from Philip Hefner, *The Human Factor: Evolution, Culture, and Religion* (TSc; Minneapolis: Fortress, 1993), 118–19; Warren S. Brown, "Cognitive Contributions to Soul," in *Whatever Happened to the Soul? Scientific and Theological Portraits of Human Nature*, ed. Warren S. Brown, Nancey Murphy, and H. Newton Malony (TSc; Minneapolis: Fortress, 1998), 99–125.

7. Francisco J. Ayala, "Human Nature: One Evolutionist's View," in *Whatever Happened to the Soul? Scientific and Theological Portraits of Human Nature*, 31–48 (esp. 40–41); Brown, "Cognitive Contributions."

8. Joe M. Kapolyo, *The Human Condition: Christian Perspectives through African Eyes* (Downers Grove, Ill.: InterVarsity, 2005); Ismael Garcia, *Dignidad: Ethics through Hispanic Eyes* (Nashville: Abingdon, 1997).

9. Charles Taylor, *Sources of the Self: The Making of the Modern Identity* (Cambridge, Mass.: Harvard University Press, 1989), 211.

10. William James, *The Varieties of Religious Experience: A Study in Human Nature, Being the Gifford Lectures on Natural Religion Delivered at Edinburgh in 1901–1902* (London: Longmans, Green, 1902), 189.

11. A. D. Nock, *Conversion: The Old and the New in Religion from Alexander the Great to Augustine of Hippo* (Oxford: Clarendon, 1933), 7–8.

12. Francis Crick, *The Astonishing Hypothesis: The Scientific Search for the Soul* (New York: Simon & Schuster, 1994), 261.

13. Helmut Thielicke lists "three humblings": Copernicus, Darwin, and Freud (*Being Human . . . Becoming Human: An Essay in Christian Anthropology* [Garden City, N.Y.: Doubleday, 1984], 29–32). On the relationship between the neurosciences and the anthropology we find in scripture, see Joel B. Green, *Body, Soul, and Human Life: The Nature of Humanity in the Bible* (STI; Grand Rapids: Baker Academic, 2008).

14. Wolfhart Pannenberg, *Systematic Theology*, vol. 2 (Grand Rapids: Eerdmans, 1994), 182. Pannenberg anticipated this position in his earlier works, *What Is Man? Contemporary Anthropology in Theological Perspective* (Philadelphia: Fortress, 1970), 45–53; and *Anthropology in Theological Per-*

spective (Philadelphia: Westminster, 1985). See Nancey Murphy, *Bodies and Souls, or Spirited Bodies?* (CTI; Cambridge: Cambridge University Press, 2006).

15. Alister E. McGrath, *Scientific Theology*, vol. 1 of *Nature* (Grand Rapids: Eerdmans, 2001), 197. For a recent survey of ways in which creation of humanity "in the divine image" has been interpreted, together with a contemporary proposal, see Stanley J. Grenz, *The Social God and the Relational Self: A Trinitarian Theology of the Imago Dei* (MCT; Louisville, Ky.: Westminster John Knox, 2001).

16. See, e.g., J. Richard Middleton, "Image of God," in *Dictionary of Scripture and Ethics*, ed. Joel B. Green (Grand Rapids: Baker Academic, 2011), 394–97.

17. I have discussed Philo and later interpreters further in Joel B. Green, *Practicing Theological Interpretation: Engaging Biblical Texts for Faith and Formation* (Theological Explorations for the Church Catholic; Grand Rapids: Baker Academic, 2011), 86–95. See the important interpretive work in J. Richard Middleton, *The Liberating Image: The* Imago Dei *in Genesis 1* (Grand Rapids: Brazos, 2005). Cf. Walter Brueggemann, *Theology of the Old Testament: Testimony, Dispute, Advocacy* (Minneapolis: Fortress, 1997), 451–52; Colin E. Gunton, "Trinity, Ontology and Anthropology: Towards a Renewal of the Doctrine of the *Imago Dei*," in *Persons Divine and Human: King's College Essays on Theological Anthropology*, ed. Christoph Schwöbel and Colin E. Gunton (Edinburgh: T&T Clark, 1991), 47–61; Christoph Schwöbel, "Human Being as Relation Being: Twelve Theses for a Christian Anthropology," in *Persons Divine and Human*, 141–70.

18. Robert A. Di Vito, "Old Testament Anthropology and the Construction of Personal Identity," *CBQ* 61 (1999): 217–38.

19. Genesis 3 has been the object of a wide range of psychological analyses, and these are surveyed and assessed in D. Andrew Kille, *Psychological Biblical Criticism* (GBS:OTS; Minneapolis: Fortress, 2001).

20. Horst Dietrich Preuss, *Old Testament Theology*, 2 vols. (OTL; Louisville, KY: Westminster John Knox, 1996), 2:171.

21. William P. Brown, *The Ethos of the Cosmos: The Genesis of Moral Imagination in the Bible* (Grand Rapids: Eerdmans, 1999), 160–61.

22. Ray S. Anderson, *Theology, Death and Dying* (London: Basil Blackwell, 1986), 46. Cf. John Goldingay, "Death and Afterlife in the Psalms," in

Judaism in Late Antiquity, part 4: *Death, Life-after-Death, Resurrection and the World-to-Come in the Judaisms of Antiquity,* ed. Alan J. Avery-Peck and Jacob Neusner; *Handbook of Oriental Studies, vol. 1: The Near and Middle East,* 49 (Leiden: Brill, 2000), 61–85; Roland E. Murphy, "Death and Afterlife in the Wisdom Literature," in *Death, Life-after-Death, Resurrection, and the World-to-Come,* 101–16.

23. See Robin C. Cover, "Sin, Sinners (Old Testament)," in *ABD* 6:31–40 (esp. 38).

24. E.g., Josh 7:20; 1 Sam 15:24; 2 Sam 12:13; 19:21; 24:10; Pss 41:5; 51:6; et al.

25. E.g., Num 14:40; 21:7; Judg 10:10, 15; 1 Sam 7:6; 12:10; 1 Kgs 8:47; et al.

26. See below, ch. 4.

27. See Rom 8:19-22, 38-39; 1 Cor 15:24-26; Eph 1:21; 6:12; Col 1:16; 2:9-15; 1 Pet 3:22.

28. See Rikki E. Watts, *Isaiah's New Exodus and Mark* (WUNT 2/88; Tübingen: Mohr Siebeck, 1997).

29. The secondary literature on this theme is extensive and growing. For a useful summary of the discussion, see Nicholas Perrin, "Exile," in *The World of the New Testament: Cultural, Social, and Historical Contexts,* ed. Joel B. Green and Lee Martin McDonald (Grand Rapids: Baker Academic, 2013), 25–37. More broadly, cf., e.g., Craig A. Evans, "Aspects of Exile and Restoration in the Proclamation of Jesus and the Gospels," in *Jesus in Context: Temple, Purity and Restoration,* ed. Bruce Chilton and Craig A. Evans (AGJU 39; Leiden: Brill, 1997), 263–94; Michael F. Fuller, *The Restoration of Israel: Israel's Re-gathering and the Fate of the Nations in Early Jewish Literature and Luke-Acts* (BZNW 138; Berlin: de Gruyter, 2006); Michael A. Knibb, "The Exile in the Literature of the Intertestamental Period." *HeyJ* 17 (1976): 253–72; N. T. Wright, *The New Testament and the People of God* (COQG 1; Minneapolis: Fortress, 1992).

30. See Joel B. Green, "Healing and Healthcare," in *The World of the New Testament: Cultural, Social, and Historical Contexts,* ed. Joel B. Green and Lee Martin McDonald (Grand Rapids: Baker Academic, 2013), 330–41.

31. Cf. H. Kruse, "Die 'dialektische Negation' als semitisches Idiom," *VT* 4 (1954): 385–400.

32. See M. Eugene Boring, *Mark: A Commentary* (NTL; Louisville, Ky.: Westminster John Knox, 2006), 204–5.

33. Williams, *Doing without Adam and Eve*, 151.

34. See Timothy B. Cargal, *Restoring the Diaspora: Discursive Structure and Purpose in the Epistle of James* (SBLDS 144; Atlanta: Scholars Press, 1993), 81–82.

35. See Luke L. Cheung, *The Genre, Composition and Hermeneutics of James* (PBTM; Carlisle: Paternoster, 2003), 206–13.

36. See Andrew Chester, "The Theology of James," in *The Theology of the Letters of James, Peter, and Jude,* by Andrew Chester and Ralph P. Martin (NTT; Cambridge: Cambridge University Press, 1994), 1–62 (especially 39–41).

37. John Wesley, *Explanatory Notes upon the New Testament* (London: Epworth, 1976 [1754]), 857.

38. E.g., *2 Apocalypse of Baruch 54.14-19; Liber antiquitatum biblicarum* 13.8.

39. See the helpful discussion in Mark E. Biddle, *Missing the Mark: Sin and Its Consequences in Biblical Theology* (Nashville: Abingdon, 2005), 33–44.

40. Cf. Udo Schnelle, *The Human Condition: Anthropology in the Teachings of Jesus, Paul, and John* (Minneapolis: Fortress, 1996), 63–66.

41. See, e.g., 1 Cor 1:26-29; 3:18-19; 4:9-13; 5:9-11; et al.

42. So Werner Georg Kümmel, *Man in the New Testament* (London: Epworth, 1963), 87.

43. Aleksandr I. Solzhenitsyn, *The Gulag Archipelago: 1918–1956* (London: Book Club, 1974), 163.

44. Ted Peters, *Sin: Radical Evil in Soul and Society* (Grand Rapids: Eerdmans, 1994). On what follows, see also David Atkinson, "What Difference Does the Cross Make to Life?" in *Atonement Today: A Symposium at St. John's College, Nottingham,* ed. John Goldingay (London: S.P.C.K., 1995), 253–71.

Chapter Two: Yahweh, the Healer

1. This kind of problem is expressed well in Scot McKnight's renunciation of what he calls "a soterian gospel" (*The King Jesus Gospel: The Original Good News Revisited* [Grand Rapids: Zondervan, 2011]); rather than rehabilitate the language of "salvation" (σωτηρία, *sōtēria*) in conversation with the New Testament, he rejects that language on account of its associations today with an anemic understanding of the good news.

2. Related material is conveniently collected in Wendy Cotter, *Miracles in Greco-Roman Antiquity: A Sourcebook* (London: Routledge, 1999), 11–53. More generally, see Ceslas Spicq, *Theological Lexicon of the New Testament*, 3 vols. (Peabody, Mass.: Hendrickson, 1994), 3:344–49.

3. How to define "sickness" is controverted; I have adapted this definition from Robert A. Hahn, *Sickness and Healing: An Anthropological Perspective* (New Haven: Yale University Press, 1995), 22.

4. See Hahn, *Sickness and Healing*, 28; more generally, Bryon J. Good, *Medicine, Rationality, and Experience: An Anthropological Perspective* (Lewis Henry Morgan Lectures 1990; Cambridge: Cambridge University Press, 1994).

5. Trinh Xuan Thuan, *Chaos and Harmony: Perspectives on Scientific Revolutions of the Twentieth Century* (Oxford: Oxford University Press, 2001), 294.

6. Larry O. Hogan, *Healing in the Second Tempel [sic] Period* (NTOA 21; Göttingen: Vandenhoeck & Ruprecht, 1992).

7. See, e.g., Exod 7:3; Deut 4:34; 7:19; 26:8; 29:3; 34:11; Jer 32:20-21; Dan 4:2-3; 6:27; Acts 2:19, 22, 43; 4:30; 5:12; 6:8; 7:36; 8:6, 13; 14:3; 15:12.

8. Cf. Matt 9:22; Mark 5:34; 10:52; Luke 8:48; 18:42.

9. This is emphasized in Martin C. Albl, "'Are Any among You Sick?' The Health Care System in the Letter of James," *JBL* 121, no. 1 (2002): 123–43.

10. On the range of New Testament metaphors for salvation, cf. Brenda A. Colijn, *Images of Salvation in the New Testament* (Downers Grove, Ill.: InterVarsity, 2010).

11. For this reading, see Richard Bauckham, "Jesus and the Wild Animals (Mark 1:13): A Christological Image for an Ecological Age," in *Jesus of Nazareth: Lord and Christ: Essays on the Historical Jesus and New Testament Christology*, ed. Joel B. Green and Max Turner (Grand Rapids: Eerdmans, 1994), 3–21.

12. See Reinhard Feldmeier, *The First Letter of Peter: A Commentary on the Greek Text* (Waco, Tex.: Baylor University Press, 2008), 127–30; Leonhard Goppelt, *A Commentary on 1 Peter* (Grand Rapids: Eerdmans, 1993), 81–83.

13. The verb δικαιόω *(dikaioō,* "to justify") appears only these three times in James, each time in a passive form.

14. Christopher J. H. Wright, "Old Testament Ethics: A Missiological Perspective," *Catalyst* 26, no. 2 (2000): 5–8 (8).

15. ἡγιασμένοις ἐν Χριστῷ Ἰησοῦ, κλητοῖς ἁγίοις, *hēgiasmenois en Christō Iēsou, klētois hagiois.*

Chapter Three: Yahweh, the Liberator

1. Richard A. Horsley, *The Liberation of Christmas: The Infancy Narratives in Social Context* (New York: Crossroad, 1989), 111.

2. Tremper Longman III, "Warfare," in *NDBT,* 835–39 (esp. 836–37). See further, Tremper Longman III and Daniel G. Reid, *God Is a Warrior* (SOTBT; Grand Rapids: Zondervan, 1995).

3. This is appropriately emphasized in Stephen B. Chapman, "Holy War," in *DSE,* 369–70.

4. Cf., e.g., Exod 29:46; Lev 11:45; 19:36; 22:33; 25:38; 26:13; Num 15:41; 23:22; 24:8; Deut 1:30; 5:6; 8:14; 13:5; et al.

5. Norbert F. Lohfink, *Option for the Poor: The Basic Principle of Liberation Theology in the Light of the Bible* (Berkeley, CA: Bibal, 1987), 27–52.

6. See also Exod 4:23; 7:16; 8:1; 9:1, 13; 10:3, 26; 14:12. Cf. Göran Larsson, *Bound for Freedom: The Book of Exodus in Jewish and Christian Traditions* (Peabody, Mass.: Hendrickson, 1999), 5–15.

7. The outline of what follows is adapted from Brueggemann, *Theology of the Old Testament,* 173–76.

8. Larsson, *Bound for Freedom,* 102.

9. See, e.g., Kay Young and Jeffrey L. Saver, "The Neurology of Narrative," *SubStance* 30 (2001): 72–84; William Hirstein, *Brain Fiction: Self-Deception and the Riddle of Confabulation* (Cambridge, Mass.: MIT Press, 2005).

10. E.g., Brian Stock, *Listening for the Text: On the Uses of the Past* (Baltimore, Md.: The Johns Hopkins University Press, 1990; Philadelphia: University of Pennsylvania Press, 1997); David Lowenthal, *The Past Is a Foreign Country* (Cambridge: Cambridge University Press, 1985).

11. David J. Bryant, *Faith and the Play of Imagination: On the Role of Imagination in Religion* (SABH 5; Macon, Ga.: Mercer University Press, 1989), 5; cf. Mark Johnson, *The Body in the Mind: The Bodily Basis of Meaning, Imagination, and Reason* (Chicago: University of Chicago, 1987), xx: "a basic image-schematic capacity for ordering our experience."

Notes to Pages 68–77

12. Cf. Rikki E. Watts, "Exodus," in *NDBT,* 478–87 (esp. 482–84).

13. See the exploration of this theme in David W. Pao, *Acts and the Isaianic New Exodus* (WUNT 2/130; Tübingen: Mohr Siebeck, 2000).

14. Robert N. Bellah et al., *Habits of the Heart: Individualism and Commitment in American Life* (Berkeley: University of California Press, 1985); see further Bellah et al., eds., *Individualism and Commitment in American Life: Readings on the Themes of Habits of the Heart* (San Francisco: Harper & Row, 1987).

15. Jean M. Twenge, W. Keith Campbell, and Brittany Gentile, "Changes in Pronoun Use in American Books and the Rise of Individualism, 1960–2008," *Journal of Cross-Cultural Psychology* 44, no. 3 (2013): 406–15.

16. E.g., C. H. Reynolds and R. V. Norman, eds., *Community in America: The Challenge of Habits of the Heart* (Berkeley: University of California Press, 1988).

17. Suzanne Gordon, *Prisoners of Men's Dreams: Striking out for a New Feminine Future* (Boston: Little, Brown, 1991), 4.

18. Cain Hope Felder, ed., *Stony the Road We Trod: African American Biblical Interpretation* (Minneapolis: Fortress, 1991).

19. Justo L. González, *Santa Biblia: The Bible through Hispanic Eyes* (Nashville: Abingdon, 1996). For the emphasis on community in American-Hispanic theological reflection more broadly, see, e.g., Miguel H. Díaz, *On Being Human: U.S. Hispanic and Rahnerian Perspectives* (Maryknoll, N.Y.: Orbis, 2001); García, *Dignidad.*

20. Cf. Joseph LeDoux, *Synaptic Self: How Our Brains Become Who We Are* (New York: Viking, 2002).

21. See Robert Wuthnow, *Sharing the Journey: Support Groups and America's New Quest for Community* (New York: Free, 1994).

22. Matt 4:1-11; Mark 1:13; Luke 4:1-13; and, e.g., Matt 11:2-6; 12:22-30; Mark 1:21-28; 3:22-27; 5:1-20; 7:24-30; 9:14-29; Luke 7:18-23; 11:14-23; 13:10-17. On this larger motif, see, e.g., Sydney H. T. Page, *Powers of Evil: A Biblical Study of Satan and Demons* (Grand Rapids: Baker, 1995); Graham H. Twelftree, *Jesus the Exorcist: A Contribution to the Study of the Historical Jesus* (Peabody, Mass.: Hendrickson, 1993); Richard H. Bell, *Deliver Us from Evil: Interpreting the Redemption from the Power of Satan in New Testament Theology* (WUNT 216; Tübingen: Mohr Siebeck, 2007).

152

23. Cf. Daniel G. Reid, "Principalities and Powers," in *DPL*, 746–52 (esp. 748–49).

24. Cf. J. Louis Martyn, *Theological Issues in the Letters of Paul* (Nashville: Abingdon, 1997), 125–40.

25. In recent years, the argument that Jesus was a revolutionary was proposed most seriously by S. G. F. Brandon in *Jesus and the Zealots: A Study of the Political Factor in Primitive Christianity* (Manchester: Manchester University Press, 1967); his case and others like it were thoroughly addressed by Ernst Bammel and C. F. D. Moule, eds., *Jesus and the Politics of His Day* (Cambridge: Cambridge University Press, 1984). Today, positions on this question are much more nuanced. For introductions to the discussion from competing perspectives, see, e.g., Richard A. Horsley, *Jesus and Empire: The Kingdom of God and the New World Disorder* (Minneapolis: Fortress, 2003) (Jesus' call to covenant renewal was inseparable from his prophetic denouncement of Roman imperial rule); Christopher Bryan, *Render to Caesar: Jesus, the Early Church, and the Roman Superpower* (Oxford: Oxford University Press, 2005) (contra Horsley, "the biblical tradition challenges all human power structures not by attempting to dismantle them or replace them with other human power structures but by consistently confronting them with the truth about their origin and purpose" [p. 9]).

26. This kind of work was pioneered outside biblical and theological studies, e.g., in Michel de Certeau, *The Practice of Everyday Life* (Berkeley: University of California Press, 1984); James C. Scott, *Domination and the Arts of Resistance: Hidden Transcripts* (New Haven: Yale University Press, 1990; *Weapons of the Weak: Everyday Forms of Peasant Resistance* (New Haven: Yale University Press, 1985).

27. Representative of some of the earlier voices that named the tension between the Christian movement and Rome are Walter E. Pilgrim, *Uneasy Neighbors: Church and State in the New Testament* (OBT; Minneapolis: Fortress, 1999); Richard J. Cassidy, *Christians and Roman Rule in the New Testament: New Perspectives* (CNT; New York: Crossroad, 2001).

28. See Joel B. Green, *The Gospel of Luke* (NICNT; Grand Rapids: Eerdmans, 1997), 120–38.

29. Richard Bauckham, *The Theology of the Book of Revelation* (NTT; Cambridge: Cambridge University Press, 1993), 91.

Chapter Four: How Can We Be Saved?

1. Cf. Mark 1:14; Acts 20:24; Rom 1:1; 15:16; 2 Cor 11:7; 1 Thess 2:2, 8, 9; 1 Tim 1:11; 1 Pet 4:17.

2. See Isa 40–55; cf. Watts, *Isaiah's New Exodus,* 80–81.

3. Cf. David M. Knipe, "The Temple in Image and Reality," in *Temple in Society,* ed. Michael V. Fox (Winona Lake, Ind.: Eisenbrauns, 1988), 105–38; Francis Schmidt, *How the Temple Thinks: Identity and Social Cohesion in Ancient Judaism* (TBS 78; Sheffield: Sheffield Academic Press, 2001).

4. Cf. Menahem Haran, "Temple and Community in Ancient Israel," in *Temple in Society,* 17–25 (quotation from p. 23).

5. Jacob Milgrom, *Leviticus,* 3 vols. (AB; New York: Doubleday, 1991–2001); idem, *Studies in Cultic Theology and Terminology* (SJLA 36; Leiden: Brill, 1983). See further, B. Lang, "כפר," in *TDOT* 7:288–303; Gary A. Anderson, "Sacrifice and Sacrificial Offerings (Old Testament)," in *ABD* 5:870–86. Over the past century, scholars have debated whether sacrifice was concerned with "expiation" (i.e., sacrifice as the means by which God frees and cleanses people from the onus and blemish of sin) or with "propitiation" (sacrifice as a means of assuaging God's anger). Not only does Leviticus itself make no connection between sacrifice and God's anger, but the linguistic evidence prioritizes a definition of atonement as "to wipe away" or "to cleanse"; cf. Richard E. Averbeck, "כפר," in *NIDOTTE* 2:689–710.

6. Cf. Gordon J. Wenham, "The Theology of Old Testament Sacrifice," in *Sacrifice in the Bible,* ed. Rogert T. Beckwith and Martin J. Selman (Grand Rapids: Baker, 1995), 75–87; James D. G. Dunn, "Paul's Understanding of the Death of Jesus as Sacrifice," in *Sacrifice and Redemption: Durham Essays in Theology,* ed. S. W. Sykes (Cambridge: Cambridge University Press, 1991), 35–56. Lang, "כפר."

7. See Perrin, "Exile"; relevant material has also been helpfully surveyed in Craig A. Evans, "Jesus and the Continuing Exile of Israel," in *Jesus and the Restoration of Israel,* ed. Carey C. Newman (Downers Grove, Ill.: InterVarsity, 1999), 77–100 (esp. 78–91).

8. See, e.g., Jer 4:14; 31:31-34; 1 Macc 3:18-22; 4:11; 9:46; 2 Macc 1:11, 25; 2:17-18; 7:1-42; 8:27-29; 1QM.

9. N. T. Wright, *Jesus the Victory of God* (COQG 2; Minneapolis: Fortress, 1996), 228.

10. Throughout this section, I have adapted material from Joel B. Green, "Kingdom of God/Heaven," in DJG², 468–81.

11. See, e.g., Gustaf Dalman, *The Words of Jesus Considered in Light of Post-Biblical Jewish Writings and the Aramaic Language* (Edinburgh: T&T Clark, 1902); more recently, Bruce D. Chilton, *God in Strength: Jesus' Announcement of the Kingdom* (SNTU B1; Freistadt: F. Plöchl, 1979).

12. This is demonstrated in Jonathan T. Pennington, *Heaven and Earth in the Gospel of Matthew* (Grand Rapids: Baker Academic, 2009).

13. R. B. Wright, "Psalms of Solomon: A New Translation and Introduction," in OTP 2:639–70 (quotation from pp. 665, 667).

14. Cf. John J. Collins, "The Kingdom of God in the Apocrypha and Pseudepigrapha," in *The Kingdom of God in 20th-Century Interpretation,* ed. Wendell Willis (Peabody, Mass.: Hendrickson, 1987), 81–95; Dale C. Allison Jr., "Kingdom of God," in *EDEJ*, 860–61

15. David Wenham, *The Parables of Jesus* (TJL; Downers Grove, Ill.: InterVarsity, 1989), 22.

16. See Watts, *Isaiah's New Exodus.*

17. See above, ch. 2.

18. See Joel B. Green, "Good News to Whom? Jesus and the 'Poor' in the Gospel of Luke," in *Jesus of Nazareth: Lord and Christ: Essays on the Historical Jesus and New Testament Christology,* ed. Joel B. Green and Max Turner (Grand Rapids: Eerdmans, 1995), 59–74 (esp. 69–74).

19. See Luke 1:51, 53; 6:24; 8:41, 49; 12:13-21; 13:14; 14:12-14; 16:19-31; 18:18-30.

20. See Luke 3:12; 5:27-32; 7:29; 15:1-2; 18:9-14.

21. Cf. Luke 1:77; 3:3; 5:20-21, 23-24; 7:47-49; 11:4; 12:10; 13:10-17; 17:3-4; 23:34; 24:47; Joel B. Green, *The Theology of the Gospel of Luke* (NTT; Cambridge: Cambridge University Press, 1995), 78–79, 113–17.

22. Cf. John 8:28; 12:32-33; 18:32.

23. See John Driver, *Understanding the Atonement for the Mission of the Church* (Scottdale, Pa.: Herald, 1986); Mark D. Baker and Joel B. Green, *Recovering the Scandal of the Cross: Atonement in New Testament and Contemporary Contexts* (2nd ed.; Downers Grove, Ill: IVP Academic, 2011).

24. Brian Rapske, *Paul in Roman Custody* (A1CS 3; Grand Rapids: Eerdmans, 1994), 126–27.

25. The jailor's offer of hospitality is itself an illegal act, according to Rapske (*Paul in Roman Custody*, 390–92), and this underscores the shift in his allegiances.

26. Peter L. Berger and Thomas Luckmann, *The Social Construction of Reality: A Treatise in the Sociology of Knowledge* (New York: Doubleday, 1966), 160.

27. See Lars Hartman, *'Into the Name of the Lord Jesus': Baptism in the Early Church* (SNTW; Edinburgh: T&T Clark, 1997), 130.

Chapter Five: The End of Salvation

1. For discussion and further bibliography, see Green, *Gospel of Luke*, 554–63.

2. William R. Stoeger, "Scientific Accounts of Ultimate Catastrophes in Our Life-Bearing Universe," in *The End of the World and the Ends of God: Science and Theology on Eschatology*, ed. John Polkinghorne and Michael Welker (Harrisburg, Pa.: Trinity, 2000), 19–28.

3. Paul D. Hanson, "Introduction," in *Visionaries and Their Apocalypses*, ed. Paul D. Hanson (Philadelphia: Fortress, 1983), 1–15 (quotation from p. 3).

4. See Wilkinson, *Christian Eschatology.*

5. E.g., Rev 1:4; 2:13; 3:21; 4–5; 6:16; 7:9; et al.

6. For general orientation on this subject, see Thomas Finger, "Eschatology and Ethics," in *DSE*, 276–79.

7. Richard Baukham, "The Relevance of Revelation," *Catalyst* 24, no. 4 (1996): 1–3 (quotation from p. 1).

8. Paul Ricoeur, cited in "Reflections," *Christianity Today* (7 February 2000): 84. See the helpful summary in Kevin J. Vanhoozer, *Biblical Narrative in the Philosophy of Paul Ricoeur: A Study in Hermeneutics and Theology* (Cambridge: Cambridge University Press, 1990), esp. 23–25.

9. Robert W. Jenson, *Systematic Theology*, 2 vols. (Oxford: Oxford University Press, 1997–99), 2:145.

10. Cf. James D. G. Dunn, *The Epistles to the Colossians and to Philemon* (NIGTC; Grand Rapids: Eerdmans, 1996), 222.

11. See Valerie M. Warrior, *Roman Religion* (CIRC; Cambridge: Cambridge University Press, 2006), 32–40.

12. Paul's thought is developed more fully, and helpfully, in terms of ancient science in Alan G. Padgett, "The Body in Resurrection: Science and Scripture on the 'Spiritual Body' (1 Cor 15:35-58)," *WW* 22 (2002): 155–63.

13. Cf. Richard N. Longenecker, "Is There Development in Paul's Resurrection Thought?" in *Life in the Face of Death: The Resurrection Message of the New Testament* (MNTS; ed. Richard N. Longenecker; Grand Rapids: Eerdmans, 1998), 171–202.

14. In Acts, see 2:21, 40, 47; 3:16; 4:9, 12, 14; 5:16, 31; 7:10, 25, 34; 8:7; 9:34; 10:38; 11:14; 12:11; 13:23, 26, 47; 14:9; 15:1, 11; 16:30, 31; 17:25; 23:24, 27; 26:17; 27:20, 31, 34, 43, 44; 28:1, 4, 8, 9, 27, 28.

Bibliography

Albl, Martin C. "'Are Any among You Sick?' The Health Care System in the Letter of James." *JBL* 121, no. 1 (2002): 123–43.

Allison Jr., Dale C. "Kingdom of God." Pages 860–61 in *The Eerdmans Dictionary of Early Judaism*. Edited by John J. Collins and Daniel C. Harlow. Grand Rapids: Eerdmans, 2010.

Anderson, Gary A. "Sacrifice and Sacrificial Offerings (Old Testament)." Pages 870–86 in vol. 5 of *Anchor Bible Dictionary*. Edited by David Noel Freedman. 6 vols. New York: Doubleday, 1992.

Anderson, Ray S. *Theology, Death and Dying*. London: Basil Blackwell, 1986.

Anonymous. "Reflections." *Christianity Today* (7 February 2000): 84.

Atkinson, David. "What Difference Does the Cross Make to Life?" Pages 253–71 in *Atonement Today: A Symposium at St. John's College, Nottingham*. Edited by John Goldingay. London: S.P.C.K., 1995.

Averbeck, Richard E. "כפר."Pages 689–710 in vol. 2 of *New Dictionary of Old Testament Theology and Exegesis*. Edited by Willem A. VanGemeren. 5 vols. Grand Rapids: Zondervan, 1997.

Ayala, Francisco J. "Human Nature: One Evolutionist's View." Pages 31–48 in *Whatever Happened to the Soul? Scientific and Theological Portraits of Human Nature*. Edited by Warren S. Brown, Nancey Murphy, and H. Newton Malony. TSc. Minneapolis: Fortress, 1998.

Baker, Mark D., and Joel B. Green. *Recovering the Scandal of the Cross: Atonement in New Testament and Contemporary Contexts*. 2d ed. Downers Grove, Ill.: IVP Academic, 2011.

Bammel, Ernst, and C. F. D. Moule, eds. *Jesus and the Politics of His Day*. Cambridge: Cambridge University Press, 1984.

Bauckham, Richard. "Jesus and the Wild Animals (Mark 1:13): A Christological Image for an Ecological Age." Pages 3–21 in *Jesus of Nazareth:*

Lord and Christ: Essays on the Historical Jesus and New Testament Christology. Edited by Joel B. Green and Max Turner. Grand Rapids: Eerdmans, 1994.

———. "The Relevance of Revelation," *Catalyst* 24, no. 4 (1996): 1–3.

———. *The Theology of the Book of Revelation.* NTT. Cambridge: Cambridge University Press, 1993.

Bell, Richard H. *Deliver Us from Evil: Interpreting the Redemption from the Power of Satan in New Testament Theology.* WUNT 216. Tübingen: Mohr Siebeck, 2007.

Bellah, Robert N., Richard Madsen, William M. Sullivan, Ann Swidler, and Steven M. Tipton. *Habits of the Heart: Individualism and Commitment in American Life.* Berkeley: University of California Press, 1985.

———, eds. *Individualism and Commitment in American Life: Readings on the Themes of Habits of the Heart.* San Francisco: Harper & Row, 1987.

Berger, Peter L., and Thomas Luckmann. *The Social Construction of Reality: A Treatise in the Sociology of Knowledge.* New York: Doubleday, 1966.

Biddle, Mark E. *Missing the Mark: Sin and Its Consequences in Biblical Theology.* Nashville: Abingdon, 2005.

Boring, M. Eugene. *Mark: A Commentary.* NTL. Louisville, Ky.: Westminster John Knox, 2006.

Brandon, S. G. F. *Jesus and the Zealots: A Study of the Political Factor in Primitive Christianity.* Manchester: Manchester University Press, 1967.

Brown, Warren S. "Cognitive Contributions to Soul." Pages 99–125 in *Whatever Happened to the Soul? Scientific and Theological Portraits of Human Nature.* Edited by Warren S. Brown, Nancey Murphy, and H. Newton Malony. TSc. Minneapolis: Fortress, 1998.

Brown, William P. *The Ethos of the Cosmos: The Genesis of Moral Imagination in the Bible.* Grand Rapids: Eerdmans, 1999.

Brueggemann, Walter. *Theology of the Old Testament: Testimony, Dispute, Advocacy.* Minneapolis: Fortress, 1997.

Bryan, Christopher. *Render to Caesar: Jesus, the Early Church, and the Roman Superpower.* Oxford: Oxford University Press, 2005.

Bryant, David J. *Faith and the Play of Imagination: On the Role of Imagination in Religion.* SABH 5. Macon, Ga.: Mercer University Press, 1989.

Cargal, Timothy B. *Restoring the Diaspora: Discursive Structure and Purpose in the Epistle of James.* SBLDS 144. Atlanta: Scholars Press, 1993.

Cassidy, Richard J. *Christians and Roman Rule in the New Testament: New Perspectives.* CNT. New York: Crossroad, 2001.

Chester, Andrew. "The Theology of James." Pages 1–62 in *The Theology of the Letters of James, Peter, and Jude.* By Andrew Chester and Ralph P. Martin. NTT. Cambridge: Cambridge University Press, 1994.

Cheung, Luke L. *The Genre, Composition and Hermeneutics of James.* PBTM. Carlisle: Paternoster, 2003.

Chilton, Bruce D. *God in Strength: Jesus' Announcement of the Kingdom.* SNTU B1. Freistadt: F. Plöchl, 1979.

Colijn, Brenda B. *Images of Salvation in the New Testament.* Downers Grove, Ill.: IVP Academic, 2010.

Collins, John J. "The Kingdom of God in the Apocrypha and Pseudepigrapha." Pages 81–95 in *The Kingdom of God in 20th-Century Interpretation.* Edited by Wendell Willis. Peabody, Mass.: Hendrickson, 1987.

Cover, Robin C. "Sin, Sinners (Old Testament)." Pages 31–40 in vol. 6 of *Anchor Bible Dictionary.* Edited by David Noel Freedman. 6 vols. New York: Doubleday, 1992.

Cotter, Wendy. *Miracles in Greco-Roman Antiquity: A Sourcebook.* London: Routledge, 1999.

Crick, Francis. *The Astonishing Hypothesis: The Scientific Search for the Soul.* New York: Simon & Schuster, 1994.

Dalman, Gustaf. *The Words of Jesus Considered in Light of Post-Biblical Jewish Writings and the Aramaic Language.* Edinburgh: T&T Clark, 1902.

De Certeau, Michel. *The Practice of Everyday Life.* Berkeley: University of California Press, 1984.

Díaz, Miguel H. *On Being Human: U.S. Hispanic and Rahnerian Perspectives.* Maryknoll, N.Y.: Orbis, 2001.

Di Vito, Robert A. "Old Testament Anthropology and the Construction of Personal Identity." *CBQ* 61 (1999): 217–38.

Driver, John. *Understanding the Atonement for the Mission of the Church.* Scottdale, Pa.: Herald, 1986.

Dunn, James D. G. *The Epistles to the Colossians and to Philemon.* NIGTC. Grand Rapids: Eerdmans, 1996.

———. "Paul's Understanding of the Death of Jesus as Sacrifice." Pages 35–56 in *Sacrifice and Redemption: Durham Essays in Theology.* Edited by S. W. Sykes. Cambridge: Cambridge University Press, 1991.

Evans, Craig A. "Aspects of Exile and Restoration in the Proclamation of Jesus and the Gospels." Pages 263–94 in *Jesus in Context: Temple, Purity and Restoration.* Edited by Bruce Chilton and Craig A. Evans. AGJU 39. Leiden: Brill, 1997.

————. "Jesus and the Continuing Exile of Israel." Pages 77–100 in *Jesus and the Restoration of Israel*. Edited by Carey C. Newman. Downers Grove, Ill.: InterVarsity, 1999.

Felder, Cain Hope, ed. *Stony the Road We Trod: African American Biblical Interpretation*. Minneapolis: Fortress, 1991.

Finger, Thomas. "Eschatology and Ethics." Pages 276–79 in *Dictionary of Scripture and Ethics*. Edited by Joel B. Green. Grand Rapids: Eerdmans, 2011.

Ford, David F. *Theology: A Very Short Introduction*. Oxford: Oxford University Press, 1999.

Francalacci, Paolo et al. "Low-Pass DNA Sequencing of 1200 Sardinians Reconstructs European Y-Chromosome Phylogeny." *Science* 341, no. 6415 (2013): 565–69.

Fuller, Michael F. *The Restoration of Israel: Israel's Re-gathering and the Fate of the Nations in Early Jewish Literature and Luke-Acts*. BZNW 138. Berlin: de Gruyter, 2006.

Garcia, Ismael. *Dignidad: Ethics through Hispanic Eyes*. Nashville: Abingdon, 1997.

Goldingay, John. "Death and Afterlife in the Psalms." Pages 61–85 in *Judaism in Late Antiquity*, part 4: *Death, Life-after-Death, Resurrection and the World-to-Come in the Judaisms of Antiquity*. Edited by Alan J. Avery-Peck and Jacob Neusner. Handbook of Oriental Studies—1: The Near and Middle East 49. Leiden: Brill, 2000.

————. "Old Testament Sacrifice and the Death of Christ." Pages 3–20 in *Atonement Today: A Symposium at St. John's College, Nottingham*. Edited by John Goldingay. London: SPCK, 1995.

————. "Your Iniquities Have Made a Separation between You and God." Pages 39–53 in *Atonement Today: A Symposium at St. John's College, Nottingham*. Edited by John Goldingay. London: SPCK, 1995.

González, Justo L. *Santa Biblia: The Bible through Hispanic Eyes*. Nashville: Abingdon, 1996.

Good, Bryon J. *Medicine, Rationality, and Experience: An Anthropological Perspective*. Lewis Henry Morgan Lectures 1990. Cambridge: Cambridge University Press, 1994.

Goppelt, Leonhard. *A Commentary on 1 Peter*. Grand Rapids: Eerdmans, 1993.

Gordon, Suzanne. *Prisoners of Men's Dreams: Striking out for a New Feminine Future*. Boston: Little, Brown, 1991.

Green, Joel B. *Body, Soul, and Human Life: The Nature of Humanity in the Bible*. STI. Grand Rapids: Baker Academic, 2008.

———. "Good News to Whom? Jesus and the 'Poor' in the Gospel of Luke." Pages 59–74 in *Jesus of Nazareth: Lord and Christ: Essays on the Historical Jesus and New Testament Christology*. Edited by Joel B. Green and Max Turner. Grand Rapids: Eerdmans, 1995.

———. "Kingdom of God/Heaven." Pages 468–81 in *Dictionary of Jesus and the Gospels*. Rev. ed. Edited by Joel B. Green. Downers Grove, Ill: IVP Academic, 2013.

———. *The Gospel of Luke*. NICNT. Grand Rapids: Eerdmans, 1997.

———. "Healing and Healthcare." Pages 330–41 in *The World of the New Testament: Cultural, Social, and Historical Contexts*. Edited by Joel B. Green and Lee Martin McDonald. Grand Rapids: Baker Academic, 2013.

———. *Practicing Theological Interpretation: Engaging Biblical Texts for Faith and Formation*. TECC. Grand Rapids: Baker Academic, 2011.

———. *The Theology of the Gospel of Luke*. NTT. Cambridge: Cambridge University Press, 1995.

Grenz, Stanley J. *The Social God and the Relational Self: A Trinitarian Theology of the Imago Dei*. MCT. Louisville, Ky.: Westminster John Knox, 2001.

Gunton, Colin E. "Trinity, Ontology and Anthropology: Towards a Renewal of the Doctrine of the *Imago Dei*." Pages 47–61 in *Persons Divine and Human: King's College Essays on Theological Anthropology*. Edited by Christoph Schwöbel and Colin E. Gunton. Edinburgh: T&T Clark, 1991.

Hahn, Robert A. *Sickness and Healing: An Anthropological Perspective*. New Haven: Yale University Press, 1995.

Hanson, Paul D. "Introduction." Pages 1–15 in *Visionaries and Their Apocalypses*. Edited by Paul D. Hanson. Philadelphia: Fortress, 1983.

Haran, Menahem. "Temple and Community in Ancient Israel." Pages 17–25 in *Temple in Society*. Edited by Michael V. Fox. Winona Lake, Ind.: Eisenbrauns, 1988.

Hartman, Lars. *'Into the Name of the Lord Jesus': Baptism in the Early Church*. SNTW. Edinburgh: T&T Clark, 1997.

Hefner, Philip. *The Human Factor: Evolution, Culture, and Religion*. TSc. Minneapolis: Fortress, 1993.

Hirstein, William. *Brain Fiction: Self-Deception and the Riddle of Confabulation*. Cambridge, Mass.: MIT Press, 2005.

Hogan, Larry O. *Healing in the Second Tempel [sic] Period*. NTOA 21. Göttingen: Vandenhoeck & Ruprecht, 1992.

Horsley, Richard A. *Jesus and Empire: The Kingdom of God and the New World Disorder*. Minneapolis: Fortress, 2003.

————. *The Liberation of Christmas: The Infancy Narratives in Social Context.* New York: Crossroad, 1989.

James, William. *The Varieties of Religious Experience: A Study in Human Nature, Being the Gifford Lectures on Natural Religion Delivered at Edinburgh in 1901–1902.* London: Longmans, Green, 1902.

Jenson, Robert W. *Systematic Theology.* 2 vols. Oxford: Oxford University Press, 1997–99.

Johnson, Mark. *The Body in the Mind: The Bodily Basis of Meaning, Imagination, and Reason.* Chicago: University of Chicago, 1987.

Kapolyo, Joe M. *The Human Condition: Christian Perspectives through African Eyes.* Downers Grove, Ill.: InterVarsity, 2005.

Kille, D. Andrew. *Psychological Biblical Criticism.* GBS:OTS. Minneapolis: Fortress, 2001.

Knibb, Michael A. "The Exile in the Literature of the Intertestamental Period." *HeyJ* 17 (1976): 253–72.

Knipe, David M. "The Temple in Image and Reality." Pages 105–38 in *Temple in Society.* Edited by Michael V. Fox. Winona Lake, Ind.: Eisenbrauns, 1988.

Kruse, H. "Die 'dialektische Negation' als semitisches Idiom." *VT* 4 (1954): 385–400.

Kümmel, Werner Georg. *Man in the New Testament.* London: Epworth, 1963.

Lang, B. "כבר." Pages 288–303 in vol. 7 of *Theological Dictionary of the Old Testament.* Edited by G. Johannes Botterweck. 15 vols. Grand Rapids: Eerdmans, 1974–2006.

Larsson, Göran. *Bound for Freedom: The Book of Exodus in Jewish and Christian Traditions.* Peabody, Mass.: Hendrickson, 1999.

LeDoux, Joseph. *Synaptic Self: How Our Brains Become Who We Are.* New York: Viking, 2002.

Lohfink, Norbert F. *Option for the Poor: The Basic Principle of Liberation Theology in the Light of the Bible.* Berkeley, Calif.: Bibal, 1987.

Longenecker, Richard N. "Is There Development in Paul's Resurrection Thought?" Pages 171–202 in *Life in the Face of Death: The Resurrection Message of the New Testament.* Edited by Richard N. Longenecker. MNTS. Grand Rapids: Eerdmans, 1998.

Longman III, Tremper. "Warfare." Pages 835–39 in *New Dictionary of Biblical Theology.* Edited by T. Desmond Alexander and Brian S. Rosner. Downers Grove, Ill.: InterVarsity, 2000.

Longman III, Tremper and Daniel G. Reid. *God Is a Warrior.* SOTBT. Grand Rapids: Zondervan, 1995.

Lowenthal, David. *The Past Is a Foreign Country.* Cambridge: Cambridge University Press, 1985.

Martyn, J. Louis. *Theological Issues in the Letters of Paul.* Nashville: Abingdon, 1997.

McFarland, Ian A. *In Adam's Fall: A Meditation on the Christian Doctrine of Original Sin.* CCT. Malden, Mass.: Wiley-Blackwell, 2010.

McGrath, Alister E. *Scientific Theology.* Vol. 1: *Nature.* Grand Rapids: Eerdmans, 2001.

McKnight, Scot. *The King Jesus Gospel: The Original Good News Revisited.* Grand Rapids: Zondervan, 2011.

Middleton, J. Richard. "Image of God." Pages 394–97 in *Dictionary of Scripture and Ethics.* Edited by Joel B. Green. Grand Rapids: Baker Academic, 2011.

———. *The Liberating Image: The Imago Dei in Genesis 1.* Grand Rapids: Brazos, 2005.

Milgrom, Jacob. *Leviticus.* 3 vols. AB. New York: Doubleday, 1991–2001.

———. *Studies in Cultic Theology and Terminology.* SJLA 36. Leiden: Brill, 1983.

Murphy, Nancey. *Bodies and Souls, or Spirited Bodies?* CTI. Cambridge: Cambridge University Press, 2006.

Murphy, Roland E. "Death and Afterlife in the Wisdom Literature." Pages 101–16 in *Judaism in Late Antiquity,* part 4: *Death, Life-after-Death, Resurrection and the World-to-Come in the Judaisms of Antiquity.* Edited by Alan J. Avery-Peck and Jacob Neusner. Handbook of Oriental Studies—1: The Near and Middle East 49. Leiden: Brill, 2000.

Nock, A. D. *Conversion: The Old and the New in Religion from Alexander the Great to Augustine of Hippo.* Oxford: Clarendon, 1933.

Padgett, Alan G. "The Body in Resurrection: Science and Scripture on the 'Spiritual Body' (1 Cor 15:35-58)." *WW* 22 (2002): 155–63.

Page, Sydney H. T. *Powers of Evil: A Biblical Study of Satan and Demons.* Grand Rapids: Baker Academic, 1995.

Pannenberg, Wolfhart. *Anthropology in Theological Perspective.* Philadelphia: Westminster, 1985.

———. *Systematic Theology.* 3 vols. Translated by Geoffrey W. Bromiley. Grand Rapids: Eerdmans, 1988–98.

———. *What Is Man? Contemporary Anthropology in Theological Perspective.* Philadelphia: Fortress, 1970.

Pao, David W. *Acts and the Isaianic New Exodus.* WUNT 2/130. Tübingen: Mohr Siebeck, 2000.

Pennington, Jonathan T. *Heaven and Earth in the Gospel of Matthew.* Grand Rapids: Baker Academic, 2009.

Perrin, Nicholas. "Exile." Pages 25–37 in *The World of the New Testament: Cultural, Social, and Historical Contexts.* Edited by Joel B. Green and Lee Martin McDonald. Grand Rapids: Baker Academic, 2013.

Peters, Ted. *Sin: Radical Evil in Soul and Society.* Grand Rapids: Eerdmans, 1994.

Philo. *Philo.* 10 vols. Translated by F. H. Colson and G. H. Whitaker. LCL. Cambridge, Mass.: Harvard University Press, 1926–62.

Pilgrim, Walter E. *Uneasy Neighbors: Church and State in the New Testament.* OBT. Minneapolis: Fortress, 1999.

Poznik, G. David et al. "Sequencing Y Chromosomes Resolves Discrepancy in Time to Common Ancestor of Males versus Females." *Science* 341, no. 6415 (2013): 562–65.

Preuss, Horst Dietrich. *Old Testament Theology.* 2 vols. OTL. Louisville, Ky.: Westminster John Knox, 1996.

Prince, Gerald. *Narrative as Theme: Studies in French Fiction.* Lincoln: University of Nebraska Press, 1992.

Rapske, Brian. *Paul in Roman Custody.* A1CS 3. Grand Rapids: Eerdmans, 1994.

Reid, Daniel G. "Principalities and Powers." Pages 746–52 in *Dictionary of Paul and His Letters.* Edited by Gerald F. Hawthorne, Ralph P. Martin, and Daniel G. Reid. Downers Grove, Ill.: InterVarsity, 1993.

Reynolds, C. H., and R. V. Norman, eds. *Community in America: The Challenge of Habits of the Heart.* Berkeley: University of California Press, 1988.

Schmidt, Francis. *How the Temple Thinks: Identity and Social Cohesion in Ancient Judaism.* TBS 78. Sheffield: Sheffield Academic Press, 2001.

Schnelle, Udo. *The Human Condition: Anthropology in the Teachings of Jesus, Paul, and John.* Minneapolis: Fortress, 1996.

Schwöbel, Christoph. "Human Being as Relation Being: Twelve Theses for a Christian Anthropology." Pages 141–70 in *Persons Divine and Human: King's College Essays on Theological Anthropology.* Edited by Christoph Schwöbel and Colin E. Gunton. Edinburgh: T&T Clark, 1991.

Scott, James C. *Domination and the Arts of Resistance: Hidden Transcripts.* New Haven: Yale University Press, 1990.

———. *Weapons of the Weak: Everyday Forms of Peasant Resistance.* New Haven: Yale University Press, 1985.

Solzhenitsyn, Aleksandr I. *The Gulag Archipelago: 1918–1956.* London: Book Club, 1974.

Spicq, Ceslas. *Theological Lexicon of the New Testament.* 3 vols. Peabody, Mass.: Hendrickson, 1994.

Stock, Brian. *Listening for the Text: On the Uses of the Past.* Baltimore, Md.: The Johns Hopkins University Press, 1990; Philadelphia: University of Pennsylvania Press, 1997.

Stoeger, William R. "Scientific Accounts of Ultimate Catastrophes in Our Life-Bearing Universe." Pages 19–28 in *The End of the World and the Ends of God: Science and Theology on Eschatology.* Edited by John Polkinghorne and Michael Welker. Harrisburg, Pa.: Trinity, 2000.

Taylor, Charles. *Sources of the Self: The Making of the Modern Identity.* Cambridge, Mass.: Harvard University Press, 1989.

Thielicke, Helmut. *Being Human . . . Becoming Human: An Essay in Christian Anthropology.* Garden City, N.Y.: Doubleday, 1984.

Thuan, Trinh Xuan. *Chaos and Harmony: Perspectives on Scientific Revolutions of the Twentieth Century.* Oxford: Oxford University Press, 2001.

Twelftree, Graham H. *Jesus the Exorcist: A Contribution to the Study of the Historical Jesus.* Peabody, Mass.: Hendrickson, 1993.

Twenge, Jean M., W. Keith Campbell, and Brittany Gentile. "Changes in Pronoun Use in American Books and the Rise of Individualism, 1960–2008." *Journal of Cross-Cultural Psychology* 44, no. 3 (2013): 406–15.

Vanhoozer, Kevin J. *Biblical Narrative in the Philosophy of Paul Ricoeur: A Study in Hermeneutics and Theology.* Cambridge: Cambridge University Press, 1990.

Warrior, Valerie M. *Roman Religion.* CIRC. Cambridge: Cambridge University Press, 2006.

Watts, Rikki E. "Exodus." Pages 478–87 in *New Dictionary of Biblical Theology.* Edited by T. Desmond Alexander and Brian S. Rosner. Downers Grove, Ill.: InterVarsity, 2000.

———. *Isaiah's New Exodus and Mark.* WUNT 2/88. Tübingen: Mohr Siebeck, 1997.

Wenham, David. *The Parables of Jesus.* TJL. Downers Grove, Ill.: InterVarsity, 1989.

Wenham, Gordon J. "The Theology of Old Testament Sacrifice." Pages 75–87 in *Sacrifice in the Bible.* Edited by Roger T. Beckwith and Martin J. Selman. Grand Rapids: Baker, 1995.

Wesley, John. *Explanatory Notes upon the New Testament.* London: Epworth, 1976 [1754].

Wilkinson, David. *Christian Eschatology and the Physical Universe*. London: T&T Clark, 2010.

Williams, Patricia A. *Doing without Adam and Eve: Sociobiology and Original Sin*. TSc. Minneapolis: Fortress, 2001.

Wright, Christopher J. H. "Old Testament Ethics: A Missiological Perspective." *Catalyst* 26, no. 2 (2000): 5–8.

Wright, N. T. *Jesus and the Victory of God*. COQG 2. Minneapolis: Fortress, 1996.

———. *The New Testament and the People of God*. COQG 1. Minneapolis: Fortress, 1992.

Wright, R. B. "Psalms of Solomon: A New Translation and Introduction." Pages 639–70 in vol. 2 of *Old Testament Pseudepigrapha*. Edited by James H. Charlesworth. 2 vols. Garden City, N.Y.: Doubleday, 1985.

Wuthnow, Robert. *Sharing the Journey: Support Groups and America's New Quest for Community*. New York: Free, 1994.

Young, Kay, and Jeffrey L. Saver. "The Neurology of Narrative." *SubStance* 30 (2001): 72–84.

Index of Scriptures

175

Apocrypha
Tobit

Sirach

1 Maccabees

2 Maccabees

4 Maccabees

Index of Modern Authors

Index of Subjects

CPSIA information can be obtained at www.ICGtesting.com
Printed in the USA
LVOW13s1218050514

384446LV00005B/5/P